More Praise for *WISH IT LASTED FOREVER*

"For Dan Shaughnessy the Larry Bird Celtics of the mid-1980s stand apart. Yes, they were distinctively great. Yes, they were a very colorful group. An abundant source of material. But for the scribe, this was the key: He, and they, were essentially contemporaries. He hung with them, lost cash in free throw shooting contests with them, and experienced it all with the exuberance and fresh perspective of youth. This is the story of a great team, rendered in an immersive style. It's also a writer's coming-of-age story. Looking back on that team and time, it was Bill Walton who said, 'I wish it lasted forever.' He was speaking for the scribe as well."

> —Bob Costas, twenty-eight-time
> Emmy Award–winning sportscaster

"Peels back the curtain on the pulsating Celtics teams of the 1980s with insight, candor, and a brashness that earned Shaughnessy the nickname 'Scoop.' A revealing account of his own trials and tribulations among one of the most celebrated collections of basketball stars ever assembled."

> —Jackie MacMullan, coauthor, with Larry Bird
> and Earvin Magic Johnson, of *When the Game*
> *Was Ours*

"Dan Shaughnessy has long been an insider and has great knowledge of the game, which is on display in this look back at teams I played on. He has irritated the hell out of me, but has entertained me at the same time."

> —Cedric Maxwell, Boston Celtics, 1977–85,
> MVP of the 1981 NBA Finals

"A fantastic read ... In its combination of off-court camaraderie and on-court intensity, Shaughnessy's epic ode to the Bird-McHale-Parish Celtics evokes both *Cheers* and *Hoosiers*. *Wish It Lasted Forever* is about the obvious—historic rivalries, legendary athletes, and a remarkable string of championship seasons—but it's also about an element of life as important as wins and losses: forever friendships formed by a group of guys playing a game."

—Mike Barnicle, senior contributor to *Morning Joe* and former columnist for the *New York Daily News, Boston Herald,* and *Boston Globe*

"Another book on Larry Bird? Yes, and it's delicious. Of course, it's not just Bird—the whole gang's here. Shaughnessy takes us back to a time when writers hung around with athletes: same flights, same hotels, same trips to the game—they were the ultimate boys on the bus. For Celtics fans, this book is Springsteen's 'Glory Days'—oh, he's in here, too."

—Lesley Visser, Hall of Fame sportscaster

WISH IT LASTED FOREVER

LIFE WITH THE LARRY BIRD CELTICS

DAN SHAUGHNESSY

SCRIBNER

New York   London   Toronto   Sydney   New Delhi

Scribner
An Imprint of Simon & Schuster, Inc.
1230 Avenue of the Americas
New York, NY 10020

First Scribner hardcover edition November 2021

SCRIBNER and design are registered trademarks of The Gale Group, Inc.,
used under license by Simon & Schuster, Inc., the publisher of this work.

For information about special discounts for bulk purchases,
please contact Simon & Schuster Special Sales at 1-866-506-1949
or business@simonandschuster.com.

The Simon & Schuster Speakers Bureau can bring authors to your live event.
For more information or to book an event, contact the Simon & Schuster Speakers Bureau
at 1-866-248-3049 or visit our website at www.simonspeakers.com.

Manufactured in the United States of America

1   3   5   7   9   10   8   6   4   2

Library of Congress Cataloging-in-Publication Data has been applied for.

ISBN 978-1-9821-6997-8
ISBN 978-1-9821-6999-2 (ebook)

For Danny, Nico, Matty, Jack, and Lucy,
who were playing and sleeping in our cozy COVID bubble
while Papa was upstairs writing most of this one.

When you're part of something that special, it changes you.
You spend the rest of your life trying to get that back.
When you're doing it, it seems like it's going to last forever.
When it ends, you realize how fragile, how tenuous,
and how fleeting it all is.

—Bill Walton, Boston Celtic, 1985–87

CONTENTS

CONTENTS

INTRODUCTION

They are men in their sixties now, and all these years later there is still lively interaction, busting of chops, hugs of celebration, and sometimes sorrow. When you go through what these guys went through, winning the way they won, and laughing the way they laughed, green thread runs deep and connections don't fade.

Periodically, Indiana Pacers administrative assistant Susy Fischer will take a call for consultant Larry Bird, ask, "Who's calling please?," then hear the person on the other end say, "Tell him it's the best player who ever played for the Celtics."

This means that M. L. Carr is on the line. Bird's assistant is in on the joke.

"Hi, M.L.," Fischer will say. "Let me see if Larry is in."

Carr is the player who supplied protection when Bird was a rookie in the NBA. Anybody who wanted to get tough with Bird had to deal with M.L. A federal prison guard before he was a Celtic, Carr likes to say, "You can't rattle me. I was in the big house. I told Maurice Lucas and all those other 'enforcers' that they'd have to go through me first. Those guys and those little NBA arenas were nothing compared with what I'd already dealt with."

In a serious moment of reflection, Medicare-eligible Bird admits, "M.L. was my best teammate. He always had my back."

M. L. Carr was "Froggy"—a nickname bestowed by Cedric Maxwell after he observed the way Carr's legs bowed before he went

1

up for a shot or rebound. Fans didn't know about Froggy. It was an insider thing—the same with every team ever assembled. At every level, whether high school, college, or the pros, team members and those around them speak a locker room shorthand that they alone understand. Forty years later, hearing an old nickname or signature phrase is enough to transport a teammate back in time, the same way the smell of cinnamon toast puts you back in your mom's cramped kitchen when you were five years old.

In 2021, if M. L. Carr walks through a crowded arena and hears "Froggy," he knows that one of his former teammates is nearby. The only guys who call him Froggy are Bird, Maxwell, Kevin McHale, Danny Ainge, and other Celtics from the early 1980s.

Maxwell was "Cornbread" to NBA America, "Bread" to his teammates. Robert Parish was "Chief," an homage to the gigantic, silent Indian in *One Flew Over the Cuckoo's Nest*. All Celtics fans knew Maxwell's and Parish's nicknames, but only folks in the inner sanctum knew that assistant coach Chris Ford was "Doc," Rick Robey was "Footer," Gerald Henderson was "Sarge," and Rick Carlisle was "Flip." Diminutive *Boston Herald* Celtics beat reporter Mike Carey was "Smurf."

I was "Scoop."

"You was always getting the damn scoop," says Maxwell, who serves as a color analyst on Celtics radio broadcasts in 2021. "We knew we had to be careful around you."

In 1984, after a forgettable NBA regular season game in which veteran guard Quinn Buckner struggled, I told *Boston Globe* readers that Buckner played "like a man with no clue."

Maxwell, custodian of all the Celtics nicknames, loved it.

"Bucky is the man with no clue!" he hollered at practice the next day. "He is Inspector Clue-seau!"

"All these years later, Max still brings that shit up," says Buckner, now a color analyst for Indiana Pacers broadcasts. "I'll see him in the press dining room before we play the Celtics, and he'll yell across the room, 'There he is, Inspector Clue-seau!'"

"I'll tell you one thing," McHale says today. "When I see any of those guys across a room, I just get a gigantic smile on my face. It's weird, and I noticed it years ago. If I see any of those guys a block away—Bill Walton, Max, Danny, M.L.—I get this visceral response. Something changes in me. I just get this big smile and this real sense of calm and cool and friendship. It's hard to explain, but there's something special that was there, and it remains with me."

When I told Walton I was writing about my days with the Larry Bird Celtics of the 1980s, he said, "You cannot overemphasize in your book how much fun this was. It was better than perfect. Everybody couldn't wait to get to practice every day. Everybody couldn't wait to get to the airport, to get on the bus, to get to the games. Empty the thesaurus when you write this. You have license to print whatever superlative you can find. The basketball was superb and the community was remarkable. The people in my neighborhood in Cambridge and all the Celtics fans—the guy running the parking lot outside the Garden, the people in the restaurants, the people running the airport, and the people in the tollbooths at the tunnels. It was just such a joy. It was what you dream about and I wish it lasted forever."

CHAPTER 1

"WE RAN PEOPLE OFF THE FLOOR"

In my younger and more vulnerable years (yes, that's a crib from *The Great Gatsby*), I spent many hours thinking about the Boston Celtics. Sports fans who grew up in New England in the 1950s and 1960s were grateful for Red Auerbach, Bill Russell, Bob Cousy, and the Celtics. The NBA of that short-shorts era wasn't the global entertainment entity it is today, but the Celtics were our sports salvation in a sea of mediocre teams plagued by administrative buffoonery.

Our dads spoke glowingly of Ted Williams and a Red Sox team stocked with stars who'd come back from World War II and *almost* won the 1946 World Series, but that felt like ancient history. The Red Sox of our Eisenhower/Kennedy/Johnson youth were a big bowl of bad, largely racist and managed by a chorus line of thirsty, old-school tobacco spitters who allowed losing baseball in a country-club environment. Baby boomer fans knew little of the team's bleak history. We just knew that the Sox were never any good, always cannon fodder for the Mickey Mantle–Whitey Ford New York Yankees. The old-timey Sox played under signage reading THE RED SOX USE LIFEBUOY SOAP, and our obvious follow-up was "But they still stink." It was always *stink* in those days. *Suck* would have gotten us a week in the cooler. The Red Sox of the early 1960s annually finished eighth or ninth in a ten-team American League. We were routinely at the bottom of the junior circuit alongside the Kansas City Athletics and the Washington Senators.

The Red Sox of my youth drew anemic crowds and never played .500 baseball. Only 1,247 attended when Sox righty Dave Morehead pitched a no-hitter at Fenway Park in 1965. Over and over we heard that the Sox hadn't won a World Series since 1918, when Babe Ruth roamed the Fenway lawn. That factoid rolled off tongues like the Midnight Ride of Paul Revere.

There was no NFL in Boston in the 1950s or '60s. New England's professional football team was the Sam Huff–Frank Gifford New York Giants. With Chris Schenkel behind the mike, Giants games were telecast into Greater Boston homes every Sunday. The Boston Patriots, original members of the upstart American Football League, were born in 1960, but it was more than a decade before they were taken seriously. The Pats played at Boston University, Fenway Park, Harvard Stadium, and Boston College. They even played a home game in Birmingham, Alabama. They managed to advance to the AFL Championship Game in 1963, but lost to the San Diego Chargers, 51–10.

The Patriots' first two trips to the Super Bowl did little to improve the franchise's loser image. The 1985 Pats made it to Super Bowl XX in New Orleans but were routed by William "Refrigerator" Perry and the Chicago Bears, 46–10. It was, at the time, the worst blowout in Super Bowl history. Eleven years later, the Pats returned to the Super Bowl, this time losing to the Packers, 35–21. Those twentieth-century New England Patriots were nothing like the Bill Belichick–Tom Brady dynasty of the new millennium.

The Boston Bruins of my youth were often worse than the Sox and Pats, regularly finishing in fifth or sixth place in the original six-team National Hockey League. Drawing loyal hockey fans from Charlestown, Southie, and the North Shore of Boston, the Spoked-B's welcomed big crowds to the Boston Garden, but there wasn't much cheering in the 1950s and early '60s. The Canadiens took Boston out of the playoffs six times in the 1950s. The Bruins missed the playoffs in the first eight years of the 1960s, almost impossible given that they were playing in a six-team league in which four teams annually qualified for the postseason. The best player on the team was goalie

Eddie Johnston, who lost a franchise-record 40 games in 1963–64. Bostonians regularly filled the Garden because they loved hockey, but the local team didn't compete until 1966, when teen angel Bobby Orr arrived from Parry Sound, Ontario (aluminum siding for the Orr's family home sealed the deal). Orr pushed the Bruins into the playoffs a couple of years later and, in 1970, delivered Boston its first Stanley Cup since 1941.

The math is pretty simple: from 1941 to 1970, Boston celebrated zero championships in baseball, football, and hockey.

This is why the Celtics hold a special place in the hearts and minds of New Englanders who grew up in the age of Elvis Presley, Walter Cronkite, and Woodstock. While the Red Sox, Patriots, and Bruins disappointed annually, the Celtics were champions just about every year, an evergreen gift to our region's title-starved fans.

I'm forever amazed by the Celtics of my youth. While the Sox, Pats, and Bruins struggled, the Celtics gave us a taste of what life was like for New York baseball fans and Montreal's hockey krishnas. The Celtics of the fifties and sixties have never been fully appreciated, in part because the NBA wasn't yet a major sport and the game was only beginning to take root in cities across America. Fueled by Larry Bird, Magic Johnson, Michael Jordan, and the 1992 US Olympic Dream Team, the NBA in the 1990s became a global sports attraction and today enjoys popularity second only to the mighty NFL. In the fifties and sixties, the NBA was a minor league with little national television presence. The NBA played four-team *doubleheaders* and sometimes featured the Harlem Globetrotters to attract fans. The league had teams in Rochester, Syracuse, Fort Wayne, and Tri-Cities, Iowa. *Yahoo*.

Few fans get to come of age with a professional team that wins the championship *every year*. I did. The Boston Celtics won their first NBA crown in 1957, lost in the Finals a year later, then won eight straight NBA championships—one in each of Red Auerbach's final eight years on the bench.

It was a New England spring ritual—like Easter, forsythia in bloom, and clunky storm windows coming off the sides of houses.

The Celtics were NBA champs when I entered first grade in Groton, Massachusetts, elementary school in 1959, and I was in high school by the time they abdicated. Who else gets to make this claim? Picking out your favorite Celtics championship team of that era was like pausing over a freshly opened box of chocolates. *Hmmm. What will it be today? Shall we experience the first one in 1957 when Tommy Heinsohn scored 37 with 23 rebounds to win Game 7 in double overtime against the Hawks? Or perhaps sample the 1965 title when John Havlicek stole the ball in Game 7 of the conference finals?*

The success of the Auerbach-Russell Celtics had a universality that wasn't lost on New England's fans and young ballplayers. Our region's amateur coaches and gym teachers were blessed with a model squad that produced a nightly clinic of team-over-self basketball. Impressionable young players paid attention to everything the Celtics did. Russell, the best player on the team, never complained about "touches." He inhaled every rebound, made the quick outlet pass, and raced down to the other end of the floor to play defense. When he blocked a shot, Russell didn't swat the ball into the second row of the stands to impress the girls. He knew it was better to control and corral the shot, then get the fast break going. Russell beat opponents with his athletic prowess *and* his mind.

In an interview at the *Boston Globe* in the 1990s, Russell told me that one of his favorite competitive moments came when he was able to win a regular season game with a mind trick against Lakers guard Archie Clark:

"We were behind by two points with just a few seconds left and they had the ball. All they had to do was dribble out the clock. Now I know that Archie Clark is a scorer and would not be able to resist a chance for an easy basket. So when they inbounded, I created a path to the basket for him, knowing he'd go for the easy points. Sure enough, he went for the hoop and I came up from behind and blocked it. We got the ball back and scored and won in overtime."

The big fella delivered his trademark cackle when he was done telling that one. The vignette perfectly explains the man and the team.

Green godfather Auerbach annually paid Russell one dollar more than the physically superior Wilt Chamberlain—a statement that Russell was worth more than Wilt even without scoring 50 points per game. Three of the Celtics starters—Russell, Satch Sanders, and K. C. Jones—were defensive specialists. Red reminded us that it didn't matter who started the game; it mattered who was on the floor at the finish. With Hall of Famers coming off the bench—first Frank Ramsey, later John Havlicek and Kevin McHale—Red invented the sixth man. Celtics box scores were democratic, regularly featuring six or seven players in double figures. Boston's winners never had a league scoring champ. They ran six simple plays, over and over. If a Celtics point guard called out, "Zipper," it meant that one of the sharpshooters would rub off a low-block pick, come out past the foul line, catch a pass, and toss up a fallaway jumper. It was okay that the other team knew what was coming. They still couldn't stop it.

Leadership was collaborative. Auerbach regularly called time-out and asked his players, "Anybody got anything?"

"That made us play even harder," recalled Heinsohn, who was part of the Celtics from 1956 until his death in December of 2020. "If you designed the play, you had the pride of authorship. You wanted your play to work."

Celtics players were lean and hungry. Auerbach preached fast break offense at all times. In an era when many teams would sacrifice early-season games by playing themselves into condition, the Celtics got into shape during preseason and won November games on sheer conditioning.

"We ran people off the floor," said Cousy.

There was none of the infinite wealth of today's NBA. Players had off-season jobs (Heinsohn sold insurance, Cousy operated a driving school). Winners' playoff shares were important. Before postseason games, Ramsey, who became a Kentucky bank president after his NBA career, scribbled the amount of a winner's share on the locker room blackboard and announced, "Y'all are playing with mahhh money!"

A decade before the Civil Rights Act, the Celtics successfully dealt with issues of race. No one got offended when Auerbach made references to *schvartzes*, a Yiddish term that is not traditionally a compliment.

"It means Black," Red said. "It's an insult according to who says it."

In 1950, Auerbach drafted the NBA's first Black player, Duquesne's Chuck Cooper. Red was the first NBA coach to start five Black players: Russell, Tom Sanders, Willie Naulls, Sam Jones, and K. C. Jones in 1964. He hired the first Black head coach in American team sports when he made Russell player-coach in 1966.

At the peak of their championship run in the 1960s, the Celtics were cited for their racial harmony in a speech Red Sox GM Dick O'Connell delivered at an annual brotherhood breakfast at Fenway Park:

"Right now you're sitting in a sports building talking about brotherhood," said O'Connell. "May I suggest the best example is right down the street from here. There's a team over there in the Boston Garden made up of Blacks and whites, Catholics and Protestants, coached by a Jew, and they've been World Champions for a long time now. Everyone's running around looking for theories and searching into history for explanations. If you want a perfect example of what we've been talking about, just look at the Celtics."

"Our thing was somewhat connected to what I call the foxhole syndrome," ninety-two-year-old Cousy said in 2021. "When you're in a foxhole and the bullets are flying all over the place, the last thing on your mind is the color of the person next to you that will hopefully save your ass. That is the ultimate bonding. Winning that championship was all we thought or cared about. So, once the whistle blew, race and personality would go out the window. You would bond with the other four guys out there, and everything else became secondary. It also induces a sense of camaraderie. The most racist city we used to visit was St. Louis. Russell had to walk through the crowd to come onto the court and occasionally we'd hear the N-word. There was a greasy spoon across from the hotel where we stayed, and when we'd walk in after a game, they'd say the Black guys can't eat there, and we'd say, 'Hey, this shit shouldn't be eaten by *any* human beings,' and we'd all turn and walk out together."

The Boston Garden, home court of the Celtics, was the first basketball palace universally known by American sports fans. When the pro game was coming of age, gradually gaining network-television exposure, the Celtics were the best team in the sport and included Cousy, "Mr. Basketball," the first NBA player to appear on the cover of *Sports Illustrated*. Boston's Houdini of the Hardwood was league MVP in 1957.

Built in 1928, the old Boston Garden was one of the original dual-purpose barns in major metropolitan cities designed to feature hockey, basketball, circuses, concerts, and all other forms of indoor entertainment. Basketball courts had to be portable, and in 1946 Celtics owner Walter Brown commissioned a Brookline, Massachusetts, company to build a floor that could be set down and taken up daily. Originally built from oak scraps from wood cut from a forest in Tennessee, the 264 five-by-five Garden panels were arranged in alternating fashion, producing the trademark oak parquet pattern common in many early twentieth-century New England homes. Watching black-and-white televisions, sports fans across America—including young Bill Walton and Larry Bird—learned to identify Boston games because of the Garden's distinct floorboard pattern. Boston's beloved sports palace was demolished in the 1990s, replaced by the generic TD Garden, but the portable parquet floor remains part of the Celtics identity, like the Gothic frieze that adorned the upper deck of the original Yankee Stadium. The Celtics court is famous for dead spots where the ball won't bounce back into a dribbler's hand. Opponents claim only the Celtics know the secrets of the parquet's irregular bounces, but none of that is true. The floor is assembled and disassembled dozens of times every season when the arena is converted from hockey to basketball by the Garden's "Bull Gang." Bird says the dead spots changed from game to game, depending on how tightly the Bull Gang fastened the floor bolts.

Another Celtics trademark is stately banners hanging from the iron rafters above the court, flags dedicated exclusively to championship seasons. There have never been EASTERN DIVISION CHAMPIONS banners hanging in the Boston Garden. Ever competitive, and resentful of the Bruins, Auerbach mocked the hockey team's ADAMS DIVISION CHAMPS banners when the Celtics were at their height of popularity in the 1980s. Individuals are also cited. Beginning with Cousy's number 14 in 1963, twenty-one Celtics' numbers have been retired to the rafters. It's a swollen assembly that inspires ridicule from Celtics haters and NBA rivals.

One of the magic numbers of the original Celtics dynasty was 13,909, the attendance figure assigned to any sellout at the old Garden. This number never accounted for hundreds of hardscrabble fans who snuck under turnstiles or gained entry by handing a couple of bucks to a friendly usher. Another Celtics tradition was Russell throwing up before every big playoff game. Neither glorious, nor healthy, it was nonetheless a revered Celtics postseason ritual.

The World Champion Celtics wore green or black high-top sneakers ("cheaper and they don't show the dirt," said Auerbach) and played in a gimmick-free environment. No rock music blared from the tinny public address system. During time-outs, Auerbach permitted cornball organist John Kiley to play "Stout-Hearted Men," and "Roll Out the Barrel," but the patriarch forbade artificial noise when the ball was in play. There were no celebrity fans, fuzzy mascots, or cheerleaders. The first dolled-up Celtics Dancers didn't set foot on the parquet floor until November of 2006, a week after Auerbach's death.

Absence of glamour and phony trappings made the Celtics cool. When the champs visited the Kennedy White House in 1963, forward Satch Sanders signed off, telling JFK, "Take it easy, baby."

The team's radio play-by-play voice was Johnny Most, an ultimate homer, who said he gargled with Sani-Flush. Most bled green for forty-eight minutes of every broadcast, sitting high above courtside, making villains of every Celtics opponent ("Rudy LaRusso just crawled out of a sewer!"). Most's "Havlicek stole the ball!" call was our twentieth-century "The British are coming!" and triggered a best-selling LP. Johnny was a heavy smoker who set his pants on fire mid-broadcast in the 1980s.

Smoke fueled the Celtics dynasty. Many Garden fans smoked in the arena, and Auerbach's cigar emerged as the original trash talk of American sport. Boston's arrogant coach lit up a Hoyo de Monterrey near the end of every win.

"When the league was picking on me, I tried to think of something that would aggravate the higher-ups," said the coach. "I wasn't having much luck until one day I lighted up a cigar during a game. Afterward, I got a little note, saying, 'It doesn't look good for you to be smoking cigars on the bench.' I haven't been without one since."

"We hated that thing," said Cousy. "As soon as he'd light up, the other guys wanted to kill us. He'd sit there all comfortable on the bench, and we were out there on the floor taking all the abuse. We had to play much harder to keep the lead because the other team wanted to make him stick that cigar up his ass!"

Red's cigar was the beginning of NBA trash talk, the ultimate taunt—something the Larry Bird Celtics turned into performance art in the 1980s.

When no-smoking regulations took hold in the 1970s and '80s, Legal Sea Foods' owner, Roger Berkowitz, made an exception for Auerbach. Under "daily catch," each Legal menu stipulated that there was no smoking allowed in the eatery, "except for Red Auerbach." When Red lit up at Legal's, he took delight in getting in the face of offended customers and showing them his Legal exemption.

Rooting for the Celtics was part my childhood in rural New England in the 1960s. We nailed backboards to hoops, trees, and telephone poles, then pretended we were Cousy, Russell, Heinsohn, Satch, and the Jones boys. In December and January we cut the tips off gloves and played with frosted fingertips. Occasionally, we'd make a trip into Boston. In the spring of 1963, I saw the Celtics in person for the first time because Cousy was retiring and my dad wanted me to be able to say that I saw him play. Four years later, I took the train in from Ayer, Massachusetts, during school vacation week and watched an NBA doubleheader: 76ers-Knicks, followed by Celtics-Warriors. Two games featuring four NBA teams for the princely sum of three bucks.

My brother, Bill, six years older than me, was a star high school player in our small town of Groton (population 4,000). When Bill told me he'd made the varsity basketball team, I asked him what position he played, and he said, "Center. Same as Bill Russell." Bill Shaughnessy was a whopping six foot one. Decades later, while killing time at a Phoenix hotel bar after a Celtics-Suns game, my brother regaled future Hall of Famer Dennis Johnson with tales of his high school basketball prowess. DJ—a six-four NBA guard—looked down at the top of my brother's head and said, "Come on, Bill, what position did you really play?"

Going to my brother's high school games was my first experience with loud, crowded gyms. The high school gym on winter Friday nights was the most exciting place in town. I was too young to attend Bill's weeknight contests, but the high school was only a half mile across a small valley from our house, and the gym lights were visible through my bedroom window when I lay in bed. I remember staring at the glow from those distant translucent windows, wondering about the magical performances that might even then be occurring inside the warm, loud gym.

Basketball is the game for everyman. You can always play, even if you're alone—a great benefit in a small town with vast acreage and few houses. You could always work on your game, narrating play-by-play in your head like Johnny Most. I was never very good. I had heavy legs, and my deadly shooting touch seemed to disappear when the shots mattered (yes, I was a choke artist), but making varsity basketball in my sophomore year of high school was life changing. Billy Crystal wrote of this in *700 Sundays*, thanking his high school coach for keeping him on the squad, saying, "It remains the nicest thing anyone has ever done for me."

My favorite color is orange—the color of the ball and the rim.

Basketball was born in Springfield, Massachusetts, just seventy-three miles from Groton, and I agree with Dennis Hopper's "Shooter" Flatch, the drunken dad in *Hoosiers*, who said basketball is "the greatest game ever invented."

It's a sport you can carry into old age. I stopped playing pickup games twenty years ago, but as long as you can stand and shoot, you can play. Old-man driveway basketball is meditation on asphalt.

In the COVID-19 spring of 2020, ESPN's *Last Dance* featured Michael Jordan's career, entertaining locked-down Americans and reviving interest in the 1980s NBA. With no live action, television networks dug into video vaults and broadcast grainy replays of ancient NBA championships. This meant rebroadcasts of Celtics classics from the 1980s, when I was the team's beat reporter for the *Boston Globe*. Night after night, I saw my twenty-nine-year-old self, wearing gigantic Michael Caine glasses, sitting a few feet from the Celtics bench, typing feverishly as Bird hit another step-back jumper. Press row was adjacent to the bench. I could hear Robert Parish yelling, "By yourself!," when Cedric Maxwell switched off to guard Kareem Abdul-Jabbar on a mismatch in the low post.

In the lockdown days of 2020, I spent hours shooting hoops in my driveway, thinking about a long-ago time when writing about the Boston Celtics was my everyday job for four seasons. Newspaper coverage still mattered to professional sports teams in the 1980s, and the Celtics accommodated scribes from Boston's daily rags. This meant we flew with the players on early-morning commercial flights, waited for bags, and rode the buses with the team. We stayed in the same (then mediocre) hotels. There were lots of breakfasts, lunches, and late-night beers with Larry Bird and his teammates. At the empty gyms before practices, we even occasionally shot a few hoops while players were being taped. Covering the Celtics under those conditions was like being on the team—without the fame, money, or groupies.

"You lived with us and we liked that," Bill Walton said in 2021. "We enjoyed that because diversity and inclusion makes for better everything. The fact that you guys were all there made it more interesting. You always brought fresh questions, enthusiasm, and ideas. It made us better."

When the NBA returned in late July of 2020, play resumed in a 220-acre ESPN Orlando Sports Complex known as the Bubble. It was an age of masks, social distancing, and isolation aimed at preventing coronavirus transmission. It cost $54,000 to send a reporter into the Bubble, and only ten independent outlets paid the fee. Bubble scribes were required to sign waivers pledging that if they spotted a player or a coach outside of official media access periods, they wouldn't approach. The contract eliminated all possibility of reporters informally interacting with players and coaches and pulled the final curtain on the access that had made covering teams fun and informative in the Stone Age when Bird and Maxwell roamed the earth. Hardworking reporters who cover the Celtics today will never get to know Jaylen Brown or Jayson Tatum the way we knew Bird, Walton, and Dennis Johnson.

This is that story.

CHAPTER 2

"ACCEPTING THOSE BEERS WOULD MAKE HIM BEHOLDEN TO YOU"

NBA teams on the road in 2021 stay at the Four Seasons, the Ritz, or the nearest available resort. They fly in private jets and consume only the finest wines, meats, and cheeses. They never touch their own luggage and rarely interact with fans or media. They live in a bubble, and we're not talking about the COVID-19 Bubble at Disney World in 2020.

In late October of 1982, the Boston Celtics, on the eve of their thirty-seventh season, checked into a musty Holiday Inn in Richfield, Ohio. Each room at the Holiday Inn featured color television, air-conditioning, and individually wrapped bars of soap only a little thicker than a book of matches. The Holiday Inn's "minibar" was the vending machine near the steamy, rank indoor pool by the lobby bathrooms. The cheap drapes in the rooms fluttered when the wind whipped outside the hotel. Snowflakes sometimes feathered through window seams. Guests were required to pull their room door shut to secure the lock.

In 1982, no one was stalking this joint in search of NBA superstars. The Larry Bird Celtics were already established as champions and basketball royalty. They'd won the franchise's fourteenth banner just seventeen months earlier, and there was every reason to believe they'd be going back to the Finals for several seasons to come. But there were no New England transplants living in Shaker Heights trying to

17

find the Celtics in the dank lobby of the Holiday Inn; no autograph-seeking greenflies, no overdressed, high-heeled young women in search of a wealthy basketball star. The Richfield Holiday Inn catered to bored businessmen and conventioneers.

The Holiday Inn was a couple of miles from the twenty-thousand-seat Richfield Coliseum, a spacious oval situated halfway between Cleveland and Akron. Harvey Greene, public relations director of the Cavaliers in the early 1980s, often drove out-of-town sportswriters back to the Holiday Inn after games because cabs wouldn't come to the arena late at night.

"My biggest fear working for the Cavs was the drive home from the Coliseum late at night during the winter," said Greene. "The first part of that drive was the one-mile stretch from the Coliseum to the Holiday Inn on a narrow, winding, desolate two-lane road through a thick forest in almost total darkness. I was always afraid I'd either hit a deer or skid on an ice patch off the road and into a ditch, never to be found. Toward the end of that drive, the Holiday Inn would magically appear in front of me like a beacon, bathed in the only light to be seen in that desolation. There was nothing else around. It reminded me of the approach leading up to the Bates Motel."

On the eve of the first game of the 1982–83 season, the Holiday Inn's restaurant/bar, Barney Google's, was empty except for Larry Bird and Quinn Buckner, who sat at one end of the bar near the overhead television. The Celtics had held their final practice of the preseason earlier that day before boarding a Northwest Airlines flight to Cleveland.

It had been an emotional week as Celtics players said goodbye to teammates Chris Ford and Eric Fernsten, both members of the 1980–81 championship squad. Fernsten was a popular, seldom-used big man, cut because the Celtics used their 1982 first-round pick on the six-eleven but extremely limited Darren Tillis. A terrific practice player who'd been Bird's teammate for the first three years of Bird's career, Fernsten was released just a few hours before the flight to Cleveland.

Ford was a ten-year veteran who'd played four seasons in Boston. He planned on playing at least one more year, but lost his backcourt job to NBA veteran Buckner, who'd been acquired in an off-season deal with the Bucks. Ford had started at guard alongside Tiny Archibald when the Celtics won the championship in 1981. Teammates called Ford "Doc," a nickname slapped on Ford by Cedric Maxwell when the gravity-challenged Ford made a Julius Erving–like cradle-rocking dunk attempt during an otherwise forgettable practice.

That's how it works in team sports. At every level. An insignificant moment can stay with a player forever. In my high school in the 1960s, a kid named Dave Martin screwed up the end of a practice, missing a layup that would have sent everybody home for the day. When Dave's layup clanged off the rim—adding another twenty minutes to practice—a teammate screamed, "Jesus, Martin!," which became Dave Martin's name for the rest of his Groton life. More than forty years after the silly episode, I came out of a restroom at the Fours across the street from the Garden and encountered a young man with his sixtysomething dad. The young man said, "Dan, we're from Groton. This is my father, Dave Martin."

"Jesus?" I asked.

Affirmative.

An Atlantic City native who starred at Villanova, Chris Ford lives forever in trivia lore as the first man to make an NBA three-point shot. He wound up doing Celtics radio commentary the year he was cut by Bill Fitch, then rejoined the team as an assistant coach and eventually became head coach. On October 28, 1982, Bird, for the first time in his career, was grappling with the reality that Ford and Fernsten were not his teammates.

I'd made a point to introduce myself to Bird at media day and talked to him in reporter scrums during a preseason that included road trips to San Antonio and Nashville. The young Celtics superstar was shy and abrupt, clearly not comfortable with new people. He didn't speak with reporters during his celebrated senior season at Indiana State. He endured interviews like a child getting a polio vaccine.

Bird was a national sensation when he led Indiana State to a 33-0 season and the NCAA title game against Magic Johnson's Michigan State Spartans in 1979. The Larry-Magic NCAA Final will forever be the highest-rated basketball television broadcast of all time. Bird never got over losing that game and was still carrying the hurt after winning NBA Rookie of the Year in 1980 and his first championship in 1981. He'd established himself as one of the best players in the NBA, but he was still obsessed with beating Magic.

Buckner was no stranger to fame and success. He grew up near Chicago where he was a high school state champ, then cocaptained Bobby Knight's 1976 NCAA champion Hoosiers, still the last undefeated team in NCAA history. He cocaptained the USA's gold-medal-winning team at the 1976 Summer Olympics. Selected by Milwaukee with the seventh overall pick in 1976, he played six seasons for the Bucks before he was traded to Boston. His Indiana/Knight/Midwest connections and winning pedigree made him an ideal teammate and drinking buddy for Larry Bird.

I knew enough not to approach when I saw Bird and Buckner at the bar. I was the new guy. Worse, I was a reporter. They had a lot of catching up to do. Probably swapping Bobby Knight stories. Still, it had been a long day and I was thirsty and had my newspapers to keep me company. I nodded in their direction as I pulled out a stool and took a seat at the loser end of the bar. Buckner nodded back. Bird took a swig from his bottle of Bud and looked straight ahead.

When the barkeep approached, I ordered something for myself and asked him to send a couple of beers to the fellows at the other end. When Buckner and Bird got their beers, Buckner raised his bottle and again nodded in my direction. Still nothing from Larry.

Ten or fifteen minutes passed and nobody else came into the bar. Bird and Buckner were safely out of earshot and everything was cool.

Until I blundered.

I haven't thought about this in almost forty years and wish I could go back in time and change the moment, but I can't.

Before I settled my tab and got up to leave, I sent another round their way. It was a moment of nervousness and insanity, violating every social and professional drinking code known to man. My face turns crimson just thinking about it.

At that juncture of my professional life, I'd been around famous athletes for more than seven years. I'd spent four seasons on the road with the perennial pennant-winning Baltimore Orioles—a team that included Hall of Famers Earl Weaver, Brooks Robinson, Jim Palmer, Cal Ripken, and Frank Robinson. I'd had lunch with Reggie Jackson—at his request. I'd interviewed Ted Williams and Joe DiMaggio and engaged in conversations with Richard Nixon and Ted Kennedy. I was neither starstruck nor clumsy around famous people. I was three years older than Bird, for God sakes. So how could I have been so ham-handed and stupid?

When the barkeep made the approach with my pathetic offer of another round, Bird shook his head. I cringed. A new writer sending down one beer was suspicious, but tolerable. Offering a second round was a boundary violation. They must have been thinking, "What's this new guy trying to do? Does he think he can buy his way into the inner sanctum?"

It was the most humiliating rejection I'd felt since my first high school mixer when Temple Bruner shook her head after I'd shuffled across the cafeteria floor to ask her to slow dance to "A Whiter Shade of Pale."

Bird was right. I deserved to have my shot blocked. I'd established that the new guy was a tone-deaf weirdo who couldn't be trusted. The Celtics' biggest star, predisposed to keep his distance from writers, now had good reason to steer clear of me. And the Celtics hadn't even played their first game of the season yet.

"I can tell you what that was," Buckner told me thirty-seven years later. "Larry was advanced with his thinking. Was then. Is now. Accepting those beers would make him beholden to you. He didn't want that to be a debt he'd have to pay if you asked him a question he didn't want to answer. He wanted to have control."

Larry Joe Bird was born in rural southern Indiana on December

7, 1956 (the same day Bill Russell and K. C. Jones left the Melbourne Olympics with gold medals), the fourth of Joe and Georgia Bird's six children. He had two older brothers, Mike and Mark, and an older sister, Linda. After Larry, Georgia gave birth to two more boys, Jeff and Eddie. Larry's dad, Joe Bird, was uneducated but had been a fairly good basketball player before he left high school and went to work in his early teens. He served his country in the Korean War and bounced from job to job when he came home. The work he liked best was finishing instruments at the Kimball Piano and Organ plant. When Larry was a small boy, one of the pianos Joe Bird worked on was supposed to be featured on a national television show, and the family gathered around their tiny black-and-white TV to see Dad's piano on television. The segment never aired.

Like her husband, Georgia Bird changed jobs a lot. She worked at a chicken farm, a shoe factory, and a nursing home. She was a waitress and a cook. But there was never money for a family car, and the Birds were always moving. Larry remembered the embarrassment of his family running up $700 worth of credit at a local store. All of the Bird boys took turns living with their maternal grandparents, John and Lizzie Kerns. John and Lizzie's house was near a streetlight, which allowed the boys to play their basketball games at night. When they weren't playing ball or doing chores, the Bird kids were hunting mushrooms, a favorite southern-Indiana pastime. Bird's favorite TV show was *Bonanza*, which featured a family that lacked for nothing.

Larry grew to be the tallest boy in his first-grade class and was forever trying to keep up with his sports-minded older brothers. Younger brothers often make the best ballplayers. Ask youth sports coaches. Children who grow up chasing older siblings "play up," and it's an advantage when they finally start playing against kids their own age. Call it the George Brett syndrome (the Hall of Fame third baseman had three ball-playing older brothers). Larry Bird was a classic case. He played ball because his older brothers played ball. Mark and Mike made him tough, and better than most kids his own age. They had a ritual of wiping their hands on the soles of their sneakers for better floor traction, something Larry did instinctively until the day he retired.

Jim Jones, a former University of Indiana baseball player, ran the youth basketball program in French Lick and had a big impact on Bird's early days. Larry played in Jones's Biddy Ball program when Larry was in the third grade. Jones taught the boys how to box out and shoot free throws. He encouraged the right-handed Bird to learn to use his left hand, which came fairly naturally to a boy who wrote and ate left-handed. Jones stressed fundamentals and practice, twin pillars of Larry Bird's game.

When he was thirteen, Bird enrolled in Springs Valley High School after his family moved to French Lick (population 2,000). He was six-one as a sophomore, but lost almost all of that season due to a broken ankle. Unable to run, he practiced his passing from a stationary position while propped up by a crutch. He wore number 33 because that was the number Mark Bird had worn. Larry was six-three by his junior year and lived for basketball, leading a breakfast club of teammates who got up at 6:30 a.m. to go to the gym and practice free throws every morning before school. One of his best friends, "Beezer" Carnes, rarely showed for the extra work. Springs Valley coach Gary Holland and Bird warned Beezer that it would cost him someday. Sure enough, in a regional final of the Indiana high school basketball tournament Beezer missed the front end of three one-and-ones and cost Springs Valley the game.

"I just looked at him and he knew," Bird remembered.

By his senior season Larry Bird was six-seven, playing every position and rarely missing a free throw. His play lured the legendary Knight to French Lick during the 1973–74 high school season. Knight was Hoosier hoop royalty, and scouts from the northern part of Indiana generally didn't think much of players from the southern part of the state.

Bird averaged almost 30 points per game in his final season. He hoped to draw interest from Kentucky's blue-chip program and made the 135-mile recruiting visit to Lexington with his parents, but Wildcat coach Joe B. Hall concluded Bird would have trouble getting his shot off in the SEC. Instead of Bird, Hall recruited another large player who was even slower: New Orleans's Rick Robey. It was a slight Bird never forgot.

With Kentucky out of the picture, Bird narrowed his choices to Indiana and Indiana State. In the spring of his senior year of high school, he chose Knight's more prestigious program, much to the delight of Georgia Bird. Larry would be the first in the family to graduate college, and he'd be playing less than fifty miles from home.

Late in the summer of 1974, Larry's uncle drove him to Bloomington and dropped him off at college. Still seventeen, Bird arrived on campus with $75, one pair of slacks, and one pair of sneakers. He was intimidated by the size of the lecture halls and the wardrobe of his roommate, fellow recruit Jim Wisman. Knight didn't have time for freshmen, and Bird didn't get much love from the star players on campus (Big Man on Campus Kent Benson would live to regret this years later when Bird torched him in the NBA). Indiana's freshmen recruits were frozen out of Assembly Hall workouts, so Bird occasionally played two-on-two outdoors with varsity stars Scott May and Bobby Wilkerson. It was there that Bird borrowed and refined May's step-back jumper. A weapon designed to create space for a player without great leaping ability, May's step-back was the most critical lesson Bird learned from his brief experience at Bloomington.

Bird was intimidated by what he experienced on campus. The preppie young people at IU were nothing like folks back home in French Lick and West Baden. They had money and polish. Bird had neither. He still hadn't been in an airplane.

After twenty-four days, Bird put his stuff in a duffel bag and hitchhiked back to French Lick without notifying Knight.

Buckner was touring overseas with a US amateur team during Bird's short time in Bloomington.

"I never saw Larry at Indiana," Buckner said. "My brother, Lorin, was two years behind me at IU, and when I got back from the tournament, I asked him, 'Where's Bird?,' and he said, 'Quinn, I think I saw him on Route Thirty-Seven South with his luggage. I think he went home!'"

When Bird showed up in French Lick, his mother didn't speak to him for a month. He moved in with his grandmother and took a town job cutting trees, sweeping streets, painting signs, unplugging sewers, and collecting garbage. He started playing basketball in local leagues, and it wasn't long before Indiana State came back with the same scholarship offer Bird had turned down a year earlier.

Meanwhile, Joe Bird's drinking led to divorce, and the depressed father of six moved in with his own parents, kept drinking, and had trouble making child-support payments. After the 1974 holidays came and went, it was all too much.

In his autobiography, *Drive*, written with the *Globe*'s Bob Ryan, Bird wrote of his father's suicide:

> He said, "Things will be better off for you, your mom, Eddie, and Jeff if I go ahead and take my life." . . . I could tell from looking in his eyes that he was going to do it. . . . I don't think he spent a lot of time thinking about it. I believe he made the decision quickly. He was a couple of weeks behind on his pay-ments to Mom, and the police were sent out to my grandfather's house to get him. He said, "Can I have until this afternoon to get some bills straightened out?" And they said, "Fine." But he knew that was the end of it. He had said he would never spend a day in jail; he was too proud for that. . . . He went to the bar, ordered half a pint—that's what they tell me—and then went back to my grandfather's house to drink it. He called Mom up and told her exactly what he was going to do. . . . He got off the phone, took a shotgun, and killed himself. . . . I know in my mind he thought he was doing something to help the family financially. It wasn't insurance money, but Social Security. My mom received some money from his being in the service and it did help us out. But I would have given anything to just go on living the way we were than to have to lose my father.

It was all part of Bird's tumultuous "gap year." Still a teenager, the gifted but troubled young man in a short time lost his dad, enrolled at Indiana State, married and divorced high school classmate Janet Condra, became a father (Janet gave birth to Corrie after the divorce), and met Dinah Mattingly, his lifelong partner, whom he'd marry in 1989.

Bird regretted his hasty first marriage and was never a presence in the life of his daughter, Corrie.

"That was a very rough time in my life," he wrote, ". . . what with my father's death, changing colleges, and the entire marriage/divorce/baby situation. I remember thinking, 'What's going on with my life?'"

NCAA guidelines forced Bird to sit out his freshman season at State, but he practiced with the team and the Sycamores knew what was coming in 1976–77 when he finally hit the court. State went 25-3 with Bird averaging 32.8 points, third best in the nation and good enough for third-team All-America. Before the start of his junior season, he was featured on the cover of *Sports Illustrated*, flanked by a pair of ISU cheerleaders and accompanied by the headline "College Basketball's Secret Weapon." *Sports Illustrated* was a kingmaker in those days, and the cover changed Bird's life.

The Sycamores slumped in Bird's junior season, finishing second in the Missouri Valley Conference and losing to Rutgers in the NIT, but Bird was a first-team All-American. In April, he played with Michigan State's Magic Johnson on the USA's World Invitational Tournament team coached by Joe B. Hall. Once again, Hall disrespected Bird's talents, regularly playing him (and Magic) behind Kentucky stars—including Robey and Kyle Macy—who were not as good.

"That was the first time I got to meet Larry," Robey said. "We were together about a month. We trained in North Carolina. I got to know him pretty good then. Larry just had that attitude and will to win, and it rubbed off on all of us. Magic and Bird always got on Coach Hall cuz he started his UK players ahead of them. Larry never forgot about that."

The tournament was scouted by Red Auerbach, who understood the Kentucky bias. Bird reminded Auerbach of a six-nine Cousy.

Bird pledged to play his senior season at Indiana State, but the

Celtics didn't care. They were coming off a 32-50 season and had two first-round picks in the 1978 draft. Bird was draft-eligible because he was originally in the NCAA class of 1978, but a team drafting Bird risked wasting the selection if it was unable to sign Bird before the 1979 draft. Multiple teams, including Indiana and Portland, met with Bird in an effort to get him to commit if they selected him, but Bird wouldn't do it. He wanted to go back for his senior season at Indiana State and said he would entertain professional offers only after his senior season. Any team drafting him in 1978 would have to live with the risk. He went golfing on the morning of the 1978 NBA draft.

Undaunted, Auerbach believed he could sell the Celtics mystique. On June 9, 1978, Celtics vice president Jan Volk represented the Celtics in New York while Auerbach hosted a draft party at the Blades and Boards Club in the old Garden. Five teams—Portland (Mychal Thompson), Kansas City (Phil Ford), Indiana (Robey), New York (Michael Ray Richardson), and Golden State (Purvis Short)—passed on Bird. With the decks clear, after a sigh of relief, Volk selected Bird with the sixth pick of the draft. Boston used its other first-round pick on Portland State's Freeman Williams.

It was the beginning of a twelve-month recruiting effort that went to the deadline.

While the 1978–79 Sycamores were on their way to 33-0, they received regular visits from Celtics family members, including Auerbach, Heinsohn, Cowens, and K. C. Jones. Meanwhile, the Celtics won fewer games than Indiana State, finishing 29-53 for the second-worst record in franchise history.

When the Indiana State season ended, Auerbach tried to get Bird to play the final eight games of the 1978–79 NBA season with the last-place Celtics. Bird declined. He'd promised his mom he'd get his degree, and he had to complete student-teaching obligations to fulfill graduation requirements. This sent him to West Vigo High School in Terre Haute, where he served as a physical-education and health teacher. Bird's duties included teaching a class of special-needs students, plus courses in CPR and driver's education. No doubt, there are adults in rural southern Indiana who today tell friends they once had Larry Bird as a driver's ed instructor.

In the spring of 1979, a group of Terre Haute businessmen formed a committee to help Bird find an agent. They screened as many as forty-five candidates and came up with Bob Woolf, a Boston-based glad-hander who'd represented scores of professional clients and been dumped by many. Auerbach hated Woolf.

"They couldn't stand each other," Bird said years later. "Red was always a little pissed that I chose Woolf and stayed with him. It was funny as hell."

There was ample speculation, never proven, that Woolf won the right to represent Bird by offering a discount for his services. The agent was down on his luck in 1979 and knew his career would soar on the wings of Bird. Negotiations with the Celtics were predictably combustible, but one week before the deadline, the parties agreed to terms on a five-year, $3.25 million contract. One of Bird's first purchases was a modest brick ranch home ($137,000) with a two-car garage on Newton Street near Route 9 in Brookline—catty-corner from the home of Bob Woolf. Newton Street neighbors got used to seeing a six-nine blond man cutting the grass.

Dinah Mattingly, the woman in Bird's life who'd helped the young man keep everything together while so many things happened when he was nineteen, accompanied Bird to rustic Camp Milbrook in Marshfield, Massachusetts, for his first rookie camp in August of 1979. Bird was unimpressed with the outdoor courts, claiming some of the rims weren't precisely ten feet off the ground. Paying no attention to the objections of his rookie phenom, Auerbach blew a puff of smoke, looked at Mattingly, and huffed, "What is *she* doing here?"

For the second time in ten years, Auerbach was rebuilding the Celtics. He was assembling his third dynasty, a team that would win the final three championships of his lifetime. He had Bird and was readying to add Robert Parish, Kevin McHale, Danny Ainge, Dennis

Johnson, and Bill Walton. All but Ainge are in the Basketball Hall of Fame, and they became the core of the 1985–86 Boston Celtics, perhaps the best NBA team of all time. Every one was a steal.

In 1979, Bird was the only one already in place, joining a team that went from bad to great more quickly than any other team in the history of the sport. After winning only 29 while they were waiting for Bird, the 1979–80 Celtics went 61-21, an improvement of 32 wins — at the time the greatest single-season turnaround in league history.

Former Cavaliers coach Bill Fitch was Boston's new boss in 1979–80, and his arrival marked the first time Auerbach went outside the Celtics family to hire a head coach. Fitch was an Iowa native with zero connections to the Celtics or Boston. Red's bringing Fitch to Boston was like Vito Corleone turning over his family business to the non-Italian consigliere Tom Hagen.

Fitch was tough and affable, an ex-marine who bragged about his days coaching baseball and basketball at Creighton University, where his star player in both sports was future St. Louis Cardinals Hall of Famer Bob Gibson. Fitch had been head basketball coach at North Dakota State, Bowling Green, and the University of Minnesota, making his NBA bones as coach of the expansion Cavaliers. He took the Cavs to the playoffs three times in nine seasons and was NBA Coach of the Year in 1976. He was a control freak and an authority figure. Auerbach correctly believed that Bird would respond well to Fitch's discipline.

Bird knew little about the NBA and had never heard of Fitch. When Fitch chatted with Bird at a club function before the start of practices, Bird thought he was talking with a Celtics fan, and Fitch had to tell him, "Larry, I'm Bill Fitch. Your new coach."

Fitch got Bird's attention in an early preseason practice when the coach observed notorious layabout Curtis Rowe jogging and fired Rowe on the spot. A star and champion at UCLA, Rowe was an NBA bowser, known for telling teammates that wins and losses don't show up on your paycheck.

Not all of the other Celtics were on board with Fitch's autocratic style. Maxwell was a third-year player who'd demonstrated he belonged in the league but was periodically unmotivated. Another important starter was nine-year guard Tiny Archibald, a wildly talented and famously moody point guard who had once led the NBA in scoring and assists in the same season. Robey—Joe B. Hall's favorite—was acquired from Indiana, but the important big man in this lineup was Dave Cowens, perhaps the most underrated of all Celtics superstars.

Entering his tenth season, Cowens was wearing down physically and emotionally. He'd been a league Rookie of the Year and Most Valuable Player. He'd won two championship rings, including one from 1974 when he outplayed the half-foot-taller Kareem Abdul-Jabbar in a Game 7 win in Milwaukee. Cowens dove on the floor and demanded hard work from teammates, officials, and team employees. He was a fan favorite and a Renaissance man. He grew up on a Christmas tree farm in Kentucky, lived in a cabin in the woods, wore flannel shirts, and once took a job driving a cab around Boston just for the fun of it. The night he won his first NBA championship, Cowens over-celebrated and woke up the next morning on a park bench on the Boston Common.

M. L. Carr was the other new guy in Bird's first pro camp. He'd played his college ball at tiny Guilford (in North Carolina), in Israel, and for two ABA franchises before joining the NBA's Detroit Pistons. In between basketball jobs, Carr worked as a guard at the Lewisburg federal prison in Pennsylvania. After four good solid seasons with the Pistons, he earned free agency and signed with the Celtics.

"I tried to hide M.L. in Israel, but the goddamned American Basketball Association found out about him," Auerbach said. "He just had a winning way about him."

Carr was a six-six swingman who could defend and get into the heads of opponents. He did not need the ball to beat you. He would be a perfect "glue guy" for the next Celtics dynasty.

The addition of Carr came with future considerations that changed the course of Celtics history. How those extras changed the Celtics' future takes a few lines to explain.

In the spring of 1979, the Celtics were owned by Kentucky Fried Chicken magnate John Y. Brown, who formerly owned the ABA's Kentucky Colonels and had no use for Auerbach's vision. In February of '79, Brown—in an effort to impress his fiancée, former Miss America Phyllis George—acquired Buffalo Braves scoring champ Bob McAdoo in a deal with the Knicks. Brown made the trade without consulting Auerbach, who threatened to resign. McAdoo played only twenty games for the last-place Celtics. When the dismal season ended, Brown sold the Celtics to Harry Mangurian, who became one of Auerbach's favorite Celtics owners. In the summer of '79, Auerbach, back in power, made a deal with Pistons coach and general manager Dick Vitale, trading McAdoo as compensation in return for free agent Carr and two first-round picks, including Detroit's first pick in 1980.

Things worked out well for all parties. Brown married Phyllis George and went on to become governor of Kentucky. George became a television superstar with the NFL on CBS and a beloved first lady of Kentucky. Vitale was fired by the Pistons after twelve games in 1979, but found fame and fortune as ESPN's voice of college basketball. McAdoo played only fifty-eight games with the Pistons, but wound up winning two rings with the Lakers before he was inducted into the Basketball Hall of Fame. The 1979–80 Pistons went 16-66, which made their top pick—owned by Boston in 1980—the first pick in the entire draft. Auerbach used the pick to assemble two-thirds of the greatest frontcourt in NBA history.

Auerbach believed Minnesota's Kevin McHale was the best player in the '80 draft, but he knew the Warriors coveted Purdue center Joe Barry Carroll. Golden State had the number three pick. Believing McHale would still be available at number three, Auerbach swapped his top pick and the number thirteen pick to the Warriors in exchange for Golden State's top pick, plus hidden-gem center Robert Parish. Auerbach acquired the player he wanted in the first place—McHale—plus Parish as a throw-in. All for Joe Barry Carroll. Parish wound up playing more NBA games than anyone else in history and winning four championship rings—one more than either Bird or McHale.

31

Auerbach received full credit for the swindle, which created a problem at the top of the Celtics pyramid. In 1979, Fitch was far more current regarding NBA player personnel, and Fitch was the one who coveted Parish. The Chief was good in his four seasons with the Warriors, but Fitch saw potential greatness. Parish ran the court better than any other NBA center and, in the best Celtics tradition, didn't need the ball to beat you. He was stoic and selfless. What Parish lacked was a strong supporting cast and a coach who could motivate. The Celtics had both.

Maneuvering to select Bill Russell in the 1956 draft is the most important move of Auerbach's career. It required dealing Ed Macauley and Cliff Hagan to St. Louis (the Hawks had the second overall pick) and cutting a second deal with the Rochester Royals to guarantee they wouldn't select Russell with their number one pick. NBA owners in the 1950s made deals like this all the time. NBA owners were arena landlords, interesting in winter programming that would pay the heating bills. Rochester's Lester Harrison and Boston's Walter Brown were two such owners. In exchange for not taking Russell, the Royals were promised an annual visit from the Ice Capades, a popular skating show owned by Brown. This is how the Rochester Royals wound up selecting the immortal Sihugo Green instead of Bill Russell with the first pick of the 1956 draft.

The second-best move of Auerbach's GM career was the gamble to select Bird and wait a year to sign him.

Red's bronze medal performance was the Carr/McAdoo/Carroll/Parish/McHale parlay. With special thanks for John Y. Brown, Phyllis George, and Dick Vitale.

Playing without Parish and McHale in his rookie season, Bird made the Celtics contenders again immediately.

"You could tell the first day," said Cowens, who played his final Boston season the year Bird was a rookie (much as veteran Cousy had teamed with rookie Havlicek for one transition year). "People always say he wasn't fast, but Bird was quick. He had a great first step and could get by people. And he could handle the ball with that first step.

He had a quick mind and a quick release. There wasn't anything that he did not do well. He was a really tough cover for the other team."

Bird quickly established himself as NBA-ready with his full arsenal of shooting, passing, rebounding, and diving after loose balls. He averaged 21 points, 10 rebounds, and won Rookie of the Year in 1979–80. Starting point guard Archibald recovered from an Achilles problem and averaged 14 points a game, and Maxwell led the league in field goal percentage. Owing to Bird's popularity, the Celtics started selling out every home game. They swept the Houston Rockets in the first round of the playoffs, but were beaten in the second round by a Philly team that featured Julius Erving, Caldwell Jones, Bobby Jones, and Darryl Dawkins.

With Parish and rookie McHale on board the following year, the Larry Bird Celtics won their first championship in the spring of 1981. The lasting memory of that title run was an epic, seven-game Eastern Conference final against the same Sixers who'd beaten Boston during Bird's rookie year. The Celtics trailed the series, three games to one and came back from a 6-point deficit to win Game 5. Game 6 in Philadelphia is remembered for an episode when Maxwell lunged into the stands for a loose ball and wound up getting into a fight with a Sixers fan. A blocked shot by McHale sent the series back to Boston, where the Celtics and Sixers engaged in hand-to-hand combat for the full forty-eight before Bird won it with an 18-foot bank shot.

Boston won the '81 Finals against Moses Malone and the Houston Rockets in six games. Malone spiced up the series after Game 4 when he said he could recruit four nobodies from his hometown of Petersburg, Virginia, and still beat the Celtics. When the Celtics took a huge lead in Game 5, Maxwell found Malone and said, "You'd better find those damn boys from Petersburg because the ones you got right now ain't working for you."

Max bagged the Finals MVP Award when the Celtics won the championship in Game 6 in Houston, and a champagne-drenched Bird pulled a stogie from Auerbach's hand and put it in his own mouth while he flashed a V-for-victory sign. Days later, when the

Celtics gathered at City Hall Plaza for a championship rally, Bird spotted a banner in the crowd that read MOSES EATS SHIT and told the crowd, "You're right. Moses does eat shit."

In the spring of 1982, the Celtics made it back to the Eastern Conference finals and engaged in another seven-game brawl with Philadelphia. For a second straight spring, the Celtics fell behind, 3-1, then rallied to force a seventh game at the Garden. Boston fans taunted the spooked Sixers with signage ridiculing Philly's players as choking dogs, but Dr. J. and Co. were up to the task and beat the Celtics decisively. When the imminent defeat was obvious, Celtics fans sent the Sixers to the finals with a gracious chant of "Beat LA."

The squandered opportunity stayed with Bird.

"After I won the first one, I thought I was gonna win five or six in a row," he said. "I thought we had a good enough team."

It was on to the 1982–83 season, which started at the woebegone Richfield Coliseum and ended in disarray.

CHAPTER 3

"CHIEF JUST HAD A DISDAIN FOR YOUR ASS"

L ike the Celtics franchise, the *Boston Globe* sports staff was a pow-erhouse in the early 1980s. The *Globe*'s roster featured ten writers who'd eventually be honored in their respective Halls of Fame. The *Globe* had Will McDonough on football, Peter Gammons on base-ball, Bob Ryan on basketball, Fran Rosa on hockey, and Bud Collins on tennis. These men invented Sunday notes columns, which would become staples of major metropolitan daily newspapers in the final golden decades of the print press. The *Globe* had Lesley Visser, who would become a television pioneer and make it to the football Hall of Fame; Jack Craig, the first sportswriter who dedicated a column to sports television; and Pulitzer Prize winner John Powers—the last word on every Olympics. Leigh Montville was among the best col-umnists in the country before he became a *Sports Illustrated* feature writer and bestselling author. Photographer Stan Grossfeld, who trav-eled with the Celtics during the playoffs, won two Pulitzers in the 1980s. Ron Borges came on board to cover the Patriots and boxing. The *Globe*'s summer interns were Jackie MacMullan and Ian Thom-sen, who went on to become authors, television personalities, and basketball experts. We had what Earl Weaver called "deep depth."

Sports Illustrated in 2009 declared, "From the mid-1970s to the early '80s, the *Globe* contained arguably the greatest collection of reporting talent ever assembled in a sports section, one that was unrivaled in its time and is sure never to be duplicated."

Vince Doria, who took over as *Globe* sports editor in 1978, recalled, "The *Globe* dominated Boston in those days. It was the voice of the city. It was making a ton of money and plowing that money back into the product. Everybody read the *Globe*. I can't tell you how many people I would run into who'd say, 'I don't like the *Globe*. I don't like its politics. But I buy the paper anyhow to read the sports.'"

Along with Visser and hockey Hall of Famer Kevin Paul Dupont, I graduated from college in 1975 and covered high school sports for the *Globe*. It was an honor to sit alongside annual Massachusetts Sportswriter of the Year Ray Fitzgerald, and to have conversations with McDonough, Ryan, Gammons, and the rest. When those gods of the industry ripped pages from their typewriters and discarded them into trash cans, we'd fetch them out of the baskets and take them home to learn.

It was nearly impossible for a twenty-three-year-old to crack that lineup, so in 1977 I went to the *Baltimore Evening Sun* to cover the Orioles. The job required complete immersion in the beat, flying around the country with a big league team, riding buses with the players, staying in the same hotels, covering their games, emotions, contracts, and conflicts from spring training through the end of the World Series. I moved from the *Sun* to the *Washington Star* in 1979, but didn't stop covering the Orioles until the *Star* went out of business in the summer of 1981. I rejoined the *Globe* staff in '81, and Doria offered me a chance to cover the Celtics when Ryan—the de facto Commissioner of Basketball—took a job at a Boston television station.

Following Ryan at the *Globe* was like filling in for Lou Gehrig at first base for the Yankees. I'd sat next to Ryan at Celtics home games and couldn't believe how well he knew the players, coaches, and referees. I was sitting next to Ryan at a Celtics-Bullets game when a ticky-tacky foul was called on Bullets' enforcer Rick Mahorn and Washington coach Gene Shue wheeled toward the press table, pointed his finger at Ryan, and yelled, "That call is *your* fault, Bob

Ryan! *Your* fault!" Ryan had written about Mahorn mugging people, and Shue believed that the power of Ryan's pen was influencing NBA officials.

"Bob can watch us for a week and figure out all of our plays," gushed Bird.

The gushing was mutual. I was at Ryan's side on press row when veteran guard Dennis Johnson dribbled toward the press table in midgame and said, "Hey, Bob, can you keep it down about Larry—we got *a game* going on out here!"

If you approached Ryan from behind while he was chatting with NBA commissioner David Stern and uttered, "Excuse me, Commissioner?," both men would turn around.

The Celtics were the hottest team in Boston in 1982. They'd won a championship in Bird's second season and were at the start of a fifteen-year sellout streak that would reach 662 consecutive games. They had the banners, the parquet floor, Auerbach, and Boston's most popular athlete since Bobby Orr. A generation of young New England basketball fans mimicked Bird's unique habit of wiping his hands on the soles of his sneakers on his way onto the floor. The Celtics were must-see TV and an almost impossible ticket unless you had connections or wads of cash.

Basketball was a natural beat for me. I knew the history of the Auerbach/Cousy/Russell Celtics because I'd lived it as a fan. I'd read Cousy's *Basketball Is My Life* and *The Last Loud Roar*. In middle school, I'd bought Johnny Most's record album, *Havlicek Stole the Ball*. While riding the bench for the Groton High varsity, I covered the team, writing under the pseudonym Lancer. In our season opener on a December Friday in Littleton, I came off the bench and missed a couple of free throws at the end of a close game. Correspondent Lancer had no choice but to rip benchwarmer Shaughnessy for choking at the line.

During my Holy Cross years, I covered three summers of the Boston Neighborhood Basketball League for the *Globe*. The BNBL took me to sixteen Boston neighborhood playgrounds, part of a *Globe* initiative to diffuse racial tension during the combustible days of court-ordered desegregation. I covered college hoops in Baltimore and Washington and occasionally traveled with the Bullets. I'd sat along-side Bullet rookie Mitch Kupchak (he knew a lot about baseball) on a road trip to Atlanta and rode the bus with the Bullets the night they won their only NBA championship in Seattle in 1978. Writing about pro basketball was fun. NBA players and coaches were smart, accessible, and colorful. It was easy to bring the sport to life.

The NBA of 1982 would be unrecognizable to any young person around the game today. It was simply not a major American spectator sport. Baseball had been replaced by the mighty NFL as our national pastime, but both sports were still far ahead of the NBA in revenues, TV ratings, and relevance. Seventeen of twenty-three NBA teams lost money in 1982. In 1981 and 1982, NBA Finals weeknight games weren't broadcast on prime-time television by CBS. Replays of the games were dumped into the late-night slots because they were played during the May sweeps and CBS didn't want to bump regularly scheduled prime-time programming in favor of a fringe sport. The NBA delayed the start of its 1981–82 season to avoid clashing with the World Series and to push the start of the Finals past the coveted May sweeps.

Six months before I went on the Celtics beat, I anchored a five-part *Globe* investigative series dealing with the troubles of the NBA. The nine-week project was designed to shine a light on a struggling product. When my calls to Commissioner Larry O'Brien raised red flags in the league office, O'Brien dispatched to Boston his executive vice president: David Stern. None of us had ever heard of Stern. We assumed he was a front-office bean counter who'd feign transparency, then try to steer us away from a negative series. Cordial and erudite, the Columbia-educated Stern arrived at Morrissey Boulevard on a February Friday morning and came upstairs for breakfast in the executive dining room of the *Globe*'s massive Dorchester headquarters. Among those in attendance: Doria, project editor Alan Richman, reporters Larry Whiteside, Jack Craig, Ryan, and me.

I was armed with the negative data and went for the jugular, requesting numbers on how much money the league was losing and how many teams were in danger of folding. After a barrage of pointed questions, Stern looked at my boss and said, "Where'd you get this guy?"

In an effort to disarm us, Stern suggested each reporter submit written requests.

I was looking for financial information. Craig had questions about the league's television deals. Ryan—who'd long held that NBA official Bob Rakel was a menace to the league—used Stern's offer to have some fun and settle an old score: the top request on Ryan's wish list to Stern was "A letter of resignation from Bob Rakel."

When Craig pushed Stern to explain the NBA's weak television ratings, Stern countered that the NBA had attracted more viewers than indoor soccer. With that, our emotional and theatrical sports-TV reporter fell to the floor, pounded his fists into the carpet, and yelled, "Indoor soccer? Please!"

Ryan casually turned to me and said, "Whatever happened to decorum?"

Stern had reason to cite indoor soccer. In that same year, the US Army opted to spend TV sponsorship dollars on indoor soccer rather than the National Basketball Association.

Two months of work produced a five-part series, entitled "The National Basketball Affliction. The NBA: A Major League with Major Problems." Our series logo was an image of a shattered glass backboard. We kicked off the series with my story on conflicts of interest regarding multiple team owners, including the Clippers' Donald Sterling and the Lakers' Jerry Buss.

"A decade ago, pro basketball was being ballyhooed as 'the Sport of the 70's,' a game that would appeal to the masses," we told readers. "But that predicted popularity never materialized. Instead, the National Basketball Assn. finds itself struggling with astronomical salaries, television disinterest, and at least a half-dozen franchises in severe financial straits."

An entire segment of the five-day series was devoted to player salaries. Another to television. Another to race.

Our deep dive into the death of the NBA was not prophetic. Stern succeeded O'Brien as NBA commissioner in 1984 and, with considerable help from Bird, Magic Johnson, and Michael Jordan, built the league into the multibillion-dollar, global, wildly popular league that it is today.

When Craig died in 2010, I called Stern to ask if my recollection of Jack's magic carpet moment was accurate.

"Oh, it happened," said Stern. "He threw himself on the floor. I remember him holding his heart. You guys were writing that the NBA was out of business and broken, and I laid out my rosy history. I still have the clippings from that series in my desk drawer."

This spirited and somewhat contentious relationship with Stern was one of my few connections to the NBA when I was assigned the Celtics beat in the summer of 1982. In an age before infinite data and advanced metrics, Ryan bequeathed his stack of eight-by-eleven spiral-bound yearbooks in which he'd logged game-by-game stats for every Celtics player. It was expected that I'd carry on Ryan's arduous note-taking.

Before doing anything else, I needed to establish a working relationship with Arnold "Red" Auerbach.

Red was sixty-four and hadn't coached a game in fifteen years. His statue in Faneuil Hall Marketplace had yet to be sculpted, but his reputation was already bronzed. He was the most successful coach and the best team builder in the history of American sports. He was gruff, confident, combative, and had no time for chitchat. There was a soft side, but first you had to earn a spot in his circle of trust. Much like his star player, Red wasn't warm with new people.

I grew up worshipping Red, but had doubts about how we'd get along professionally. I'd worked with veteran NBA reporter Steve Hershey at the *Washington Star*, and he'd told me Red moved the *Star*'s press seat to the upper levels of the Garden after Hershey wrote something critical of the Celtics. Red always cared about what was written about him in the Washington newspapers because his wife, Dorothy, was a DC native who never moved to Boston after Red took the job with the Celtics in 1950. When Hershey was banished to the Garden's third level after his negative story, the *Globe*'s Powers tried to intervene on Hershey's behalf, only to be told by Red, "You're Irish. You should understand. You fuck me, I fuck you!"

Enter Will McDonough; a son of South Boston and lifelong friend of gangster Whitey Bulger, Willie was the last of the old-school, news-breaking sports scribes of twentieth-century Boston. Like Red, Willie was all about loyalty and trust. McDonough played every sport as a youth, and as a reporter he developed close relationships with players, coaches, GMs, and owners. He spoke their language. He protected the people he liked and crushed the ones that turned on him ("You fuck me, I fuck you!"). He punched out NFL cornerback Raymond Clayborn when the two argued in the Patriots locker room in 1977 (like Red, Willie was taught to punch first and ask questions later), and he had the thickest Rolodex in Boston sports.

Willie and Red played racquetball weekly and did favors for each other. When Red drove to Harrisonburg, Virginia, to recruit seven-four Ralph Sampson in 1980, McDonough rode shotgun. In 2002, Willie got Red to hire Willie's son, Ryan, as a Celtics intern. Ryan McDonough was general manager of the Phoenix Suns by the time he turned thirty-two.

In the summer of '82, Willie pulled me aside in the *Globe* offices and said, "I talked to Red. I told him you're okay. So it's gonna be all right."

In August, Auerbach hosted his twenty-third annual rookie/free-agent camp at Milbrook in Marshfield, Massachusetts—the place where rookie Bird made fun of the rims in 1979. Milbrook, a former lumber mill and campsite, was owned by Jerry Volk, the father of Jan Volk, who would officially succeed Auerbach as GM in the 1980s. Jan Volk was only thirteen years old when Red had his first basketball camp in Marshfield in 1960.

Even though Milbrook was a rustic site with asphalt courts

and metal backboards, New England kids were thrilled to attend a sleepover camp for a week of basketball instruction by the great Red on Roundball. Auerbach hired collegiate ballplayers as counselors, a good way to evaluate talent for upcoming drafts (Maryland All-American Len Bias was one of Red's "counselors" in 1985). Red spent most of his time at the camp tooling around in a golf cart, but at 4:00 p.m. each day, instruction halted so that campers could watch Celtics draftees and free agents scrimmage on the substandard courts. After the afternoon session, there was a break for dinner, followed by a night scrimmage at the Marshfield High gym. Veteran Celtics sometimes played in the night sessions. It's where Cowens and M. L. Carr first tested rookie Bird in the summer of 1979.

Fitch was cordial when I interviewed him on the first day of camp. The Celtics had drafted six-eleven Darren Tillis with their top pick, and it was clear Tillis wasn't NBA-ready. Fitch tried not to sound disappointed but was obviously underwhelmed.

When the media availability was over, Auerbach approached me and said, "Want to come to dinner with us?"

Thanks, Willie.

We were off to Ming Dynasty, a fairly new establishment off Route 139, close to the high school gym. Red invited a couple of other scribes and Celtics staff members, including public relations director Jeff Twiss, a Vermont native who was in his second year with the team, and PR assistant John Creed, a former Catholic priest who served the franchise in multiple capacities as an administrative assistant. Bird was fond of telling folks, "John Creed gave up God for the Celtics."

Red ordered for the table. After some General Tso's chicken and duck sauce, it was off to the high school gym for the night session. Danny Ainge was the only Celtics veteran there on my first night. I didn't know Ainge, but had seen him try to hit against the Orioles.

When I introduced myself, Ainge asked, "Are you the guy who ripped the Red Sox pitching staff?"

Yes.

"Good," said Ainge. "I like that. We need a little bit more of that around here. A lot of those guys are my friends, and I like to have something to tease them about."

Ainge is one of the most underrated athletes in American professional sports history. Raised in Eugene, Oregon, he had two older brothers (Brett syndrome) and was great at every sport. His dad, Don Ainge, was a three-sport star who played football at the University of Oregon with future Southern Cal coach John Robinson. Don Ainge also tried out for the Red Sox and was friendly with Sox Hall of Famer Bobby Doerr, who would later scout Danny for the Toronto Blue Jays. At North Eugene High School, Ainge was the only high school athlete named a *Parade* All-American in three sports. Notre Dame recruited him as a wide receiver, and the Padres wanted to make him the first pick of the 1977 amateur baseball draft. The Padres backed off when they learned Ainge wanted to play basketball at Brigham Young, but Toronto took him in the fifteenth round, allowing Ainge to play basketball at BYU while pursuing a baseball career with the Blue Jays during the summers. In the spring of 1979, after two winters playing backcourt at BYU, twenty-year-old Ainge broke into the big leagues with the Jays. He played 211 Major League games over parts of three seasons and was three weeks into his third big league campaign when he was selected by Auerbach in the second round (thirty-first pick) of the 1981 NBA draft.

Two factors pushed Ainge from baseball to basketball: the midsummer baseball strike of 1981 and an opportunity to play with Bird. The Jays were surprised and angry when Ainge said he wanted to join the Celtics. After a court battle, the Celtics wound up paying Toronto $800,000 to acquire a career .220 hitter who'd smashed only two home runs in his big league career.

A few months after trying to hit Rich Gossage's fastball, Ainge was at his first Celtics practice, missing almost every shot with the defending world champs. Seated on a gym stage, Maxwell called out each miss.

"One for four . . . two for ten . . . three for fifteen . . . Jesus, why did we get this guy?"

"I hadn't played basketball for a long time because of the court case," Ainge said many years later. "I'd been coaching JV basketball at BYU, waiting for all of the negotiations to take place. So in that first scrimmage, I remember shooting something like five for twenty. When it was over, Fitch came up to me and said, 'Not as easy as you thought, is it, rook?' It was kind of funny to me because, in my mind, it did seem pretty easy. I'd just gotten twenty wide-open shots. I knew I'd make those shots. In my mind, Chris Ford could not guard me, so I was thinking just the opposite of what Bill was trying to make me feel."

In his first NBA season, Ainge played without his typical confidence, shooting 36 percent over 53 games. His new teammates picked on him and knocked him around, but he earned their respect when he bounced back for more.

He didn't smoke or drink, rarely swore, and was already a father of two children at the age of twenty-one. Auerbach loved to poke fun at Ainge's religion:

"Hey, Danny, tell me again—how many wives do you Mormon guys have?"

Spying Ainge playing poker with Bird and McHale, the GM teased, "Hey, Danny, I thought gambling was against the rules."

"Red, it's not gambling against these guys," said Ainge. "It's a sure thing."

Decades later, Timberwolves GM Kevin McHale traded Kevin Garnett to Celtics GM Danny Ainge, effectively delivering a seventeenth World Championship to Boston, the first ever won by a GM not named Auerbach. It wasn't gambling. It was a sure thing.

Ainge was tanned and fit when he arrived at Red's camp in the summer of '82. He'd played in the LA Summer Pro League and wanted a spot in Fitch's guard rotation along with Archibald, Gerald Henderson, and Buckner.

As the Globe's new Celtics beat reporter, I came to the job with cynicism for professional athletes, coaches, owners, general managers, and agents—a trait not always well received by players and team personnel. Fitch, who was all about control and manipulation, didn't appreciate my attitude.

"Careful with Bill," trainer Ray Melchiorre warned me. "He doesn't like the questions you're asking."

Melchiorre was in his fourth year with the team. He reported injuries to team physician Dr. Thomas Silva (a longtime Auerbach crony), addressed the daily medical needs of the players, taped ankles (four minutes per player), and took care of all team travel. Melchiorre was responsible for locating practice sites and getting the uniforms washed on the road. He told stories of drinking six-packs at laundromats around the NBA circuit with Cowens.

The daily "home" practice court was at Hellenic College in leafy Brookline. It looked like an elementary school gym with blue walls and a stage that ran along one of the sidelines. Greek Orthodox students paid little attention to the famous athletes, and the gym was just a few miles from Bird's Brookline home ("It was always open," Larry would later say, "and I could go there by myself at night"). Boston cabdrivers could never find the place, and out-of-town media reporters were ever frustrated trying to find Hellenic. Fitch loved it.

In October of '82, when the Celtics gathered for their annual preseason kickoff media day, the big news was Moses Malone's six-year, $13.2 million contract with the Philadelphia 76ers. The rebound-inhaling Malone made the Sixers instant favorites in the NBA's Eastern Conference. McHale, who was in the last year of his three-year rookie deal, said, "Moses doesn't play a running game. I've never seen him run. But he can run to the bank now."

"Where else in the world can you make money like this for two hours of work," added Parish.

We heard nothing from Maxwell, who'd pledged not to speak to the media for the entire season due to reports of missing child-support payments back home in North Carolina.

"I was pissed off about that," Maxwell said in 2021. "I didn't think that was a sports issue. It was in the Boston papers. So that was it for a while. I took it far. I didn't say a word for the whole year. Some things are private."

As the new guy, I didn't comprehend the magnitude of this loss.

Max was the best talker on a team of yappers, and his announcement augured a year of dysfunction. By the end of the 1982–83 season, Archibald would sulk his way out of town, Robey would be traded, the Celtics would be swept in a seven-game playoff series for the first time in their history, and Fitch would be gone.

Fitch closed the doors to practice after media day and announced that they'd remain closed for the rest of the first week.

I spoke with Ainge about his shooting woes after a preseason game in Portland, Maine.

"I think maybe I'm worrying too much about it and everybody else is worrying too much about it," Ainge said. "I've just got to get it out of my mind and play normally. I just can't think about it."

When the story ran, it was headlined, "Why Can't Danny Shoot?"

Ainge's teammates—ever ready to mock and ridicule kid-brother Danny—pounced.

"I know you don't write your own headlines, but that was a horseshit headline," Ainge told me the next day.

I was impressed that he confronted me privately instead of grandstanding for his teammates. I was surprised he knew that newspaper reporters don't write their own headlines. And I loved that he used the term *horseshit* because it's a word you carry forever if you spend a lot of time around baseball clubhouses. NBA, NFL, and NHL players don't say *horseshit*. It's a baseball thing.

What I did not learn until many years later was that Ainge was going through a personal crisis at the time of his second-year slump. Less than two weeks before our interview, Ainge's mother shot herself to death at the family's new home in Santa Clara. Janet Kay Ainge had breast cancer and was feeling like a burden on her family. None of the sad news appeared in any Boston paper, but a veteran beat reporter with inside sources would have known the situation and steered clear of a silly story about Ainge's field goal percentage.

The preseason finished with a swing through Texas and Tennessee. Bird remained distant, but I was able to get what I needed in group sessions. Maxwell was off-limits to everybody. The rest of the players were largely accessible. The affable Robey had some objections to characterizations of his clumsy play, but said, "I know you're just doing your job."

Robey got along with everybody. Bird called him Footer.

"I used to tell Larry I was six-eleven, but he always said, 'Hell, you're seven foot—you're a footer,'" Robey said. "That's how I became 'Footer.'"

WBZ radio reporter Jonny Miller was on the Texas trip. Afflicted with cerebral palsy since birth, Miller has a speech impediment, which never blocked his radio career. His voice is rarely heard on air, but he's a master interviewer, players trust him, and his sound bites have been broadcast to Boston sports fans for almost fifty years. His Newton home wasn't far from Bird's house in Brookline, and Jonny was the only reporter welcome at Larry's brick ranch. Only Miller knew what it was like to stand in Bird's kitchen and watch a crazed Celtics fan going through Larry's trash on collection day.

On a night when the Celtics annihilated the Spurs in San Marcos, Texas, I happened upon Miller and Parish having a late dinner at an outside café near our San Antonio hotel. Jonny invited me to join them, then retreated to his room, leaving me with the Chief for some awkward moments. I'd expected Parish to leave when Jonny departed, but he stayed and picked at a plate of fruit. I can't recall much of the forced conversation. Parish and I were both twenty-nine years old, but had little else in common.

Parish was born in Shreveport, Louisiana, in the summer of 1953, the first of four children of Ada and Robert Parish Sr.—a six-four handyman, sandblaster, and builder of storage tanks and railroad cars for Beaird Industries. Young Robert showed little interest in basketball, but was encouraged by his junior high school coach and blossomed as he grew toward his adult height of seven feet, one-half inch. At Woodlawn High School (where Terry Bradshaw had been quarterback in the 1960s), Parish practiced a turnaround "rainbow" jumper, arching his shots over a broomstick held by his coach.

Even as a high schooler, Parish didn't care much about personal statistics, a quality that served the Larry Bird Celtics well throughout the 1980s. Parish scored a school record 881 points in his junior season, despite not playing most of the second halves because Woodlawn usually won by large margins. Heavily recruited, Parish narrowed his college choice to Indiana, Florida State, Jacksonville, Illinois State, and tiny Centenary in Shreveport.

Indiana's Bobby Knight was one of the first to warn Parish that his grades and ACT scores would make a scholarship impossible until he improved his transcript. Centenary, a school of only seven hundred students, was far more flexible, granting Parish a scholarship and instant eligibility, only to pay a steep price (after a federal court case): an indefinite NCAA probation, which included bans on television appearances and postseason play.

As a freshman, Parish scored 50 points with 30 rebounds in a game against Lamar. He averaged 19.9 points and 15.3 rebounds in his sophomore season for the 21-4 Gents and was up to 24 points and 18 rebounds per game by his senior season. But Centenary was never on television, nor in the NCAA tournament, and in the eyes of the NCAA Robert Parish ceased to exist after January of his freshman season when the sanctions first went into place. He was college basketball's invisible seven-foot man.

None of this deterred professional basketball scouts. The ABA's Utah Stars drafted Parish after his freshman season, but the big center stayed at Centenary because getting a degree was important to his parents, and all agreed that the money would be there if he waited for the NBA draft after his senior season. Parish wound up earning a degree in education in the spring of 1976, and bought Robert Sr. and Ada a new home when the Warriors made him their top pick with the eighth selection of the first round.

Parish played four serviceable seasons with the Warriors, averaging more than 17 points in each of his final two years, but was occasionally unmotivated and lackadaisical. He grew to despise Hall of Fame teammate Rick Barry, but developed a lifelong friendship with veteran Warrior big man Clifford Ray. Parish also won the attention of

Cleveland Cavaliers coach Bill Fitch, which ultimately landed him in Boston.

I knew little of the Chief's backstory as I sat and struggled for talking points in that San Antonio café in October of 1982. When we chatted about his years in the Bay Area, I told him I'd seen his friend Ray in a basketball film called *Inside Moves* starring David Morse and John Savage. It included scenes shot in the Warriors' home, the Oakland–Alameda County Coliseum Arena. Ray had a small part and I suggested Parish check it out.

That turned out to be it for me and the Chief. One of the most important players of the 1980s Celtics—the man who played in more NBA games (1,611) than any player in history—Parish cut me off for good and never said why. There'd be a couple of ugly moments in our future, but mostly cold silence. Perhaps I used the wrong fork when eating my appetizer.

"Chief just had a disdain for your ass," Maxwell explained to me in 2021.

Two nights after Chief and I had our breakup dinner in San Antonio, I saw the trash-talking Celtics at their best in an exhibition versus the Sixers at the Stokely Athletic Center in Knoxville. It was Boston's first look at Malone in a Sixers jersey, and Philadelphia coach Billy Cunningham introduced six-eight rookie forward Marc Iavaroni to the rivalry. The stacked Sixers planned to start Iavaroni alongside Malone, Julius Erving, Andrew Toney, and Maurice Cheeks. Iavaroni was a raw power forward who could rebound, defend, take fouls, and never shoot the basketball. Kurt Rambis played a similar role for the star-studded Lakers.

Erving guarded Bird, which put Iavaroni on Maxwell, an uncanny low-post player with no discernible jump shot, but an array of moves and elasticity that overwhelmed lumbering players such as Iavaroni. Early in the game, the Celtics got the ball to Maxwell in the low block on five straight possessions, and each time Maxwell scored an easy bucket or got fouled. We could hear the Celtics reserves calling out from the bench, "Torture chamber," the name of the play. When

Iavaroni was mercifully removed after less than seven minutes of the first quarter, he had four personal fouls and a turnover.

Maxwell was not the only Celtics forward with great low-post moves. McHale was virtually unstoppable in the low block. His much-rehearsed up-and-under move enticed defenders to leave their feet and get suckered into fouls. When NBA referees gathered for their annual training camp before the start of the 1982–83 season, there was a crash course in McHale 101. McHale's drop-step, twisting, up-and-under move sometimes drew a traveling violation. Referees assumed he must be dragging his pivot foot to beat defenders. It turned out to be an optical illusion, as deceptive to officials as it was to defenders. The zebras studied video of McHale in slow motion and discovered that he was not traveling—he was simply a physical freak with the quickness and agility to get underhand layups without taking a third step.

"I didn't know they studied up on it," McHale said later. "But I remember in games I would sometimes tell the refs, 'Please go in at halftime and watch the tape and just watch my feet. As long as my left foot is my pivot foot, I can move my right foot seventeen times. It doesn't matter.' They'd sometimes come out and say, 'You know, you're right.'"

Two other newspaper reporters were traveling with the Celtics: Mike Fine of the *Quincy Ledger* and Mike Carey of the *Boston Herald*, both veterans of the beat, both a little older than I was. Fine got along with everybody, but his paper didn't have much reach in the Boston market. The *Herald* had always been a favored paper of the Celtics', and Carey was a favorite of every Celtics player. A short fellow with glasses, Carey was the ultimate insider, a guy who knew everything, but wrote only what the players wanted him to write. As I mentioned earlier, players called him Smurf. On road trips, he hosted player poker games in his hotel room and routinely played golf with Ainge. He was a virtual team mascot. One legendary night in Richfield, Ohio, players shaved his body hair after he'd passed out in a room at the Holiday Inn. Carey never married and seemed to exist on a diet of cigarettes and Coca-Cola. He was a wonderful guy and knew more basketball than I did, but he made my job more difficult. When I wrote something a Celtics player didn't like, I'd often hear, "Mike Carey would never have written that."

Carey served as Ainge's *agent. While Carey was covering the team.*

"Mike was everybody's friend," said Volk. "Danny didn't want an agent and he sat with me without representation, but he felt he needed to bounce it off someone, and that was Mike. I certainly wasn't offended. It was unusual, but he was Danny's friend. I didn't give it as much thought as maybe I should have. He never wrote anything that was controversial in that context. When you look back, there are so many things that we were able to do in that environment that you'd never think about doing now."

"We were all comfortable with Smurf," Ainge remembered. "I played a lot of golf with him. We went out together and he hung out with Robey and Bird and McHale. He sometimes got frustrated because if he knew something, he couldn't write it. That's the price you have to pay. So many times, we'd tell him, 'Smurf, Shaughnessy broke the story, but he found out from someone else. You either can be with us and have fun and hang out and not write the story, or you can be away from us and try to break stories all the time. It's not that complicated.'"

"We knew you didn't care about being friends," Maxwell told me. "You weren't going to go overboard with the whole 'like' thing. Mike Carey liked us. You bothered some of the guys."

The night after my clumsy "Another round for the house" moment with Bird and Buckner in Richfield, the Celtics defeated the Cavaliers, 104–93, in their regular season opener. We had a hideously early wake-up call the next morning, and it was dark when I boarded the bus outside the Holiday Inn, bound for the Cleveland airport, and a flight to Atlanta for a Saturday-night game.

There was a fairly universal seating protocol when you traveled with a pro sports team in the 1980s. The head coach and his assistants owned the first rows behind the driver. Then came the media. Then the players.

There was some commotion as we readied for the early trip to the Cleveland airport on that Saturday in October of '82. Johnny Most was late for the bus. Johnny always had to take final drags on his cigarette before boarding. Most rarely opened his wallet—and he dressed worse than sportswriters, which put him at a fashion stratum one level above homelessness. His travel bag for a ten-day road trip was no bigger than your average toaster oven.

There were rules of the road when you traveled with Johnny. If you shared a cab, you had to be prepared to pay the full fare because when the cab arrived at its destination, Johnny would say, "All I got is a fifty." His hearing was largely gone and you didn't want to stay next to Johnny's room, especially in thin-walled fleabags such as the Richfield Holiday Inn. Staying in a room next to nocturnal Johnny meant you heard his television all night. And lots of moaning. Johnny was not a fan of *Masterpiece Theatre*.

Antismoking regulations were taking hold in America in the early 1980s, but Johnny couldn't comply. Players hid his cigarettes, gave him exploding smokes, and sometimes called his room pretending to be hotel security—"Mr. Most, we know you are smoking in there and we're going to send up security if you don't put out that cigarette." Johnny fell for it every time.

When Johnny got angry with his young broadcast partner, Glenn Ordway, he'd remind Ordway, "I'm the show!"

Bird liked to sneak up behind Johnny and say, "Hey, Johnny, I'm the show!"

In our travels, anyone in the group who did anything foolish— forgetting your briefcase, losing your notebook, spilling grape juice on your shirt—was assigned "JJ" points. As in "Johnny Junior." I racked up quite a few JJs in my four years on the beat.

Celtics games made Johnny happy. The rest of the time he seemed agitated and miserable. If you greeted him with "Hey, Johnny, how's it going?," he'd slump his shoulders and grumble, "I'm a survivor, babe."

Married three times, Johnny was unlucky in love and ever in

search of female companionship on the road. His pickup line was "Hi, I'm a lonely guy."

Catcalls came from the back of the bus when Johnny finally boarded on that early morning in Richfield in '82. When Johnny was in his seat, Fitch stood up, turned toward the players at the back, and said, "I want total silence. I have a very important question to ask you guys."

The coach took a few steps back to where Most was sitting, then broke the quiet with "We have a crisis on our hands. Johnny has lost his new hearing aid. Has anyone seen a fifty-dollar hooker wearing a five-hundred-dollar hearing aid?"

"That's really fucking funny, Bill!" Most snapped. "I'm out five hundred bucks!"

The coach and the broadcasting legend worked out their differences on the flight to Atlanta. No harm, no foul.

As we waited for bags at Hartsfield Airport, I heard an odd page over the terminal intercom.

"Would Dolph Schayes please report to Delta baggage claim, carousel three, please? Dolph Schayes to carousel three."

Maxwell, McHale, Parish, and Ainge laughed when they heard the page.

Dolph Schayes was an NBA Hall of Famer in his midfifties who'd been a twelve time All Star with the Syracuse Nats. He hadn't played an NBA game since 1964 and, in the fall of 1982, was best known as the father of Utah's six-eleven center, Danny Schayes. I asked Melchiorre why Dolph Schayes was paged to our baggage claim and what was so funny about it.

"Oh, that's just a Max thing," said the trainer. "He does it to make fun of Danny. Anytime Danny is going bad, Max calls him Dolph Schayes. Max likes the way the name sounds. So you'll hear it in airports all year. I'm surprised you didn't notice that in Texas and Tennessee. Max calls that page in just about everywhere we go, and everybody cracks up when they hear it."

The Celtics were rolling with a 13-2 record when I had a lengthy talk with McHale at the end of November. He was in the third and final year of his contract and still coming off the bench, even though Atlanta coach Kevin Loughery said McHale was already one of the best ten players in the league. The twenty-four-year-old forward had rare perspective about NBA salaries:

"It's a joke that people are paid three-quarters of a million dollars a year to play basketball. My dad just about died when I told him that. He's Paul A. McHale, my main man. He retired last Friday after forty-two years of mining, and I'm turning down offers that would be more than he could have made in his whole lifetime. I'm jealous of my brother because he gets to hunt and camp and go cross-country skiing, and I can't do any of those things now. I think my life would be just as happy without a lot of money. I'd probably be in sales or business or something."

McHale liked to challenge and tease Fitch. I wondered if the coach made Boston a less appealing workplace.

"I'd like to put some things to rest about Coach Fitch and me," McHale said. "If I told you I loved him every single day, I'd be lying, and if he told you he loved me every single day, he'd be lying. Sometimes when he yells at me, I yell back, but I feel bad about it after. It's been blown way out of proportion."

The coach's need to control things put a strain on everyone. Fitch wanted to be coach, GM, traveling secretary, scout, doctor, and reporter. He wanted Dr. Robert Leach, the team's orthopedic specialist, to be at every practice—a preposterous request for the busy physician. The Celtics official in charge of arranging team travel got into a habit of making two plans for every trip. He'd present Fitch with an itinerary that he knew Fitch would reject, then switch to Plan B, which was the main plan all along.

"There was always crazy shit going on," Maxwell said. "One time Charles Bradley got into it with a security person and really got mad. Well, Bill got on the bus and said, 'God damn it, you guys are representing the Celtics. You need to be professional.' That same day, we got to a hotel and the rooms weren't ready, and Bill said to the desk clerk, 'What the fuck do you mean, the rooms aren't ready?' So I walked by him and said, 'Way to represent the team, Coach.'"

Fitch had a rule that players had to ride the team bus back to the team hotel after games—which infuriated Carr, who had friends visiting in many NBA arenas. In New York, Carr was forced to ride the team bus from Madison Square Garden back to the hotel, only to grab a cab and return to the Garden to meet his friends.

"Those were things that Bill just didn't let up on," said Maxwell. "If Bill had just allowed us to grow from boys to men, I think it would have been a lot better for him. But as a coach, it was the only way he could do it then. I like Bill, but he was just so rigid with us. He never let up. Some of the guys really hated him, but I was never going to allow Bill Fitch to get to me."

When Fitch closed practice for security purposes, prankster McHale said, "This is good. We don't want anybody in here to see us going through these same plays the Celtics have been running for thirty years."

At the Rockets' vast arena in downtown Houston, Fitch dispatched assistant coach Jimmy Rodgers to the top row of the lower bowl when he saw a suspicious character alone in the seats.

"Jimmy looked like Rocky Balboa going up those steps," McHale recalled, laughing. "When he got up there, it turned out to be a janitor blowing dope on his lunch break."

Not every Celtics player was as carefree as McHale. Nearing the end of his career, Archibald had lost a step and grudgingly surrendered his starting job to Buckner, who was underachieving in his first days in Boston. Ainge became an everyday starter, but didn't play with his trademark confidence and was tired of Fitch's critiques. When Ainge delivered a rare F-bomb in the direction of Fitch after the coach tore into Ainge for a mistake that was actually committed by Archibald, Parish and Maxwell invited Ainge to dinner.

"That was my second year and Fitch and I were having a rough time," Ainge recalled. "After that shouting match, I felt like he treated me like he treated the other guys. It was definitely a process with me and Bill. It was a rough year, but it was rough for him, too. I don't hold any grudges."

Parish and Maxwell celebrated in an Atlanta locker room after Fitch's video equipment fell off a TV and crashed to the carpet. There was a rumor that someone might have loosened the hardware on the table stand.

Buckner felt the wrath of Fitch after representing the Celtics at a Players Association meeting.

"I'd made some comments that we might go on strike," Buckner recalled. "I'd been playing a great deal, and suddenly Bill didn't play me in a game, and he said the guards on the other team were too big. I knew it wasn't true. I thought that was grossly unfair, which made me look at him differently. Bill had a streak in him like that."

In January, I was day drinking with reporter Mike Fine on an off day at the Chicago Marriott when M. L. Carr joined us for a couple of beers. Two hours later, Fine and I knew a lot more about the state of the 1983 Celtics.

"I hate him," Carr said over and over. "Everybody hates him. It will all come out."

Carr recounted an incident from a preseason game in San Antonio when he jammed one of his fingers in an attempt to take the ball away from George Gervin. When Fitch was tearing into the team at halftime, he asked Carr if he'd hurt the finger. When Carr said he thought his hand was okay, the coach snapped, "Well, I hope you hurt it, because that was a dumb play." This set Carr off, and the two never reconciled. They'd yell at each other in practice, with Fitch telling his veteran not to expect much more playing time.

"I am orchestrating his exit," Carr told us. "Everybody is tired of him. He told us he was going to keep us at practice all day today. When I heard that, I started taking the tape off my hand and said, 'That's it, boys. I'm done with practice. Anybody wants to go to the hotel, better come with me now because I'm taking the bus back to the hotel.' I'm just tired of the foolishness."

It wasn't a matter of X's and O's or substitution patterns. The Celtics were older and no longer responded to Fitch's autocratic style. Fitch had motivated Parish to become an All-Star center, but Chief didn't need the push anymore. Max had similarly tuned out, and Archibald was near the end. McHale could tolerate the coach, but his contract was up. And assistant coach K. C. Jones was loved by the Celtics players and totally disrespected by Fitch. Fitch didn't want Jones on his staff, but had been overruled by Auerbach.

When Tillis had his wallet stolen ($610) from his hotel room in Kansas City, Fitch lectured the kid in front of the team, saying he'd made "a dumb fucking rookie mistake." A month later, Fitch had his pocket picked at the team's hotel bar in Seattle.

"Hey, Bill. I heard about you getting pickpocketed," said Maxwell. "Would you call that a dumb fucking rookie mistake?"

I failed to report the Maxwell-Fitch exchange, and Bird—ever entertained by small dustups in our traveling party—mentioned it while we were waiting for bags in San Francisco ("Would Dolph Schayes please report to carousel five?").

"No balls, Dan," Bird said.

The next day, Bird took a seat without asking for an invitation when he spotted me having lunch alone at the Oakland Edgewater Hyatt.

A lifelong St. Louis Cardinals fan, he was interested in my time covering baseball ("Was Danny any good? . . . I heard Jim Rice hated you"). He'd played hours of baseball and softball with his brothers and had mangled his right index finger in a softball accident just before his rookie year with the Celtics. He had to teach himself how to shoot all over again and claimed he was never as accurate as he'd been before the injury. The finger was a crooked mess.

When a fan came to our table to ask for an autograph, Bird waved him away.

"It ain't worth it," he said. "If I start, it never stops. It's why I don't go out much. I like going to baseball games, but if I go and sign one autograph, I spend the whole game signing autographs. It ain't worth it. Too bad, because I love them baseball games."

The 1982–83 season was not a terrible year for the Celtics. They won 56 games, which would inspire a parade in some NBA cities, but they were clearly in need of a reboot. They were much better than almost every other NBA team, but their championship hopes were diminished by internal corrosion, a cluttered guard rotation, and the emergence of the indomitable 76ers. In early March, the Celtics lost four in a row and five out of six and fell 11 games behind Philadelphia.

On an off night in Milwaukee in late March, I bumped into Ainge for an early dinner, then wound up drinking with Bird, Robey, Buckner, and Carr after Ainge went to bed. Careful not to rip into Fitch like the others, Bird let his guard down talking about his early days in French Lick and his college experiences relative to those of Buckner and Robey, both of whom won NCAA championships. When a random patron approached our table, identified himself as a Kentucky fan, and shook Robey's hand, Bird said, "That's the first time Footer ever shook hands with a Kentucky booster and didn't come away with twenty dollars in his palm."

We talked about growing up in small towns with no stoplights and lots of farms. Bird said all the kids he knew were having sex early in their teens. This must have been a southern-Indiana thing—there was none of that in Groton, Massachusetts. He told me he wanted to adopt two kids. When Buckner interrupted our conversation, Bird giggled and said, "Hey, Bucky. I'm telling my life story here.

"If I didn't have older brothers who played sports, I probably wouldn't have ever played," Bird confessed. "They'd go to games with my mom and my sister, but I usually stayed home. I got my first basketball for Christmas when I was a little kid. It was one of them rubber balls that was more like a beach ball. Really light. We had a goal outside on the garage. It didn't have no net on it. I'd go out there with my ball in the winter. When I'd get cold, I'd come inside and warm up next to this potbelly stove we had in the middle of the living room. You had to warm up the ball so it would bounce again. One time I left that ball by the stove overnight, and when I got up, that sucker had this big knot on it. I was so pissed. I knew I wasn't going to get another one. I had to play with it anyway.

"The thing I liked about basketball at first was just the shooting. Watching the ball go in. My brother Mark was three years older, and I used to rebound for him at the courts around town. He'd be fifteen to sixteen feet away, and the ball would just come through the net so soft and I didn't even have to move. That caught my eye. I'd say, 'How do you do that?,' and he'd say, 'Cuz I shoot all the time.'

"I practiced a lot by myself. We didn't have a washer or dryer at home so my mom would go to the laundromat and I'd go with her to carry. There was a park across the street and I'd go over there and shoot all the time while the clothes was dryin'."

He said his high school issued varsity players one pair of sneakers before the start of the season and another pair before the tournament in February. Converse All Stars. White high-tops. The best high school basketball shoe ever made.

"Especially with them rubber soles," Bird agreed. "We'd wear 'em all day in school. They'd last forever."

Those were the basketball shoes of my benchwarming varsity days. I told Bird about the magical Groton High gym only a half mile from my house.

"Same with us," Bird said. "There was one night when I had a helluva game going. I had thirtysomething points in the first half, and people were thinking I was going to break the Orange County record. My dad was at home. He didn't go to many games. Well, my uncle called him at halftime and said, 'You'd better get down here. Your boy is going to do it tonight.' We didn't have no car, but he walked over. I ended up with fifty-four points and thirty-eight rebounds."

Imagine living a half mile from the high school gym—having a son as good as Larry Bird—and not bothering to leave the house for a home game.

When our hefty hotel-bar tab landed on the table, I reached for my wallet, but Bird said, "I got this, Dan."

It was like witnessing a total eclipse of the sun.

A week later, a bizarre home-and-home series with the Pacers unfolded on back-to-back nights. On a Tuesday at Market Square Arena, the Celtics were pounded by the moribund Pacers while Georgia Bird and her French Lick friends watched from expensive seats. When it was over, Robey pulled me aside and said, "This was pathetic. You've got to rip the shit out of us."

Mission accomplished.

Volk didn't appreciate the harsh tone.

"You seem like a nice guy," said the erudite executive. "What happens to you when you get behind the keyboard?"

Auerbach complained to his friend McDonough.

"Willie, I thought you told me this kid Shaughnessy was okay?"

The next night at the Garden, Bird went off for 53 points in a 142–116 victory over the same Pacers. It was the most points ever scored by a Celtic in a regular season game, and he did it in only thirty-three minutes.

The embarrassment in Indiana had motivated him.

"It's something you don't know if you don't live there," Bird said. "Indiana is basketball country. My mom was there and my friends were there and they all follow my career. To walk out of that arena and have everybody say 'What's wrong?' really hurt."

In the final week of the regular season, Fitch pulled me aside in a hotel lobby in Detroit and said, "I want to talk to you for a minute, Danny. You have to start writing the truth. You're too negative for a new guy. There's been more negativity this year than any other year, and nobody ever said Bobby Ryan wasn't a good writer. Do you even read what you write before it goes in the paper?"

It was about to get worse. The playoffs were coming and the sand was running out on Fitch's four-year term of office.

CHAPTER 4

"THE WORST FEELING I'VE EVER HAD PLAYING BASKETBALL"

In April of 1983, Larry Bird and the Boston Celtics had one championship on their résumé and were on deck for four straight appearances in the NBA Finals. Bird was going to win the Most Valuable Player Award in each of the next three seasons, two of which would put new banners in the Garden's rafters.

Before all that unfolded, they had to endure the drudgery and embarrassment of the 1983 NBA playoffs.

The Celtics drew the Atlanta Hawks for a first-round, best-of-three "mini" series. The Hawks had the worst record of any playoff team, and the Celtics had beaten them five times in six tries during the season. Veteran Dan Roundfield and sensational rookie Dominique Wilkins were Atlanta's best players, and they also had behemoth center Tree Rollins.

Bird suffered a groin pull late in the season, but played forty-one minutes in the finale and pronounced himself fit for the playoffs. Buckner, Robey, and Carr lingered in Fitch's doghouse. When Carr was benched for the last regular season game, Fitch said it was because Carr had jammed fingers.

"I guess I should have sat all eighty-two games because I jammed it in preseason and it's been the same all year," said Carr.

"I've never been on a team where there was an active mutiny like

61

that," Buckner recalled decades later. "It was embarrassing. I was like, 'Jeez, these guys, they hate this man.'"

"I was a young guy and just thought this is the way it is," remembered Henderson. "But the veterans, they'd already experienced other coaches. Max, Tiny, M.L., and Chief—they were tired of it."

Interviewing Red Auerbach for a pre-playoff piece, I mentioned that I was in need of a new car. Always about deal-making and patronage, Red urged me to go see his friend who ran a Toyota dealership in Wellesley and said he'd make a call for me. When I went to the shop, I couldn't get myself to say, "Red sent me," and when I saw Auerbach the next day, he asked me how things had gone at the dealership, and I confessed I hadn't dropped his name.

"Jesus Christ," he barked. "You're like a guy from the IRS. I tried to give one of those guys a key chain that cost me a buck fifty and the guy wouldn't take it."

Before the first playoff game, Maxwell received the *Boston Globe*'s Jack Barry Sportsmanship Award. Barry, who died in 1975, was a *Globe* lifer who covered the first days of the NBA and is credited with inventing the term *turnover*. Auerbach was in charge of deciding who would get the award—presented to a media-friendly player—and thought it would be amusing to give it to Maxwell after the season in which Max did not talk to the press.

The team issued a printed, pre-playoff summary of regular season highlights, which included this from December 29: "Darren Tillis robbed of $610 from hotel room in KC."

The Celtics beat the Hawks, 103–95, in Game 1. Bird played forty-six minutes, scoring 26 with 15 rebounds. Buckner, never a great shooter, canned three critical jumpers down the stretch. Fitch used only eight players. Robey, Carr, and Wedman did not play.

The team practiced at Hellenic the next two days, and I wrote features on Ainge and Buckner. When I asked Buckner about Fitch, Buckner did not want to answer, but finally said, "Bill trusts Tiny more than me, but I have to earn that." Buried in the pedestrian article was my conclusion: "Fitch has been disappointed with Buckner."

We flew to Atlanta the next day, and Carr brought his five-year-old son along for the two-night trip. When we landed, there was a new wrinkle: a "media bus" parked behind the players' bus.

"The second bus is for the media and radio-television people," Fitch said as we loaded our bags into the underbellies of the two carriages.

Plus kids, evidently.

Shaking his head in disgust, Carr walked his five-year-old son up the steps of our bus and said, "Bill says players and coaches only on our bus. So Michael's riding with you guys."

"Bill Fitch was ahead of Donald Trump in the separation of parents from their kids," Carr said in 2021. "I could not believe he did that to me and my family. They say time heals all wounds . . . not all of 'em."

We kept the little boy entertained on the ride downtown, and when we got to the hotel, Michael was reunited with his dad as we entered the lobby to get keys.

One of the perks of traveling with professional sports teams in the 1980s was speedy, no-stop check-in at hotels. Small, marked envelopes containing room keys were spread out on the front desk. From years traveling with the Orioles, I knew never to approach the desk until all the players had found their keys and gone off to their rooms. On this particular day, I couldn't find an envelope with *Shaughnessy* on it.

I was about to tell the desk clerk that there must have been some mistake when I caught a glimpse of Fitch near the bell stand holding a tiny envelope aloft, motioning for me to come over.

A call to the woodshed.

"You've got to stop this right now," the coach said when I approached for my key.

"What are you talking about, Bill?"

"You know. What you wrote about Bucky. I would never say I was disappointed with a player."

"I didn't quote you saying that you were disappointed. It's my opinion. It's my deduction on what I've seen all year. You didn't get the guy you thought you were getting. We all know. It's okay. Everybody knows."

"Don't give me that innocent look," Fitch snapped. "You've got a face like an altar boy, but you're really an executioner."

He handed me the envelope. Fitch was done with me. And after the stunt he'd just pulled with M.L. and his young son, I was pretty sure most of the players were done with him.

Boston's guards missed their first 14 shots of Game 2 as Boston fell behind by 17 en route to a 95–93 loss at the Omni. Bird heaved an airball at the buzzer. Back at the hotel bar, I asked Celtics lifer Tommy Heinsohn if the Celtics could lose this series, and he snapped, "You're damn right they can. Fitch has lost the team."

They did not lose the series. In the third and deciding game, the Celtics routed the Hawks, 98–79. The lone memorable moment of the entire series came midway through the third period when Ainge and Rollins tangled after Rollins hit Ainge with a left elbow. Ainge charged Rollins, wrapped his arms around the big man's hips and took him down, Lawrence Taylor–style. While they were rolling on the parquet, Rollins bit the middle finger on Ainge's right hand. Ainge was ejected and disappeared into the trainer's room, where he received two stitches and a tetanus shot. When the locker room opened after the Celtics' win, we rushed Ainge's locker and he softly said, "Tree bit me."

Tree Bites Man. Film at Eleven.

Ainge played fourteen NBA seasons, was a starter on perhaps the best NBA team of all time, and has enjoyed success as an NBA broadcaster, coach, and general manager. As a player, he was a chronic whiner and agitator, constantly in the middle of arguments and brawls. He was booed more than any other Celtic in the years he played with Bird, Parish, and McHale. Yet he is perhaps best remembered for something he did not do. The Tree Bites Man story got flipped, and Ainge has spent forty years correcting casual fans with bad memories.

Danny Ainge? Aren't you the guy who once bit another player?

One day after the incident, the marquee on the Ground Round next to the Cleveland Circle Cinema read TRY OUR FINGER FOOD AFTER THE MOVIES!

Auerbach said the Celtics might sue Rollins. They did not.

Boston's next opponent was the Milwaukee Bucks, winners of the Central Division, who featured veteran center Bob Lanier, forward Marques Johnson, and guard Sidney Moncrief, a six-four athletic freak from Arkansas who had dueled Bird in the NCAA tourney. The Bucks were coached by Don Nelson, a haloed ex-Celtic who had his number 19 hanging from the Garden rafters. The talented Bucks hadn't won a playoff series since 1978, but Buckner, a veteran of many Milwaukee disappointments, predicted they'd be a formidable opponent.

Milwaukee destroyed Boston, 116–95 in Game 1, a wire-to-wire slaughter that had Celtics fans booing and leaving the Garden midway through the fourth. Fitch embarrassed his starters by sending the lethargic veterans back onto the court for the ugly finish. Henderson, Bird, Maxwell, and Parish played garbage minutes generally reserved for the scrubs.

"It wasn't a bad thing to do," Bird said. "We're the ones who got us there, so we're the ones who should go out there and take the punishment."

"We had about four or five minutes out there where we just plain quit," said Fitch. "It's hard to get that to roll off my tongue. . . . I don't think our guys ever played that bad before, and they didn't know how to react to it."

"I think he lost those guys that night," Buckner said later.

Fitch called for a 10:00 a.m. practice the next day. No visitors. No media.

Bird talked to reporters outside the Hellenic gym at 9:00 a.m. and admitted, "When you come out and get beat the way we did, it's embarrassing because maybe there is something wrong with us."

This is how it ends, I thought to myself. The Celtics were like

Butch Cassidy and the Sundance Kid when Sheriff Ray Bledsoe tells them, "You're gonna die and you're gonna die bloody and all you can do is choose where."

Bird got the flu and didn't make it out of bed for Game 2. Ainge stepped up with the best game of his young career, scoring 23 in the first half, but again the Celtics were beaten at home, 95–91. Again they were booed. By this time, I was routinely characterizing Fitch as "coach-under-siege" and "Big Brother Bill."

"We were funky that year," McHale said in 2021. "We were bad. We just had a lot of stuff going on. It had run its course. Bill had jumped a lot of ass and there were a lot of raw feelings."

We flew out of Boston at 6:40 Saturday morning. The schedule called for Games 3 and 4 in Milwaukee on Sunday afternoon and Monday night.

At Saturday's afternoon practice in Milwaukee, Fitch told his team that the media had created a wedge between him and the players. Nelson, meanwhile, played Celtics tricks on the Celtics, calling Ainge a cheap-shot artist, claiming Ainge had been the instigator in the Tree fiasco. This attack was designed to make sure Milwaukee fans booed Ainge every time he touched the ball in Games 3 and 4. It was right out of the Auerbach playbook, a Fredo move that Red did not appreciate.

"It wasn't anything Red wouldn't have done," Nelson said later. "He called me a whore in the paper. I asked for forgiveness and wrote him some letters, but it took a couple of years."

As I waited for an elevator at our Milwaukee hotel on the eve of Game 3, *Globe* scribe Larry Whiteside told me, "Fitch doesn't like you. He keeps talking to me about you. He said you're dumb. He told me to keep you away from him. He said he might punch you out."

The coach was sharing this sentiment with several folks in the Celtics traveling party, and when I saw a pale-looking Bird in the hotel later that night, he said, "So when are you and Bill gonna have this big fight?"

On the morning of Game 3, the 556-page Sunday *Boston Globe* included a column by me headlined, "These Problems Go Deep." The story featured side-by-side photos of Fitch and Robert De Niro playing Travis Bickle in his crazed *Taxi Driver* role. The photo caption read *"Taxi Driver*'s Travis Bickle and Celtics coach Bill Fitch have similar compulsive tendencies."

> Like *Taxi Driver*'s Travis Bickle alone in his room watching *American Bandstand* on TV, Bill Fitch retreats to his quarters after each Celtic game and views videotape over and over . . . but it's clear that the answers to the Celtics malaise aren't in the game films and they aren't on the chalkboard alongside the X's and O's. Just as you don't treat psychological disorders with penicillin and Band-Aids, the Celtics are beyond the point where they can be saved by conventional coaching methods. . . . It is probably too late. This year may be remembered as the year when more was less and the Celtics graced the covers of *Sports Illustrated* and *Psychology Today*. . . . The smell of death is in the air.

It was Overwriting 101 and would have looked stupid if the Celtics crawled out of the 2-0 hole, beat the Bucks, and won another World Championship.

None of that happened. The series was over in less than thirty-six hours. The Celtics lost Game 3, 107–99, and endured the first four-game sweep in franchise history the next night, losing 107–93. During a pause late in Game 4, veteran official Jake O'Donnell came by the press table and said, "Did you ever see Boston play like this?"

O'Donnell's offhand remark was heard by me and a twenty-one-year-old Marquette junior guard seated to my left: Glenn Rivers. The wide-eyed college player told me he was contemplating forgoing his senior season and entering the 1983 NBA draft. I heard things worked out well for that nice young man.

When the sweep was complete, Bird shouldered the blame, saying, "It's the toughest thing that ever happened in Celtics history."

"It's nothing to be embarrassed about," countered McHale, who attempted only 29 shots in the four games and was officially a free agent. "I'm going to hold my head up high. The sun will come up tomorrow."

"I can't believe Kevin can say that," grumbled Bird. "That's a terrible way to look at this. I'm not holding my head high and neither should he."

For those who spent time around these Celtics, there was nothing surprising about the diverse responses. The two superstar forwards played alongside each other for twelve NBA seasons, appearing in five Finals and won three championships. They were the Babe Ruth and Lou Gehrig of professional basketball, but like their baseball forebears they were never particularly close. Outsiders assumed they were tight because both were blue-collar Midwesterners from small towns and big families; white superstars in a Black man's game. Neither one knew much about the NBA before becoming a star in the league.

But they were not alike.

Bird was quiet, suspicious, uncomfortable around anyone he didn't know. McHale was loud, trusting, ever the class clown. Bird seemed to enjoy seeing people flummoxed. McHale went out of his way to make strangers feel comfortable and pushed back only if he thought he was being treated as a dumb jock. He didn't like the image that he was the natural talent while Bird was portrayed as the hard worker who'd made himself great with hours of practice. McHale logged the same hours, but never talked about it.

Raised in the Iron Range of upper Minnesota, one of four children of Paul and Josephine McHale, Kevin McHale was something of a genetic mutant. He had tall uncles on his mother's Croatian side, but according to McHale, those relatives were "way removed." Kevin's dad was five-ten, his mom, five-five. His two sisters were five-six, and his brother, John, was a pedestrian six-footer.

Kevin Edward McHale, born December 19, 1957, grew to be six foot ten with the arms of a seven-footer.

"It was just me," McHale said with a sigh.

Paul A. McHale rarely missed a day of work in his four decades in the mines. Eight of his nine siblings either worked in the mines or married someone who did. Like all Hibbing boys, Kevin first played hockey, but moved indoors when it became clear his arms and legs were better suited for basketball. In his senior year of high school, he led the Hibbing Blue Jackets to the state finals, but didn't attract a lot of attention from college coaches. For all the McHales, going to college meant going to "the U," which is what everybody in the state calls the University of Minnesota. McHale wanted to be a Gopher, just like Dave Winfield, Jim Brewer, and Ron Behagen.

McHale teamed with Mychal Thompson at the U, but Minnesota was on NCAA probation most of the time McHale was a Gopher. He led the U to the finals of the NIT in his senior season, where they were beaten by Virginia's seven-four Ralph Sampson. McHale scored only 8 points in the final, but walked out of Madison Square Garden with his head held high.

"Once any game started, I was really excited and I loved to compete," he said. "But once the game was over, I mean—does whining and pissing and moaning allow you to play again? No. It was over. We didn't play well enough. . . . When we lost to the Bucks, I didn't like the fact that everyone thought the world was over because we lost four basketball games."

McHale's Zen values offended Bird's singular focus on basketball When Bird talked about McHale's talent and contributions to the Celtics, there were always subtle implications that McHale should be better. In Bird's world, McHale clearly took nights off, sometimes didn't work hard enough to get to his spot, and cruised on defense. It annoyed Bird that McHale didn't dive for loose balls—a Bird specialty. Bird's faint praise of McHale fortified the notion that McHale was a natural who didn't take the game seriously. Bird sounded sincere when he praised Parish, but never had any of that over-the-top praise for McHale.

McHale knew Bird was going to get the lion's share of the credit . . . and blame. He was okay with it. Whenever he was asked about perhaps being a bigger star on another team, his fallback was "I'd have scored a lot more points and won a lot fewer games."

"There wasn't anybody on the team who had a close relationship with Larry other than people who drank with him," Maxwell said. "Robey and Quinn maybe. It was cultivated in that way, and I don't think Kevin had that relationship with him."

Seven days after the loss in Milwaukee, Kevin and Lynn McHale had their first child, daughter Kristyn. They were basking in the glow of new parenthood while Bird seethed about the loss in Milwaukee.

"Sitting in the locker room after being swept by the Bucks was the worst feeling I've ever had playing basketball," Bird wrote in his autobiography. "We just died as a team. All the spark, all the enjoyment, all the rah-rah we had those first three years—all of a sudden it was gone."

While McHale doted on his infant daughter, Bird retreated to a summer of commitment at his new home in West Baden, which featured a full-length, outdoor basketball court. Buckner accepted an invitation to Camp Larry and arrived for daily workouts that included daily 7:00 a.m. five-mile runs, followed by hundreds of jump shots. After the run and the morning jumpers, Bird went on twenty-mile bike rides, then returned for another five hundred jumpers and free throws. He was anticipating numerous playoff springs against Magic and Kareem.

Back in Boston, Auerbach was making his own preparations for the next few playoff springs.

CHAPTER 5

"EVER NOTICE HOW QUIET IT GETS IN HERE ALL OF A SUDDEN WHEN YOU WALK IN?"

Red Auerbach was sixty-five in the summer of 1983. Before David Stern, the salary cap, the draft lottery, and stupid money changed the professional basketball landscape, Auerbach had already established himself as the best team builder in professional sports. He was the only coach/executive in any of the four major leagues who could claim he'd been part of his league's existence since the creation. He'd officially named Jan Volk as his successor as Boston GM, but pledged to stick around when Don Gaston, Alan Cohen, and Paul Dupee purchased the team from Harry Mangurian in August of 1983. Auerbach wanted to fix things after the way the Celtics fell apart against the Bucks. Less current in league matters, Red was still building the Celtics roster, still polluting the Hellenic gym with cigar smoke.

Twenty-four days after Game 4 in Milwaukee, while the Sixers were sweeping the Lakers in the Finals, Fitch abruptly resigned in a press conference at the Garden. He didn't want to be in Boston anymore. He said he was discouraged because Mangurian had announced the team was for sale. Fitch also said he didn't think Red would be sticking around much longer. It was all baloney. Fitch had

71

found a new gig in Houston and was itching to get away from the Auerbach-controlled Celtics.

I was flying between Philadelphia and Los Angeles when it went down and heard the news when I called the office on one of those clunky, $100-per-minute, chord-connected telephones that snapped in and out of the airplane's tray-table chair back. After enjoying a couple of champagne toasts at thirty-five thousand feet, I deplaned and called Will McDonough from an LAX pay phone.

"Mangurian said you're the reason," Willie told me. "Fitch thinks you're full of shit. I told him he worries too much about you and that he should be looking at some of what the other guys are writing."

McDonough's column in the next day's *Globe* stated, "What happened is that Fitch sat back and watched himself get knocked in the media for two weeks, then started to ask himself if there was any way he could get the rewards he thought he deserved here."

Fitch left Boston with a four-year record of 242-86, winning 74 percent of his regular season games and a championship. Six days later, he was hired to coach the Houston Rockets.

It was the ultimate win-win-win situation: good for the Celtics, good for Auerbach, and good for me.

Not until 1999 did Bird finally admit Fitch had overstayed his welcome.

"Three years is the max," Bird told me during his third and final season as coach of the Indiana Pacers. "Bill was a great coach, but at the end of that last year it started to get a little crazy."

On the day Fitch announced he was leaving, Auerbach said, "Our next coach will be a guy who fits our philosophy and our system. We want a guy who will run a disciplined team and do things the way we want them done."

For the fifth time since stepping away from the Boston bench in 1966, Auerbach hired one of his ex-players to coach his team. Russell, Heinsohn, Sanders, and Cowens had filled the role. Now it was K. C. Jones's turn.

At his introductory press conference, Jones said, "I've been associated with the Celtics since I've been Black."

The change had a nice symmetry. Fitch never wanted Jones on his staff, but was forced to keep him and pouted by marginalizing him. Jones had been a successful NBA head coach in Washington, taking the Bullets to the Finals in 1975, but Fitch had no use for Jones's suggestions and bristled when he got friendly with players.

Hard feelings had boiled over on draft day 1982, when Jones lunged at Fitch and pushed the head coach in front of assistant coach Jimmy Rodgers and other team officials. When Fitch fired Jones later in the Celtics executive offices, there was a second shoving match, again initiated by Jones. Jones retreated to his office after the scuffles and started calling friends around the league looking for a job. While he was dialing, Fitch came into Jones's office and told K.C. he could stay—no doubt at the insistence of Auerbach.

Jones explained his working dynamic with Fitch with this vignette: "I was working on a play with Tiny Archibald from the far side of the gym. Before I could finish, Bill called over from the other side of the court, and with all the other players looking on, he said, 'Hey, Tiny, when he gets through with that stuff, come over here and I'll show you how to do it.'"

"I didn't feel there was a lot of communication between Bill and K.C.," Henderson remembered. "They each had their style and they were very different."

Jones needed no introduction to Boston sports fans. He'd been Russell's wingman at the University of San Francisco when the Dons won 56 straight and back-to-back NCAA championships. They won gold together at the Melbourne Olympics in the fall of 1956. K.C. was a starting guard for the Russell dynasty after Cousy retired.

One can make a case that the always-in-the-spotlight K. C. Jones trails only Russell as the most decorated player in basketball history. Like Ringo Starr, Jones was surrounded by greatness, always present when the awards were handed out. After earning NCAA and Olympic gold, he was a champion in his first eight seasons as an NBA player, won another ring as assistant coach with the champion 1972 Lakers, and earned yet another as Fitch's assistant in 1981. He'd get two more as head coach of the Larry Bird Celtics.

Auerbach was feisty when camp opened in the summer of '83. He had one of "his guys" as the head coach and was confident that the Celtics were back.

"Come here, Dan," Red greeted me on the first day of rookie camp. "Bill had a problem dealing with people. It's going to be different now. No more closed practices. No more closing off the locker room to you guys. No more of that chickenshit stuff."

The departure of Fitch and hiring of Jones liberated Auerbach and made his job fun again. Red was no longer in competition for credit with his head coach.

Auerbach was anxious to get back into roster building and knew he had to start with his backcourt. Future Hall of Famer Archibald was near the end, no longer worth the trouble, and Buckner's career was trending south. Ainge was a budding star who'd slumped under Fitch, while Henderson was a steady player at both ends who wasn't going to get many shots on a team loaded with frontcourt shooters. Henderson was also going into the final year of his contract. Red needed to find a veteran, take-charge guard who could defend the likes of Andrew Toney and Magic Johnson.

On June 27, 1983, Auerbach and Mangurian summoned three Boston writers to Red's office for what seemed to be the sole purpose of ripping McHale's agent, John Sandquist. McHale was on the cusp of signing an offer sheet with the Knicks, and Red wanted us to know that Sandquist was a no-good double-dealer. Mangurian maintained that he'd made a handshake deal with McHale, which wasn't honored. The bosses were hot, and we dutifully recorded their airing of grievances.

While we were scribbling, a staffer came into Auerbach's memorabilia-cluttered office and slipped a note in front of Mangurian. The owner put the paper in front of Red, who took a puff on his Hoyo de Monterrey and said, "You guys need to leave. But if you aren't busy, why don't you stick around for a half hour?"

Thirty minutes later, Red summoned us back to his office to inform us that the Celtics had acquired Phoenix guard Dennis Johnson in exchange for Robey.

This was a whopper. How many superior NBA guards are available in the prime of their career in exchange for a rarely used backup center? Auerbach had convinced Jerry Colangelo to trade a proven, twenty-eight-year-old guard, who'd already been MVP of the Finals, for a broken-down center who wouldn't score more than 5 points in any game for the rest of his career. Robey was basically done, while DJ—a future Hall of Famer—was on his way to playing in the next four NBA Finals.

Like Bird, Dennis Johnson grew up in a big family without much money. His dad was a cement mason, his mom a social worker, and he had fifteen siblings. His path to professional basketball could never be replicated today. DJ didn't play on any pricey AAU traveling squad and never even tried out for his Dominguez High School team in Compton. He was "discovered" playing in summer league games in San Pedro with three of his brothers while he was working as a cashier and shelf stocker at a local liquor store.

Harbor Junior College coach Jim White offered Johnson a slot when he saw Johnson playing summer ball. DJ played two tumultuous seasons for White, getting kicked off the squad a couple of times, but impressed with his instincts, fearlessness, rebounding, and defense. When Harbor went 29-4 in Johnson's second season, Pepperdine assistant coach Gary Colson gave him a scholarship. With Dennis Johnson in the Pepperdine backcourt, the Waves went 22-6 and made it all the way to the second round of the West Regional against powerhouse UCLA. They were eliminated by John Wooden's Bruins, but DJ made his bones in the tournament, going head-to-head with UCLA All-Americans Richard Washington and Marques Johnson. Seattle SuperSonics coach Bill Russell made Johnson the second pick of the second round in the 1976 draft. DJ signed with the

Sonics for $27,500 and bought his mother a car. Three years later, at the age of twenty-five, he was named MVP of the NBA Finals, averaging 23 points and blocking 11 shots as the Sonics beat the Bullets for their only championship.

By the time Johnson came to the Celtics he'd been named to the league's all-defensive team five times. He could bump and run with Toney and Magic.

The Celtics gained a secondary benefit with the subtraction of Robey from Bird's nightlife. Playful Footer could stay up drinking all night, but he wasn't playing big minutes, and it was Bird who paid the price for Footer's nocturnal lifestyle.

"Anytime Fitch got mad at Larry, I got blamed," Robey admitted. "We spent a lot of time together. Even when we were home, I'd spend a lot of time at Larry's house because I was living off Route Nine in Newton, pretty near him. Those were good times for us, and whenever I see Dinah today, I still commend her for putting up with the two of us crazy dudes."

Johnson was available to the Celtics because of his own baggage. Sonics coach Lenny Wilkens labeled DJ a cancer when the young guard acted out in Seattle. Phoenix coach John MacLeod didn't like DJ walking the ball up the floor and dribbling from the point while the shot clock ran down.

"John was very set in his ways, and he had basically said he didn't want DJ anymore," explained Colangelo. "We had to move him. Boston was the only team that showed any interest."

"As a general manager you've got to avoid your coach being down on certain people," countered Auerbach.

Red waived Archibald a month after trading for DJ. Chris Ford was hired as an assistant coach, and Greg Kite, a clunky six-eleven center who'd played with Ainge at BYU, was drafted in the first round to replace Robey.

McHale's summer free agency created tension. The *Globe* published a Larry Johnson cartoon that featured a snout-nosed McHale snorting dollar bills from a trough under a headline that read, "The

Real McHale." McHale eventually agreed to a four-year, $4 million contract, but he was hurt by the negativity.

The arrival of DJ put everybody in a good mood for the start of camp as the Fitch goose step was replaced by the K. C. Jones soft shoe.

"Who ever heard of a Black guy with red hair and freckles?" Ainge said when he greeted Johnson. "I'm going to call you Chemo so that your cancer doesn't spread to the rest of us."

When Max got his first look at DJ, the veteran hollered, "Here's the guard with the biggest butt in the league."

It was the first quote from Maxwell in over a year.

Buckner was Max's next target: "Bucky knows who DJ is. That's why he got all skinny for us this year."

Perhaps owing to all those early-morning runs at Camp Larry, the muscular and blocky Buckner was seventeen pounds lighter than he'd been at the end of the '83 season.

"This is the NBA," Ainge said, loud enough for everybody to hear. "Tall, lean guys, right? Before he lost the weight, Bucky was the only player in the league who bought pants with a bigger waist size than inseam."

Buckner was a prodigious sweater who could lose five pounds of water at a single practice. At the end of a long summer day on the Hellenic floor, we sometimes heard his sneakers squishing and saw seawater leaking out of his leather sneakers. The man sweated like Chuck Berry.

In more evidence that things had changed, before the start of the first practice boom-box-toting, leggings-wearing Louise Boland strutted onto the court to lead a stretching drill to the tune of David Bowie's "Let's Dance."

The attractive young dancer got the players' attention.

"This is the only thing you can get Max to do," Auerbach said as he sat in a sideline chair, blowing a plume of smoke.

"Relaxation is the big thing," said Carr. "That's typical of what's different here this year."

It wasn't all fun and flash dance. Before the start of preseason games, Parish said he wanted to renegotiate his contract. With a salary of $650,000 per season, he was angry that McHale was getting $1 million per year.

"How can you pay a nonstarter more than a starter?" Chief asked. "It's an insult to me."

Parish stayed home when we flew to Phoenix for an eight-day preseason trip, and I came out swinging in the next day's *Globe*, starting my column with "Robert Parish is wrong."

Probably not a party starter in the home of Robert and Nancy Parish.

A day later, at the baggage claim in Tempe, Arizona ("Would Dolph Schayes please report to baggage carousel six"), Ainge pulled me aside and said, "I see where you ripped Robert and his agent. Robert's not going to like it. Mike Carey would have never done that."

Too bad. Sports reporters aren't friends of the athletes. I was conflicted about this issue when I covered the Orioles at the age of twenty-three, but by this time I knew my role. As I mentioned earlier, if the players think you're their friend, they'll expect to be protected the way friends protect one another. They'll feel betrayed when you write something they don't like. It was a bonus to be friendly and learn things away from the gym, and I certainly was okay sharing beers and personal stories if we bumped into one another because it was good for background, but the line had to be drawn. We were professional acquaintances but we were never going to be friends. To this day, I'm amazed by fans who believe the rules of journalism should be suspended for those who cover sports.

For all of his self-ridicule about being an uneducated hick, Bird seemed to have the best grasp of the reporter-player relationship. He noticed everything, loved gossip, and had a sharp needle. When I appeared in the locker room, pen and notebook ready, he liked to say, "Hey, Scoop—ever notice how quiet it gets in here all of a sudden when you walk in?"

Parish was still home when the Celtics got to LA October 11. Lakers fans were reeling from a deal that had sent popular starting guard Norm Nixon to the Clippers along with Eddie Jordan for treetop Swen Nater and rookie guard Byron Scott. Nixon's soon-to-be wife, Debbie Allen, was a Hollywood star, and Nixon had been a starter with Magic and Kareem on the Lakers' 1980 and 1982 championship teams.

When I approached Jack Nicholson and asked him what he thought of the trade, Nicholson put his arm around me and said, "I'm wearing black, ain't I?"

The Parish squabble was resolved when the Celtics shuffled deferred monies and extended his deal by a year. The team insisted it had not renegotiated, and Red explained it away, saying Parish got bad advice from his agent.

On Sunday night, October 16, when the World Champion Sixers came to Boston for a preseason game, Parish was back in Boston's starting lineup with Bird, Maxwell, Henderson, and Ainge. For reasons no one clearly understood (there were always a lot of head-scratchers with K. C. Jones), Dennis Johnson was coming off the bench. Making the veteran prove himself with his new team was a noble notion, but everybody, including Jones, knew that DJ was Boston's best guard.

Cunningham went with the starting five that had wiped out the Lakers in the Finals: Malone, Erving, Toney, Cheeks, and Iavaroni.

This wasn't a prime-time, must-see event, even in Boston. The Globe budgeted its preseason game story for the second page of the sports section because the Baltimore Orioles were closing out the World Series in Philadelphia (remember when the World Series mattered?) and the Patriots had won an afternoon home game against the San Diego Chargers. How much news value could there be in a Sunday-evening preseason basketball game at the Garden?

In the fourth minute of play, Maxwell got tangled up with Malone and fired the ball at the Sixers center. Both benches emptied. A minute later, with Parish at the free throw line, Bird mixed it up with Iavaroni as they lined up to rebound. A 1950s NBA donnybrook ensued. Punches were thrown, blood was spilled, a sport coat was ripped open, and Bird was ejected.

Red was in his usual spot (loge 1, row 6, seat 2) on the other side of the court when the fight broke out. When Auerbach learned Bird had been ejected, it triggered his Brooklyn street smarts and Fort Wayne/Tri-Cities instincts. He rose from his seat, stepped into the aisle, made his way down the steps, leveraged himself over the hockey boards, and stormed across the floor, looking for the two scab officials (NBA refs were on strike) and anyone representing the 76ers. He'd just seen his best player bounced by the oldest trick in the sport. Red literally wrote the book on this ploy (it's all there in *Basketball for the Player, the Fan and the Coach* published by Pocket Books in 1952): sacrifice one of your goons to get the other team's star thrown out of the game. Red chased Cunningham, whose nifty camel-colored sport coat split down the back. Auerbach went toe-to-toe, face-to-tummy with the six-ten Malone. When mumbling Moses looked down on Red's bald pate and scowled, Auerbach said, "Go ahead, hit me, you big son of a bitch!"

The 1983–84 Celtics may have won the NBA championship in that moment.

"It just showed the league that he isn't going to give up and that he's still the Man," Bird told me. "We laughed when it was over with, but everybody on the team really appreciated it. When it was happening, by God, we knew Red was there and we knew we had somebody behind us. And to think it was just an exhibition game."

"It was very simple," said Red. "Every time I looked up, Cunningham's in the middle of the floor and they're doing a job on our guys and the refs are doing nothing about it. So I got mad. That's all. I got mad."

"Never seen anything like that," said K.C. "And I've seen a lot in all my years here."

League vice president Scotty Stirling said, "Auerbach's actions were embarrassing and intolerable," and fined Red $2,500.

"The NBA is scared to death of Red," said striking referee Jake O'Donnell.

The morning after, Ainge walked onto the Pappas Gymnasium floor at Hellenic wearing boxing gloves.

One night before the team flew to Detroit for the season opener, players were required to appear at the annual New England Sports Lodge B'nai B'rith Salute to the Celtics at a local function hall. The event was pushed by Auerbach, who'd long cultivated support for the team from Greater Boston's Jewish community. Players attended grudgingly, but were inspired when master of ceremonies John Dennis kicked off his remarks with "Only in America could you have two thousand Jews worshipping at the feet of thirteen Black men."

Parish, Maxwell, and M. L. Carr spit out their water.

Later in the evening, Bird spoke for his teammates and said, "I really believe each one of us will not forget what happened last year."

Boston's regular season opener was played at the Pontiac Silverdome, easily the NBA's largest venue. The Silverdome accommodated close to 95,000 fans (61,983 attended a Celtics-Pistons playoff game in '88), but to Bird, it was still a "gym." In Bird's world, every NBA game was played in a gym. It didn't matter if the arena was Madison Square Garden, the Seattle Kingdome, or the Teflon-roofed Silverdome. If it had a roof, a hard court, and two ten-foot baskets, it was a gym.

Bird liked the Detroit fans, particularly Leon the Barber, who always sat behind the visitors' bench. Leon Bradley was the most famous heckler on the NBA circuit, knew many of the players personally, and kept track of all the coaches and officials. He was M. L. Carr's barber, and Celtics players thought he was hilarious. DJ draped a towel over his head when he was on the bench for the Celtics' opener. He didn't want his new bosses to see him laughing at Leon's barbs.

Bird hated Pistons center Bill Laimbeer, a cheap-shot specialist and well-known flopper, who grew up with a rich dad. Bill Laimbeer Sr. was president of a Fortune 500 glass company, and the joke around the NBA was that Bill Laimbeer Jr. was the only NBA player who didn't make more money than his father.

"I can't stand Laimbeer," Bird said. "Make sure you keep me posted when they get around to naming the All-Star reserves this winter. Laimbeer made it last year and it was awful. He'd take a seat near the front of the bus on practice day, and when I'd come on the bus, he'd say, 'Good morning, Larry,' and I'd have to say, 'Fuck you, Bill.'"

The night before the season opener in Pontiac, K. C. Jones belted out a few tunes in the suburban Michigan Hilton piano lounge. Jones was well-known to bartenders and piano players around the NBA circuit. Only Tony Bennett did a better version of "I Left My Heart in San Francisco."

The Celtics lost their opener at the Silverdome, then ripped off nine consecutive wins. One of the nine victories came in Indianapolis, where the Celtics stayed at the Hyatt Regency, which was attached to a small shopping mall. On the game day in Indy, I strolled into McDonald's with Bird before the short ride to the gym. Being with Larry Bird at a McDonald's in Indiana reminded me of the scene in *Coming to America* when a Madison Square Garden vendor discovers he is in the presence of the crown prince of Zamunda. Hoosier teens working the counter at the McDonald's were gobsmacked. Bird signed autographs for kids, none for adults. He knew what it was like to be a kid awestruck by pro ballplayers. He'd once been rebuffed when he asked for Dan Issel's autograph at a Kentucky Colonels game. Bird had no use for autograph-seeking adults, and if a desperate gentleman tried the time-tested "My wife will kill me if I don't get your autograph," Bird would send him away with "Well, I guess she's married to a dead man."

NBA officials were still on strike early in the '83–84 season and there were zebra picket lines at most arenas. When the Celtics bus rolled toward picketing referees outside Market Square Arena, Bird ordered the bus to find another route into the Pacers gym.

The Celtics beat the Pacers, but the evening's highlight for some players was a press row dustup featuring Carey and me, Smurf versus Scoop—the ultimate insider, loved and trusted by the players, versus the guy who made the room quiet when he came around.

Smurf and Scoop got into it when Carey accidently pulled the plug on my Stone Age computer.

The mid-1980s were pioneer days of electronic transmission for newspaper reporters working on location. Just a few years removed from typewriters, telephones, dictation, and Western Union, we were issued clunky plastic computer boxes known as PortaBubbles. The machines featured a small TV-type monitor that had a rubber dock with ear holes at the top. When ready to transmit, one would dial the office, then insert the telephone receiver into the dock. Bigger than a bread box, the machine was electronically powered and had limited "save" capacity. If you unplugged in midstory, everything since you last hit Save was gone.

Near the end of the Celtics-Pacers game, thinking he was unplugging his own machine, Carey bent down and ripped my cord from the power strip under the press table. My story vanished, I was on deadline, and the Celts were winning a close game in Larry's hometown. I did not react well. Carey had earned multiple JJ points, and a press row argument ensued.

"Ha, ha, Scoop," McHale said after the win. "We saw! Smurf got you! He pulled the plug! That's right out of the Peter Vecsey school-of-journalism tactics!" McHale was referencing a *New York Post* sportswriter known for his competitive streak.

McHale loved getting into the beat guys' business and had an opinion about everything. He once approached me before practice on a snowy morning in Brookline and said, "Scoop, something I've noticed about you people here in Massachusetts and the way you handle snow. Back home in Hibbing, when we see a car stuck in a snowbank, we just go up behind the car and start pushing. You don't even have to talk to the driver. Here, when people see a car stuck in the snow, they love it. They ignore the poor guy and say, 'Good, there's another guy I can beat in to work today!'"

When a local female sports anchor came to practice for interviews, McHale sidled up to me and said, "I knew it! She's big in the hips. When you just see a girl on TV, a lot of people can't tell, but growing up in Minnesota, you develop a sixth sense for that sort of thing. You're always talking to girls who're wearing giant parkas, so you have to be able to tell what they look like under all that."

In mid-November, when I was talking to Ainge about losing his starting job ("To be honest, I don't believe the Celtic system is the ideal situation for me, but I'm not going to complain," Ainge admitted), McHale interrupted us with "Enough of this, Scoop! Leave Danny alone. Let's talk about that new movie *The Big Chill*. Danny says there's no way the guy would have let his wife sleep with the college friend just because she wanted to have a baby. I disagree. What do you say?"

We were all starting families. Danny and Michelle Ainge already had two children (they'd become parents of six), the McHales had a baby girl at home (first of five children), and I'd just learned I was going to be a dad for the first time.

Dennis Johnson tested K. C. Jones early in the season. Upset that McHale didn't pass him the ball in a game against the Sixers, Johnson acted out and, when Jones barked at him in the locker room, yelled at his coach in front of the other players. Jones—who'd had a tryout as a defensive back with the Rams and had stood up to Wilt Chamberlain in his NBA days—asked DJ if he wanted to step outside.

"Dennis was a little bit of an outsider," recalled Maxwell. "And we were such a tight team. Dennis was wrong. Players normally stuck with each other on those things. We call it the Amen section. Not this time. We told DJ he was wrong and that he was going to apologize. And he did."

"I could see how Dennis could be hard on coaches," said Ainge. "But our culture was so strong that DJ didn't have to be the best player or the only leader. He could just play. So we got the best version of DJ."

On Wednesday, November 16, the Celtics, winners of nine straight, flew from Denver to Salt Lake City. After landing, we heard the usual "Would Dolph Schayes please report to baggage carousel number three."

And then . . . seconds later . . . a tall fiftysomething man with a good head of hair and an athletic spring in his step appeared at our baggage claim and said, "Hi, I'm Dolph Schayes. Somebody here looking for me?"

Absolutely incredible. A Carl Jung moment of synchronicity. After

84

years of being paged at random airports across America—when he was probably not even in the same time zone as the Celtics—Dolph Schayes actually appeared at carousel 3. It was one of my favorite moments on the Celtics beat, and I'm pretty sure it was the highlight of Cedric Maxwell's life.

A month later, the Celtics beat the Pistons in front of 24,318 fans at the Pontiac gym. Parish scored 24 with 19 rebounds. The next morning, Chief was sitting with Buckner near the Northwest gate at Detroit's Metro Airport when I plopped myself down in the empty seat to Parish's right.

"Robert," I started. "What's up? Why won't you talk to me?"

"I just don't like you," he snapped.

Was it the stuff I wrote about his holdout? Was he jealous of the coverage the *Globe* gave Bird and McHale? Was it something I said in an unguarded moment on a bus or in a hotel lobby? We all knew that Parish was easily slighted. *Sports Illustrated* folks told us of a reporter who tried to get an interview with the Chief and joked, "We've done our story on Kareem for this week," only to be rejected by Parish, who took the remark as an unforgivable insult.

"Just tell me what I did," I asked Parish. "We're grown-ups. We can talk about this."

"No. Leave me alone. Just leave me alone."

I could see Buckner was getting increasingly uncomfortable as I persisted, but we were in a safe, public space. Surely the Chief and I could work this out.

Parish wasn't having it. "Just let it go. Why can't you just let it go? You remind me of a woman. You're like my wife!"

"I honestly didn't know what you'd done," Buckner said in 2021. "Chief was a man of few words, but he made sure we knew that he didn't care for you at all."

That was my last try with the Chief. He was an important player and all of his teammates liked him. But I was done. The *Globe* had plenty of other reporters who could get quotes from Robert Parish.

My last Celtics column for 1983 was a collection of New Year's resolutions from team members. Ten of the twelve players weighed in. Bird's resolution was "To bring Rick Robey back so I can get my rebounding average back up there." The only players not represented were Parish and Dennis Johnson.

"I don't have a resolution, but yours should be trying to not have so many people mad at you," said DJ.

I think DJ secretly liked me because, like Maxwell, he saw a pro-white bias in the Boston media and took comfort in the knowledge that I had no problem criticizing Bird and McHale.

Then came the "Big Joe" weekend in Milwaukee.

Joe Hillenbrand was a former University of Minnesota football player who routinely led a group of McHale's Hibbing buddies to Milwaukee when the Celtics came to town. Big Joe was an epic drinker who weighed north of three hundred pounds. His assorted friends included "Bones" (Michael Cervoney) and "Jimbo" (Jim Sandor), McHale's cousin from Hibbing. McHale's brother John was sometimes with the group.

"Most of the trouble I got into was when those clowns came around," McHale said in 2021. "If I just say those names now, my liver starts hurting."

The Celtics came into Milwaukee early on a Saturday afternoon in mid-January after a Friday-night game in Philly. The trek from Philly to Milwaukee featured a stop in Detroit, a couple of flight delays, and an unexpected Hank Aaron sighting when we were waiting for bags in Milwaukee. When Ainge went over to say hello to the home run king, Maxwell hollered, "Hey, Danny, did he hit more homers than you?"

Aaron out-homered Ainge, 755–2, but the Hammer never drained a three-pointer over Magic Johnson.

When the Celtics bus pulled up to the downtown Milwaukee Hyatt, we spotted a Winnebago with Minnesota plates. Big Joe and the Minnesota Crew were in town.

"It was unbelievable," recalled McHale. "The Winnebago and our team bus, side by side outside the hotel."

Buckner offered to show everybody around Milwaukee, and Bird joined the group. Much beer was consumed—not a great idea given Sunday's made-for-TV noontime start. The result was predictable and ugly: the Bucks handed the Celtics their worst loss of the season, 106–87, as the Celtics shot 39 percent. Bird made only 3 of 13 shots. McHale was 0 for 8. Buckner 1 of 5. Only Ainge—never tempted by the nectar of the gods—had a strong game, scoring 18 points on 8-of-13 shooting.

"I don't remember much about that weekend, to be honest," Buckner said in 2021. "I'm sure we went to Major Goolsby's."

Everybody in the Celtics traveling group knew what had happened, and so did Don Nelson. The Bucks' coach offered to provide the Minnesota Crew with a fully stocked Hyatt suite for ensuing visits.

"It was a disaster," recalled McHale. "We'd stayed out way too late and drank and, oh, gosh. After the game, K.C. just pulled me aside and said, 'Kev, those guys aren't coming to Chicago, are they?' When the Winnebago left, I was very relieved."

A day later, Bird was named an Eastern Conference All-Star starter along with Malone, Dr. J., Isiah Thomas, and Sidney Moncrief. Sure enough, Laimbeer was named a reserve, which meant another weekend of "Good morning, Larry" followed by "Fuck you, Bill!"

The highlight of the NBA's first "All Star Weekend" in Denver was an Auerbach tantrum while coaching an old-timers squad in a Saturday matinee at McNichols Arena. Retired NBA official Norm Drucker took the brunt of Red's fire, but Auerbach had plenty more for league publicist Brian McIntyre and longtime rival coach Alex Hannum. One of Auerbach's old-timers was Dolph Schayes, still blissfully unaware that he'd been a Celtics punch line.

Overseeing All Star Weekend was forty-one-year-old David Stern, Commissioner Larry O'Brien's aide-de-camp, no stranger to Red's combative ways. Stern was about to lead the NBA into an era of unprecedented popularity and prosperity on the backs of the Celtics and Lakers with considerable help from a North Carolina junior named Michael Jordan. After Sunday's All-Star Game, Stern joined McHale and me in the lounge of the league's hotel headquarters and an over-served McHale knocked a full beer into the lap of the incoming com-missioner. Unflappable Stern ordered McHale a replacement beer. It was hard not to be a fan of the new commish.

The Celtics' annual February West Coast trip was next. This jun-ket was born in the 1960s when Celtics owner Walter Brown needed his Bruins and Celtics to vacate the barn to make room for family-friendly skating shows during Massachusetts public schools' Febru-ary vacation. The trip always brought out the best in Bird, who liked the warm weather and the run-and-gun Western Conference game. It also catered to his passing skills. Bird believed Western Conference stat crews were far more liberal in crediting assists. Call it the Magic Effect.

Far from the bad weather and clingy masses at the Boston Garden, Bird averaged 26 points, 13 rebounds, and 13 assists over forty-three minutes per night in the first three games of the trip, all victories.

During warm-ups in Portland, I got hit in the noggin by a stray Kenny Carr pass. The errant throw bounced off the side of my head, mangling my giant-frame eyeglasses. Carr felt bad and came over to apologize. Bird saw the incident from his end of the court and loved it. After torching Carr and the Blazers for 34 points, 18 rebounds, 9 assists, and 3 steals in forty-six minutes, he hunted me down in the hotel bar.

"I saw the whole thing, Scoop," he said with a big grin. "You was pissed!"

Noting my Molson Golden, he launched into a discussion on beer bottles: "No green bottles for me. I see where all them Molsons and Heinekens are popular these days, but I can't do it. It goes back to col-lege when I was at a crowded party once and I picked up somebody's green bottle and started chugging it. That third cigarette went down my throat and I just about gagged. No beer in green bottles since then."

For the Lakers portion of the West Coast trip, the Celtics stayed at the generic Airport Park Hotel in Inglewood, near the Forum. I was having lunch with my sister-in-law in the hotel lounge the day before

the Lakers game when Bird and Buckner arrived from morning practice and plopped down at our table. They weren't buying the notion
that my lunch date was a relative.

"Sister-in-law, my ass," Bird said when I saw him at the Forum the
next night. "Got you, Scoop!"

Professional athletes love it when they think they have something
on a writer.

After the Celtics lost to the Lakers, we moved on to Phoenix,
where I had more family, who could attest to the truthfulness of my
explanation about the relative in LA. The Celtics beat the Suns and
DJ outrebounded Robey, 9–1.

Two weeks later, we were back at the Milwaukee Hyatt for a
weeknight game with the Bucks (no Big Joe this time). As I sat in
the atrium lobby with Bird, McHale, and Buckner, we saw assistant
coach Ford—back from a scouting trip—hop out of a cab and rush
into the lobby with a hanger bag slung over his shoulder. In this era
before sophisticated scouting and nonstop television coverage of college basketball talents, the Celtics regularly sent assistant coaches to
study college games in preparation for the draft.

"What's up, Doc?" said McHale. "You've been gone for a couple
of days. Where've you been?"

Ford turned toward McHale and said, "I just got here from the
SEC tournament and I've been watching the guy who's going to
kick your ass for the next ten years, Kevin. He's only six-four and he's
chunky, but I've never seen anybody like him. Name's Charles Barkley."

Everybody laughed. The joke wasn't on McHale until the 1984–85
preseason when rookie Barkley showed up with the Philadelphia
76ers.

Ten days later, the Celtics beat the Knicks at Madison Square Gar-
den in a playoff preview game attended by Hibbing native Robert
Zimmerman, aka Bob Dylan. McHale made a rare start in place of
Maxwell (groin) and led the Celtics with 18 points.

McHale liked to brag about all the famous folks from Hibbing, including Roger Maris, Vincent Bugliosi, American Communist Party leader Gus Hall ("Gus could really go to his left!" said McHale), and Robert Zimmerman.

"I dedicated this game to my main man and great crooner, Bobby Dylan," McHale said. "Bobby inspired me. He was the key to the game. We're going to have to bring him to the playoffs with us."

The 1983–84 Celtics finished 62-20, clinching home court throughout the postseason. It was clear that only three teams had a chance to win the 1984 NBA championship: Boston, Philadelphia, and Los Angeles. The Lakers were the favorites. They had a deeper, healthier team than the one the Sixers had broomed in 1983. The Lakers had swept the regular season series with the Celtics. When Portland coach Jack Ramsay was asked what it would take to prevent the Lakers from winning the championship, Ramsay had only two words:

"Divine intervention."

Time for an act of God. Maybe two.

CHAPTER 6

"WE PLAYED LIKE SISSIES"

"**S**coop, get over here."

Cedric Maxwell and M. L. Carr were standing near the Boston Garden's courtside seats, cackling as the Celtics got ready for practice. Max had something he wanted to share.

It was Saturday morning, April 28, 1984, and the top-seeded Celtics were getting ready for the second round of the playoffs. The Garden was newly available for practice because the Bruins had been broomed out of the Stanley Cup playoffs by the Montreal Canadiens. The Celts were set to open against the Knicks the next day. Boston didn't learn the identity of its conference semifinal opponent until the night before practice when the Knicks beat the Pistons in a fifth-and-deciding game in overtime in Detroit. The Knicks-Pistons series was dominated by New York's six-seven forward Bernard King, who scored 42 points per game.

Wearing his I ♥ NEW YORK T-shirt, Max was in a talking mood. "Scoop, write this down. It's going to be a monumental task to try to stop Bernard King, but he ain't getting forty on us. We're going to stop the bitch."

Carr, who'd been teasing Maxwell about King's scoring binges, slapped his knee and howled.

"Bernard has scored his last forty points," said M.L. "He won't get any forties here. We've got somebody that can stop him."

"That's right." Max cradled a basketball with his right hand as he

91

sashayed down the sideline, mocking King's unusual gait. "Ain't no way any bitch who walks like this is gonna get forty off me."

The 1984 Celtics were the Dream Team of trash-talkers, but this bordered on hate speech. Maxwell was challenging King's manhood.

As the players drifted back toward their teammates, readying for prepractice stretch, Ford came over and said, "Scoop, you're not going to write that, are you? I mean, you can't. . . ."

Sorry, Doc. The next day's morning *Globe*, a massive New England voice with a Sunday circulation north of eight hundred thousand, featured a sports cover story headlined, "Celtics Baiting King." The quotes were all there, though I omitted the part where Max mimicked King's stride. When K. C. Jones confronted Maxwell with the headline, Max said, "If you're scared, get a damn dog, man."

The 1984 Celtics were telling the league that they were going to win the championship, they were going to have fun, and they didn't care if they hurt your feelings.

New Jersey's five-game, first-round upset of the 76ers cleared the path for Boston. With Philly out of the way, Boston and Los Angeles were on a collision course to meet in the Finals for the first time since 1969, when Bill Russell (eleven rings) and Sam Jones (ten) closed their careers with a Game 7 championship win in Los Angeles.

Bird and Maxwell had opposite responses when I asked about the removal of the Sixers from the playoffs.

"If we win the championship, there will be a little something missing," confessed Bird.

"I'm happy to see the chumps out of there," said Max. "Get 'em out of the way, that's what I say."

Philly was where a fan dropped the N-word on Maxwell during the 1981 conference finals, provoking Max to charge into the stands. The matter was settled out of court.

King ignored Maxwell when Max tried to shake hands before the opening tap of Game 1 against the Knicks, an 18-point Celtics victory. King was "held" to 26.

The 1984 Knicks turned out to be a tougher opponent than the

Celtics expected. New York was coached by Hubie Brown, a teacher of the game, who was aided by young assistant, Rick Pitino, best known in those days as a guy who'd played at UMass during the Dr. J. era and coached Boston University in front of small crowds on Commonwealth Avenue. The Knicks had an affable seven-foot center, Bill Cartwright, who was no match for Parish, but later gained notoriety by winning three rings with the Michael Jordan Bulls.

The Celtics crushed the Knicks again in Game 2, holding King to 13 points.

"They're in the grave right now," announced McHale. "We've got to keep pourin' dirt on 'em. We've got the shovel in our hands."

"The Knicks are like salmon," added Kevin Kernan of the *New York Post*. "They're swimming upstream—going home to die."

In New York for Games 3 and 4, the Celtics stayed at the frayed Summit Hotel at 569 Lexington Avenue. Boston's arrangement with the hotel represented another of Auerbach's time-honored deals with cronies from an earlier era.

Auerbach hated New York even though he was born and raised in Brooklyn. To his dying day, he held a grudge against the Knicks because he believed Madison Square Garden robbed his 1938 George Washington team of a prestigious National Invitational Tournament bid.

"They screwed us because they were afraid a team from a small school in DC would come into the Garden and beat one of the New York teams," Auerbach said.

Red enjoyed my tweaking King and the Knicks and was warming up to me a little. When I told him my wife was expecting our first baby in May, he gave me a box of Dutch Masters. The cigars were distributed when Sarah Shaughnessy was born during the '84 playoffs, and the sacred carton today stores batteries on a shelf in my home office closet. Every Christmas, when there's high demand for Duracell AAA's, I think of Red.

Auerbach-Shaughnessy relations were newly strained when Red banned *Globe* reporter Lesley Visser from the Celtics locker room after they lost Game 3 in New York. This unfolded a full six years after women media members were "allowed" to work NBA locker rooms and just two years after Red had attended Visser's wedding to CBS NBA announcer Dick Stockton. In Sunday's *Globe*, I presented Red with the coveted "Governor Ross Barnett Award"—a sarcastic reference to a Mississippi segregationist of the sixties.

King scored 43 when the Knicks squared the series in Game 4. This brought a crowd to Maxwell's locker.

"Oh-oh," said Max. "This is like a confessional. I'm sorry for letting Bernard King score forty-three points. I really am."

"The Bitch Is Back!" declared the *Post*.

A close series between Boston and New York with the star power of Bird and King was good for TV ratings. In Boston, President Reagan's May 9 speech to the nation was broadcast on tape delay *after* the Celtics and Knicks played Game 5 at the Boston Garden.

That game, eventually won by the Celtics 121–99, featured predictable dustups: Ainge scrapped with Knicks guard Darrell Walker, Knicks Len Elmore chased DJ, and King went jaw to jaw with Carr—who was described by a New York tabloid as "M.L. of Sam." Two nights later, King scored 44 in a 2-point Knicks win at Madison Square Garden, forcing a seventh game Sunday afternoon at the Boston Garden.

After the Game 6 loss in New York, K. C. Jones went to Jimmy Weston's on Fifty-Fourth Street for some Friday-night crooning, belting out "Misty," "San Francisco," and "You're Nobody till Somebody Loves You." Jones met Frank Sinatra at an after-party and was amazed that the Chairman of the Board knew his name. The Celtics coach pledged to learn "Summer Wind."

In the Sunday-afternoon series finale, Bird scored 39 with 12 rebounds and 10 assists in a 121–104 clincher. It's cut 3 on the B side of Bird's Greatest Hits album.

When the loser's locker room opened to the press, Brown was met by silence as he stood before reporters. No one knew how to ask Hubie about what he'd just seen.

"You guys going all Charlie McCarthy on me?" asked Brown. "Okay, I'll say it. This game was all about Larry Bird. I hope nobody underestimates Larry Bird's performance. . . . His performance was beyond description."

Boston's subsequent conference final series with Milwaukee bore no resemblance to what had happened one year earlier. Boston easily won the first two at home. Games 3 and 4 were scheduled for Saturday afternoon and Monday night in Milwaukee. This meant a free Friday night in Milwaukee.

Another road trip for Big Joe and the Minnesota Crew?

Fortunately for K. C. Jones, no wide-body camper was outside the Milwaukee Hyatt when the Celtics rolled into Brewtown on a bus from Chicago. No Big Joe. No Bones. No assorted McHales from the Iron Range.

After an early-Friday-night dinner, a few of the Celtics met at Major Goolsby's and watched the Lakers lose to the Suns in overtime in the Western Conference final series. Watching a playoff game in a noisy bar with Larry Bird wasn't much different from watching a game with your college pals. Every time a Laker got fouled while making a shot, Bird would yell, "Now you've got to make the free throw."

The not-hungover Celtics beat the Bucks for a third straight time the next afternoon. I returned to Goolsby's after the game, met McHale and a few writers, then trudged to my room and noticed the red message light blinking on the room phone. My wife, Marilou, had gone into labor two weeks early. I drove to Chicago in the dark of night, waited for O'Hare to open Sunday morning, and made it to Boston's Beth Israel Hospital in time to witness Sarah Shaughnessy come into the world. The Celtics must have missed me. They lost Game 4 the next night in Milwaukee.

I was handing out Red's Dutch Masters when the Celtics eliminated the Bucks in Game 5 at the Garden. Meanwhile, the Lakers KO'd the Suns out West, and it was game on for the Finals everyone wanted.

CBS was ecstatic. Boston-LA meant that Bird and Magic would

be meeting in a championship event for the first time since NBC set unbreakable ratings records with its broadcast of the Bird-Magic NCAA Final in 1979. At least one of them had been in the NBA Finals in each of their first four NBA seasons, but this was the first championship series featuring both.

The Celtics and Lakers were the Yankees and Dodgers of pro basketball. They'd played in seven NBA Finals from 1959 to 1969 with Boston winning every one. Lakers fans were haunted by the 1962 finale, when Frank Selvy's potential series winner clanged off the rim at the Boston Garden. LA general manager Jerry West experienced what he called the low point of his life when the Lakers couldn't beat Boston in 1969. A Celtics-Lakers Final in 1984 meant that the league's two showcase franchises accounted for 60 percent (23 of 38) of *all* NBA crowns in the first four decades of the league's existence. (In the COVID summer of 2020, the LeBron James Lakers won their seventeenth NBA crown, finally tying the Celtics for most championship banners.)

Celtics-Lakers also represented a clash of cultures easily framed by media outlets. It was ham and cheese versus sushi, stationary bikes versus Italian ten-speeds, meaty-faced Celtics fans versus Rambis Youth—a cult of slender teen boys wearing yellow T-shirts and nerdy Clark Kent glasses.

Like the city they represented, the Celtics were gritty, tough, arrogant, and loud. Their game was pass, move, pick, and block out. Their coach was a rugged ex-player who'd been a defensive specialist. The Lakers were fashionable, fast, and sprinkled with glitter. Their coach, Pat Riley, looked and dressed like a movie star.

"They were the Thoroughbreds and we were the Clydesdales," said Carr.

LA had celebrity fans Nicholson, Michael Jackson, the Fonz, and Rod Stewart. To sing the national anthem, the team invited Jeffrey Osborne, Stevie Wonder, and Dionne Warwick. Their promotions staff bombarded the senses with Laker Girls and halftime entertainment. In contrast, the national anthem at Celtics games was performed by a cornball trumpet/snare-drum jazz duo. According to an official Celtics press release, the Boston Garden's halftime entertainment featured "ballboy rolling out ball carts."

Themes of race were underscored. Boston's fundamental game versus LA's showtime. Suburban versus urban. The Celtics had three white stars: Bird, McHale, and Ainge. Except for Rambis, all the Lakers who played significant minutes were Black. It was never stated by anyone in authority, but the Celtics were white America's team while the Lakers were the favorites of the Black community. Players on both teams were aware that many people in Boston's Black community wanted the Lakers to beat the Celtics.

"The country was split," Magic told ESPN. "If you were white, you cheered for the Celtics; if you were Black, you cheered for the Lakers. . . . We go to Boston and me and Coop see these five African American men and they stop us and say, 'I hope you kill 'em. All of us in Boston, we live in Roxbury and we want you to beat the Celtics.'"

"That didn't just start with Celtics-Lakers," said Henderson, who came to Boston when Bird arrived in 1979. "I got a sense of that the first day I came to the Celtics. Traveling around the country in my first days, we were always 'the White Team' against 'the Black Team.' It was always like that. But the big difference was that we had some white boys that could fucking play. In 1984, LA had the damn 'Showtime.' It was sparkling and fun to watch and good-looking. It was the hot thing in the NBA, and we were just these guys from around the block. And the Black-white thing really took hold with a lot of the country."

Maxwell was acutely aware of the racial undercurrent. When he first played for Boston in 1977, he was stunned when friends told him to steer clear of South Boston. He sometimes spoke of a sweet, yet awkward, encounter with Kevin McHale's mom in the 1980s.

"The players on our team, we all loved each other," Maxwell told NBC Sports Boston. "It was a very unique family bond. We were so close, and when we'd see somebody else's parents, we'd just grab them and hug them like they were our mom. I remember seeing Kevin's mom—and I was close to Kevin—and I go up and I was like, 'Hey, Mrs. McHale, how are you doing?' And I go in and give her a big hug, and I remember to this day Mrs. McHale cringing. Because I knew it was the first time a Black person had ever probably hugged her because she was from Hibbing. They'd probably never seen Black people except on TV.

"In 1984, people of color weren't rooting for the Celtics against Magic and Kareem," continued Maxwell. "It wasn't just a Boston thing. I had friends asking me, 'What was wrong with you?' I have talked to Worthy and Michael Cooper about it. Basically, it was Black and white. Being a Black guy on a 'white' team was tough. We never got any credit as players. We had great Black players, but we were identified as a white team, and it was so unfair. We were just a team, but the public perception was that we were a white team. All of us who were there felt that way, except maybe M.L. He played both sides of the coin."

Apart from its racial flavor, the matchup featured an unusual contrast of basketball pedigrees. Most of LA's best players were products of blue-chip NCAA programs: Kareem Abdul-Jabbar, Jamaal Wilkes, and Swen Nater had attended UCLA. James Worthy and Bob McAdoo were North Carolina Tar Heels. Magic (Michigan State) and Byron Scott (Arizona State) were from power conferences. Boston's starting five hailed from Indiana State (Bird), Centenary (Parish), North Carolina–Charlotte (Maxwell), Virginia Commonwealth (Henderson), and Pepperdine (DJ). Anybody could build an NBA powerhouse with the best players from the blue-chip conferences. Building a champion with players from no-name schools was another tribute to Auerbach's genius.

Red bristled at any mention of a Lakers dynasty. He had fourteen championship rings and wore the one from 1969—the one that hurt LA the most.

The drama was further exaggerated by weather, geography, and grueling scheduling.

Other than an occasional World Series game affected by rain or cold weather (or a rare Super Bowl plagued by rain) every major sport today plays its championship in a climate-controlled environment. This wasn't the case in Boston in 1984. The old Boston Garden, built in 1928 and demolished in 1998, had no air-conditioning, and New England was due for a summerlike swelter in May–June of '84.

Travel and scheduling were other issues. A seven-game series starting in Boston meant the Lakers had to fly across the country six times in twelve days. The Celtics made the trek five times, always on commercial aircraft, sometimes changing planes in either Chicago or New York. The frenetic schedule and east-west dynamic made for great television, but took a toll on both teams, especially the Lakers. Starting with Game 4, the schedule called for a game or a coast-to-coast flight in each of the final seven days of the series. The rigors of the 1984 Finals inspired the NBA to change formats—from 2-2-1-1-1 to 2-3-2—the following year. It stayed that way until 2014.

For Bird, the '84 Finals presented an opportunity to bandage the wound that had never healed from the 1979 NCAA Final. For West and the Lakers, it was a chance to make amends for seven Finals lost to Boston.

"We were hearing about the leprechauns and all this crap," Worthy told ESPN years later. "Jerry West had never gone back to the Boston Garden. That pain transferred over to us."

CBS producer Ted Shaker called it a match made in sports television heaven.

The still-fresh and not-yet-sweating Lakers demolished the Celtics at the Garden in Game 1, running to a 30–12 lead and laying waste to Boston's 9-0 Garden playoff record. The final score was 115–109, but it was never close. The high-flying Lakers played at a different speed from Boston.

Little-used Celtics guard-forward Scott Wedman scored 6 points on 4 shots in twelve minutes of Game 1.

Wedman was a strange fit with the Larry Bird Celtics. Raised on a farm in Kansas, he was a late bloomer who'd received few scholarship offers and wound up at Colorado, hardly an NBA factory. He grew to be six-five, made himself a better player, and was the Kansas City Kings' first-round pick (number six overall) in the 1974 draft. A deadly marksman, Wedman became an All-Star with the Kings.

"In the early 1980s, before we traded for Scottie, we were playing against him in Kansas City and he was killing us," Henderson recalled. "He was fucking torching Larry's ass. Max, too. We couldn't stop him. We had a time-out and Fitch said, 'Can anybody stop this guy?' and M.L. raised his hand. Bill put him in the game and Scottie came off a baseline screen and M.L. nailed his ass. You could hear it from the bench. We didn't have no more trouble out of Scottie after that."

Wedman was traded to the Celtics in 1983, but Fitch and K. C. Jones never knew what to do with him. A vegetarian who carried his own bottled water (McHale always claimed he filled the bottle with tap water when Wedman wasn't looking), Wedman was twenty years ahead of his time regarding diet and fitness. Bird was slow to warm up to him. Who could trust a guy who wouldn't eat a hamburger? The only time writers ever heard from Wedman was when he refused to play in a practice gym because he was convinced there was asbestos in the gym's walls and ceiling. He was frequently accompanied by a personal massage therapist, who always wore a hat and rarely spoke.

Before Game 1 of the Finals, I saw Parish summon Wedman's therapist from the stands and disappear into the Celtics locker room. Parish returned for the start, but played poorly, fouling out in twenty-seven minutes while Abdul-Jabbar scored 32.

I chased down Wedman's healer at the next day's Garden practice. He reluctantly identified himself as Steve Krischel, said he was from Kansas City, and told me Parish had a bum shoulder.

"I couldn't do in four minutes what was necessary for Robert to play," said Krischel. "If it were up to me, I'd have said he couldn't play yesterday."

I tracked down veteran team physician Dr. Thomas Silva, who'd never been accused of being overly thorough (McHale insisted that his entire physical when he came to the Celtics was a thirty-second exam in which Dr. Silva asked him to cough). Silva's solution to most maladies was an ice pack. Players called him Dr. Ice.

"I am not aware that Robert was seen before the game, and I am not aware he had a problem before the game," huffed the good doctor. "I would not condone that action at all. Ray [trainer Melchiorre] had better do some explaining, not only to me, but to Jan and Red. That's not a good situation."

"Robert didn't really say anything before the game," Melchiorre snapped. "Then, some guy who shouldn't be in the locker room was in the room. Robert said he had some tightness in the muscles of his left shoulder, but what qualifications does this guy have? The guy looks like a plumber."

There were three days off in between Games 1 and 2 in Boston—a deadly gap for newspaper reporters trying to file daily stories—and it made the "plumber" story a perfect off-day feature. How could the Celtics allow a mystery healer into their locker room to treat Parish minutes before the first game of the Finals?

"Circulation of the *Globe* at the Copley Marriott was way up today," league publicist Brian McIntyre told me when we got to the Garden for the next practice. The Celtics locked us out for the first time all season and announced that only team medical personnel would be allowed in the locker room, effective immediately.

Dr. Silva and the Celtics weren't the only ones unhappy with me. Lakers coach Riley didn't like me reporting that the Lakers were staying at the Copley Marriott.

"Why do you put where we're staying in the paper?" asked the coach. "It brings out the crazies in Boston. We've had a bunch of false fire alarms."

I argued that it seemed like a reasonable detail to include in my notes column. But Riley was right.

We had a good relationship before the series. When Riley first became Lakers head coach in 1981–82, I'd flown to LA to profile him, and after the story ran, the coach sent me a handwritten thank-you note on Lakers stationery:

"I felt you made me appear bigger and better than I really am," Riley wrote with a Lakers-purple felt pen. "That I appreciate, and also the effort of a man doing his job, regardless of what was written."

There was none of that collegial love in the hot Boston spring of 1984. Riley was paranoid about everything. With cause. In addition to the prank fire drills, phones rang in the rooms of Lakers players at all hours, even if instructions had been left to block calls. The Lakers were sent to practice sites—arranged by the Celtics—only to find locked doors. Trusting nothing in Boston, the Lakers brought their own towels and water to the Causeway Street gym. The Garden's old-timey wiring wouldn't allow LA to bring its own air-conditioning units.

Game 2 produced a 124–121 Celtics overtime victory—one of the most dramatic and important games in the history of the Celtics.

Late-game craziness started with twenty seconds left in regulation when McHale stepped to the line with Boston trailing by 2 points. Riley instructed Magic to call time-out only if McHale made both shots.

Nervous McHale back-rimmed both free throws (ghost of Beezer Carnes). When Magic corralled the second miss, he called time-out even though McAdoo was standing next to him in the paint screaming, "No! No!"

Eighteen seconds were left on the clock.

"All of a sudden it's dead quiet in Boston Garden," CBS's Dick Stockton said while viewers saw the image of a gleeful Jack Nicholson delivering the choke sign.

Scott and Cooper congratulated each other while Riley drew up an inbounds play.

On the other bench, Carr hollered, "Come on, guys! We gotta make something happen!"

The Lakers time-out was a strategic blunder. Riley still calls it the biggest mistake of his coaching career. He knew that if the Lakers had simply let play continue after Magic rebounded the second McHale miss, Boston would have been forced to foul. Instead, the Celtics had time to set up their defense and plot for a steal.

Guarded by McHale, inbounding from the sideline near the Boston basket, Worthy passed to Magic, who was guarded by Bird. Magic got it back to Worthy, who was almost under the Celtics basket. Worthy panicked. He thought about calling a time-out, then, out of the corner of his eye, saw Scott up the floor and lobbed a crosscourt pass in Scott's direction. Henderson, who'd been guarding Scott, attacked the lazy throw like an NFL defensive back homing in on a soft pass for an easy pick. The Celtics guard never broke stride on his way to an uncontested, game-tying layup.

Henderson stole the ball! Just as Havlicek had stolen the ball on the same floor nineteen years earlier.

"You never expect anything like that is going to happen," Henderson said. "You're taught to rotate on defense, and that's what happened. I don't know what James was thinking. As soon as he got the ball, he let it go. I rotated like I was supposed to, and this big, fat cookie was up there, and all I had to do was intercept that ball and knock it toward the basket so I could make the layup before he got me. . . . That took some steam out of them."

"It was bad," Worthy told ESPN. "I'm a young player. I'd never been in an ugly environment where they are just giving it to you. M. L. Carr's got that damn towel and your heart just drops out of your body."

Tie game.

Riley called time again.

"The leprechaun at work here in the Boston Garden," CBS color commentator Tommy Heinsohn exclaimed. "A steal right when you need it!"

The final seconds of regulation in Game 2 haunt Magic the way the first time-out haunts Riley. With ten seconds left, Johnson—guarded by Maxwell—took a pass from Scott. Pounding the ball out top, Magic looked toward Abdul-Jabbar, who was guarded by Parish. The pass was there. The skyhook was there. But Magic never passed to Kareem. He kept dribbling, looking for a better option. As the clock struck 0:00, Magic forced a pass to McAdoo, too late.

The Lakers still led throughout overtime. LA led by a point with fourteen seconds left in overtime when Wedman—the invisible All-Star of the Celtics—drained a 13-foot jumper from the left corner to put the Celtics ahead for good. Scott Wedman. The guy with the plumber friend. Was the hero.

Trolling for postgame quotes after midnight, I came into a circle of scribes interviewing Wedman. When Wedman saw me enter the scrum, he raised his right hand, motioned toward me, and said, "Sorry, but I can't talk anymore until he leaves. I can't talk in front of him because of inaccuracies he quoted my friend saying."

I've had dozens of players freeze me out, but have always been able to get their words by standing with the pack. Not this time. Wedman was done until I was gone. Not wanting to impede the work of the others, knowing I could get quotes from colleagues in the room, I slinked away from the pack. Scott Wedman blocked my shot.

One day later, the Celtics gathered at Logan for United Flight 97 leaving for Los Angeles at 5:15 p.m. Seated up front in the large first-class cabin was Jack Nicholson, no longer flashing choke signs in the direction of McHale. Our in-flight movie was *Terms of Endearment*, which had just won five Oscars, including Best Picture. Nicholson, who'd won Best Supporting Actor for his portrayal of astronaut Garrett Breedlove, never looked up from his book during the airing of the film. Perhaps he didn't want to fork over $3 for the headset.

Back in coach, my flight was interrupted when Wedman came back and sat for a chat.

"I'm sorry about last night," he started. "But that story really made trouble for me and Steve. He can't come into the locker room anymore and that's really a problem. Everything was going along fine until you wrote that. But I talked to my wife about it, and we agreed that you were just doing your job and it wasn't right of me to stop talking like that. I know you have problems with a lot of the guys, but you won't have problems with me anymore."

It was the most words I'd ever heard him speak.

The Celtics and Boston media stayed at the Los Angeles Airport

Marriott for the LA portion of the Finals. Saturday's practice was at 10:30 a.m. at the Forum, and Melchiorre arranged for players and media to go back and forth on the Marriott shuttle jitneys traditionally reserved for hotel guests making the short hop to LAX.

In my Game 3 setup story, I mentioned, "The Lakers endured four more false fire alarms in their final night at the Copley Marriott and have arranged to switch to the Copley Westin for their return trip to Boston."

Dick move.

Game 3 was Sunday at 12:30, and the frustrated Lakers destroyed the Celtics, 137–104. Magic set a Finals record with 21 assists, and LA scored a championship-record 47 third-quarter points. It was a jailbreak run-and-dunk show, much to the delight of Nicholson, former Laker Girl Paula Abdul, white-tux-clad Dancing Barry (aka the Ambassador of Enthusiasm), Rambis Youth, and the rest of the Forum glitterati. The Lakers scored 58 points on fast-break layups and transition jumpers. It was the most lopsided defeat in Celtics playoff history.

"The only shot we have is if they run themselves to death and then have to forfeit," Maxwell told McHale.

The rout was punctuated during a quiet moment late in the game when Bird was at the free throw line and a Forum fan yelled, "Larry, how do you stay so white?"

Parish was in a playoff funk. Dennis Johnson played only fourteen minutes, and Heinsohn suggested on national television that DJ might have a little dog in him. Meanwhile, for reasons no one could understand, Henderson was guarding Magic, which left DJ on Scott. The official explanation was that Jones wanted his players to guard the player who was guarding them, but that simply made no sense. Auerbach had acquired Dennis Johnson so the Celtics would have someone to guard Magic Johnson in the Finals.

Bird, who shot only 44 percent in the first three games, fired up 3 airballs in Game 3 and recorded only 2 assists. His failures bolstered the pre-series theme that spidery Lakers forward Michael Cooper was Larry Bird's kryptonite.

"It's embarrassing, no doubt about it," said Bird. "We got some great players on this team, but we don't have the players with the heart sometimes that we need. And today when you see Magic slapping high fives and guys going behind their backs and shooting lay-ups on us all day long, it seems like someone would try to put a stop to it, but until we get our hearts where they belong, we're in trouble. . . . If we keep playing like this, Red's going to be switching to cigarettes. . . . We played like sissies."

How do you change it? we asked him.

"You go to the hospital and get twelve heart transplants."

CHAPTER 7

"NO MORE LAYUPS"

There were two off days between Games 3 and 4 of the 1984 NBA Finals. It gave the Celtics extra time to think about the Lakers' dominance and Bird's assault on his team's manhood.

The day before Game 4, as the team bus snaked through Inglewood on the way to practice, players noticed an unusual sales prop in front of a tire shop near the Forum.

"This mechanical gorilla was in front of the store, waving cars to come in," Maxwell recalled. "The thing looked a lot like Quinn Buckner, and everybody screamed out, 'Hey, Bucky, there's your brother.' We all laughed like hell."

Later that day, on Bird's orders, equipment manager Wayne Lebeaux went to the shop and negotiated a deal to put Buckner's jersey on the prop before Game 4.

"The guy didn't want to do it originally, but I gave him a pair of Larry's tickets," said Lebeaux. "The next day, game day, I went to the shop in the morning and put one of Quinn's number twenty-eight practice jerseys on the gorilla. The team was still back at the hotel. I told our driver to make sure he took the route that passed by the shop. And to make sure he stopped—even if the light was green."

On the ride to the Forum for game day shootaround, Maxwell was first to notice.

"The gorilla was waving his hands, wearing Bucky's jersey," said

Maxwell. "It was fucking priceless. I thought the bus was going to fucking tip over with laughter."

"Quinn went crazy," remembered Carr. "He thought it was me and Max. He started saying, 'You guys need to grow up.' Then he found out it was Larry. The only ones who knew that was coming were Larry and Wayne."

Buckner didn't like it then and he doesn't like it now. He knew the levity at his expense was helpful to the team in the moment, but it took him a while to forgive Bird. Asked about the incident in 2021, Buckner didn't want to comment.

"There was nothing vicious about it," said Carr. "It was funny and it helped us."

Certainly, the stunt wouldn't be okay today.

"Back then there was a lot of things you could get away with," said Maxwell.

"That's just how that team was," Henderson said with a sigh. "Anything to keep the group loose. After the Celtics, I played with the Pistons and won a championship with them [1990], but it was nothin' like the Celtics. The Pistons had none of that looseness. They were fuckin' so serious, man. When we lost to MJ and the Bulls [1991], those guys were cryin' like babies! It was like the world had come to an end. You would have never saw that with our group in Boston."

Down 2-1, humiliated in Game 3, the 1984 Celtics carried light hearts into the Forum before Game 4.

"There's Shank," McHale announced when he first saw me (Mc-Hale sometimes preferred Shank over Scoop). "He's got a sore shoulder from driving all those pipes through us the last couple of days."

Maxwell was equally chipper. He made fun of Jerry West touting Worthy for Finals MVP ("MVP after three games? It took me six games to do that"), then borrowed a pair of black-framed eyeglasses from a Rambis Youth and launched a shot that sailed a mile wide of the rim during early warm-ups.

None of this helped when the Celtics fell behind by 14 in the first half.

"We didn't disagree with what Larry had said," Ainge recalled in 2021. "We were down two and one and it should have been three and oh probably. We were playing like garbage. It was just a dunk-fest for them. Kevin was talking about 'no more layups,' and I said to him, 'Why don't you take a hard foul one time? I do this all the time and I get booed in every arena. Why don't you foul someone hard?'"

With the Lakers leading by 5 midway through the third, Abdul-Jabbar snatched a DJ miss and fired a baseball pass to Worthy, who was streaking up the left side. Worthy caught the pass, looked to his right, and saw Rambis racing toward the basket from the right sideline. Rambis caught Worthy's chest pass in stride and went up for what he expected would be another Showtime dunk.

Not this time.

With the words of Ainge and Bird rattling between his ears, McHale—running at full speed toward Rambis—extended his Gumby-esque left arm across Rambis's throat as Rambis launched toward the rim. The Lakers forward was upended like an NFL wide receiver, his left sneaker nearly hitting the rim before he crashed to the floor.

"As blatant a cheap shot as I have ever seen," Riley said.

Rambis bounced up and went after McHale as both benches emptied. Peacemaker Worthy pushed Rambis away from McHale and into a group of photographers seated on the floor. Buckner tackled Cooper, who was going for Henderson. While players milled about, a contrite McHale tried to make peace with Rambis, who shook his head and walked away. Since the crash had unfolded near the baseline where the press was seated, the postcollision fracas spilled into media tables and played out in front of our computers.

Asked about the moment years later, Bird joked, "That's where all the flopping started."

The play wouldn't be a punch line if it happened today. McHale's takedown would earn a flagrant foul, game ejection, and possibly a suspension for the rest of the series.

"I'd be suspended from the league for a year," McHale said with a chuckle in 2021.

In 1984, it was a personal foul on McHale, and Rambis was awarded two free throws.

In that moment, the 1984 NBA Finals went from *Footloose* to *On the Waterfront*—from Technicolor with digital special effects to grainy black-and-white newsreel.

"You could feel the whole thing turn," McHale said.

Minutes after the takedown, Bird tangled with Cooper as Bird tried to inbound after a Lakers basket. Unless it's the closing seconds of a tight game, the inbounds pass after a basket is a perfunctory, uncontested play. Not with Cooper guarding Bird. The Lakers swingman was all over the Celtics MVP, and an annoyed Bird leveraged Cooper ass-over-teakettle into the photo pit behind the baseline. There was no whistle. Seconds later, Bird and Abdul-Jabbar went jaw-to-jaw in the same spot where Rambis was upended.

"Kareem said, 'I will fuck you up, white boy,'" Maxwell recalled. "I was two feet away, and that is exactly what he said. Larry Joe Bird didn't give a shit. He was like, 'Whatever.' At that point, the series went from basketball to rollerball. Essentially, they lost their cool. We took them into deep water and they didn't know how to swim. That's when I knew we had 'em. Kareem was a thinker. You want to get into the head of the thinker, and we'd done it. I'd never seen Kareem like that. When we got into the intellectual's head, the rest of 'em were chopped liver."

Magic panicked at the end of Game 4, just as he had in Game 2. LA blew a 5-point lead in the final minute of regulation, and a Magic turnover in the closing seconds sent the game into overtime. With the score tied and thirty-five seconds left in overtime, Magic missed two free throws. The Celtics huddled and Bird said, "Give me the ball and get out of the way." With 0:14 on the clock, Bird canned a turnaround jumper over Magic in the lane.

The Lakers still trailed by 2 with ten seconds left in overtime when Worthy was fouled and had a chance to tie it. As Worthy lined up to shoot, Carr got in his grill and reminded him, "All you got to do is miss one!"

Maxwell took a spot on the rebounding line to Worthy's right. When Worthy short-armed the first free throw, effectively ending the game and squaring the series, Maxwell raised his arms over his head, walked across the key, directly in front of Worthy, brought his arms down, and gave the choke sign with his right hand. The crowd booed. The game was over. The series was tied.

"When he missed it, I just got it in my mind to go to my throat," Maxwell said. "Fuckin' chokin' out here in front of all these people. Everybody started booing and getting mad at me. And I'm like, 'All he had to do was make the free throw. I didn't miss the damn shot. He missed the shot. Why are you booing me?'"

"I had already missed the free throw," Worthy told ESPN. "Now I got to deal with this asshole coming in with the choke signal. Cedric Maxwell, who I admired as a kid. I grew up in Gastonia, North Carolina. He went to UNC–Charlotte, which was like fifteen minutes from my house. I loved him. And when he came in with that choke sign, I just lost it."

Thirty-five years after the 1984 Finals, young Celtics star Jayson Tatum chased down Maxwell in the new Garden and said, "Cornbread—man, I saw that *30 for 30*," an allusion to ESPN's retrospective series. "Damn, you're a bad motherfucker."

LA had one last chance to tie the game, but after a time-out, the annoying M. L. Carr (another North Carolina homey) intercepted yet another Worthy pass and went in for an uncontested dunk. It was the ultimate indignity for a superior Lakers team. Mocked and shocked by Boston's bullies, the high-flying Lakers scored only 2 fast-break points after McHale's third-quarter tackle.

Riley called the Celtics "thugs." A tough Irishman from Schenectady, Pat had made it to the NBA and to the top of the coaching profession on rugged play, street smarts, and mental toughness. Now he was watching his team get painted as soft. The series should have been over, a four-game Lakers sweep with Worthy as MVP. Instead it was 2-2 and going back to Boston.

"What is ingrained in their team is what you saw," he seethed.

111

"Now we know that's the way it's going to be. Now it's an ugly situation. They made a statement with that play. It was like in a gang war when the leaders meet the night before and decide on the weapons. They agree to hand-to-hand combat, then one side shows up with zip guns."

Think anybody would talk like this in a Zoom interview in 2021?

In the room at the other end of the corridor, K. C. Jones said little. The most important strategic decision of the series had been made when DJ moved over to guard Magic in the middle of Game 4, but the Celtics coach played no part in the decision.

"The truth has never been told about that situation," Henderson said in 2021. "At halftime of Game Four, I told Dennis to get on Magic. I made that choice. Not K.C. or DJ or Red. Nobody. It was me. I couldn't guard Magic because he was throwing the ball right over the top of my head. So I told DJ, 'You guard Magic because I can catch Byron Scott.' Byron was running out on DJ, and DJ couldn't keep up with him and didn't want to keep up with him. I could do that. Scott wasn't going to run out on me. And of course it was better for DJ to handle Magic because he was bigger. I didn't have any problem with that. It was just what had to happen."

DJ held Magic to 6 of 14 shooting and forced 9 turnovers in his first six quarters on Johnson after the switch.

Game 5 was set for two nights later, Friday night in Boston. No more days off. Just games, and coast-to-coast travel days.

I bumped into Rambis in the LAX gift shop the morning after Game 4. He was thumbing through a paperback and didn't want to talk to a reporter from the *Globe*. When the Lakers landed in Boston, it was well over ninety degrees with stifling humidity, and no Lakers bus was waiting at Logan. Bob Ryan and I witnessed Magic and Kareem folding themselves into the back seat of an ITOA taxi.

"How can they do that?" Ryan asked incredulously. "Kareem and Magic in the same cab? Terrible risk. They should separate those two—like the president and vice president during a national emergency!"

It was ninety-seven degrees and humid when the Lakers arrived at the Garden for Game 5.

Bird, Mr. White Heat, made 15 of 20 shots, scored 34 points, and grabbed 17 rebounds in a 121–103 thrashing of the Lakers.

How hot was it? Veteran referee Hugh Evans was overcome from the heat and watched the second half from the sideline. Carr spent time-outs fanning Bird with a dime-store trinket he'd brought to the Garden, while Buckner flapped wet towels in the faces of Parish and Maxwell. On the other bench, Abdul-Jabbar sucked on an oxygen mask—a disturbing visual for folks watching back home in LA.

"Kareem was always their biggest threat, and on that night he couldn't do anything," Buckner remembered. "The oxygen was a bad look, and you know how M.L. blows those kinds of things up."

When we asked Kareem what the Garden felt like, he said, "I suggest that you go to a local steam bath, do one hundred push-ups with all your clothes on, and then try to run back and forth for forty-eight minutes."

The game ended after midnight. Nine hours later the Celtics were on American Flight 11 out of Logan's Terminal B bound for Los Angeles.

"Well, boys, the series has changed," Maxwell told us after the next day's practice in the air-conditioned Forum. "In those first games, the Lakers were like little kids, running across the street without even looking. Now they stop at the curb, they hit the button on the Walk/Don't Walk sign. They wait for Walk. They look both ways. Then they cross."

He was in his motormouth glory.

"Don't get used to me saying all these great things much longer because when my career is over, you'll never see me again," Maxwell insisted. "I'm going to go back to North Carolina and do what I love to do—drive around in my big Cadillac all summer and watch guys work. I pull up to construction sites, hit the button to make my windows go down, then look out the window at the workers and say, 'Sorry, boys, but I got nothin' to do today.'"

The Celtics arrived for Game 6 full of confidence and bravado, talking of "Tragic Johnson" and the "LA Fakers." When they left their Forum locker room for pregame warm-ups, Carr ran down the corridor to the LA room, pounded on the door, and hollered, "Come out here and take your beating like a man! LA Fakers! You can't hide now!"

The Lakers responded with a 119–108 victory, using Celtics tactics. Worthy was called for a crackback block on Maxwell, jousted with Bird, and cocked his fist as he was restrained by teammates. Abdul-Jabbar said, "They're not the only team with pride."

Bird took only 11 shots and said, "My teammates wouldn't give me the ball."

Leaving the Forum, Nicholson pledged, "Tell Paul Revere to hang the lantern in the church because I'll be there Tuesday."

"Everything is back there to be had," said Riley. "History. The Boston Garden. Retired numbers. Championship banners. We have a chance to do something no other team has ever done. Go back to Boston Garden and win a championship on that parquet floor. So they got a lot of pressure on them."

In my final dispatch from LA, I wrote, "The Lakers will be staying at the Parker House, their third hotel of the series—an NBA record."

Incorrigible.

Waiting for a Sunday-night red-eye to Boston, after thirty-four hours in Los Angeles, Bird slept on the LAX terminal floor, using a Converse equipment bag for a pillow.

On board, *Globe* columnist Leigh Montville struck up a conversation with a striking young fashion model seated in coach. Elle Macpherson wasn't yet famous, but told Montville some of her photos were about to be published in a major publication. After takeoff, Macpherson found an empty row, stretched across three seats, and slept most of the way to the East Coast, sucking her thumb the whole time.

We landed at Logan at rush hour Monday morning. The Celtics went home to their beds while the Lakers settled into the Parker

House near Beacon Hill. LA publicist Josh Rosenfeld told us that the Lakers were considering IVs for all players before Game 7. They were obsessed with the Garden conditions, convinced that Auerbach arranged to have the heat turned on and cold water shut off in their rustic locker room.

My Game 7 *Globe* advance spared no hyperbole:

"Welcome to Hoop Heaven. One hundred miles from the spot where basketball was invented, the Boston Celtics and Los Angeles Lakers will play for the NBA championship tonight. It's Game 7 in Boston Garden. Bring T-shirts, cutoffs and a pair of thongs. This series may have raised the pro game to its zenith. All expectations have been fulfilled. Stars have starred, migraines have come and gone, fists have been raised in anger, Academy Award winners have taunted fans, and the teams have played six games and two overtimes without establishing any semblance of a pattern."

The Celtics were 6-0 lifetime in NBA Finals Game 7s, winning three at the expense of the Lakers.

An unruly, postmidnight celebration outside the Garden was expected if the Celtics won, so the team arranged for players to meet at Hellenic and ride vans to the Garden. Bird carpooled to the practice site with Quinn and Rhonda Buckner. When their team-issued van got to the Garden, the old gym was toasty, but not nearly as hot as it had been for Game 5.

At my *Globe* seat in the Garden's upstairs pressroom, I found a blank form to be filled out for a potential trip to the White House the next day. Auerbach, ever connected in Washington, had arranged for the Celtics to visit President Reagan if they won. The DC game plan involved getting to Logan by 9:00 a.m. for a 10:20 flight to National Airport (now Reagan International) just a few hours after Game 7. It was ambitious and uncomplicated. In 1984, there was no time for controversy and no red-state/blue-state debate over the current occupant of the Oval Office.

After filling out the government paperwork, I went downstairs to the locker room, where the Celtics were amazingly rested, composed, and still pranking one another. Carr, who'd been hit in the face with a cup of liquid thrown from the stands in LA, wore Kareem-taunting goggles, while Ainge went around the room with a stethoscope, checking everyone's heartbeat to see who was nervous.

After placing the instrument on Maxwell's chest, Dr. Danny said, "Your heart's going strong."

Max's play in the first six games had been unremarkable. He scored no more than 16, and no less than 6, points in any game. But he was angry about what he considered a vicious cheap shot by Worthy in Game 6 and told his teammates, "Hop on my back, boys! I'll take y'all home."

Maxwell backed it up, scoring 24 points with 8 rebounds and 8 assists in a 111–102 Game 7 win. He made 11 of 13 free throws in the first two quarters as the Celtics bolted to a 58–52 halftime lead. His 24-point effort made him the Celtics' high scorer for the only time all season. Once in 105 games. And he saved it for Game 7 of the Finals.

"James Worthy went on to have a much better NBA career than me," Maxwell said. "He was a better player than me. But in that moment, I had him. On that night, I had him in my back pocket. He knew it and I knew it."

The Celtics never trailed after the early minutes of the second quarter and led by as many as 14 in the second half. DJ scored 22, giving him 20 or more in each of his last four games after his no-show in Game 3. Parish had 16 points and 16 rebounds in forty-one minutes, and Ainge came off the bench for 10 points. Bird scored 20 and won the Finals MVP.

Fans surged to the court's perimeter, breaching the boundary as the two teams tried to play the final seconds. It was farcical and dangerous—Altamont Raceway stuff. Dozens of Boston fans were actually standing in bounds for the final minute of play, further infuriating Riley, who'd been told there'd be additional security for Game 7. This was the opposite of security. It felt as though Celtics management had hired a bunch of costumed fans who just wanted to absorb the glory with Larry and Co. After the final buzzer, Henderson pushed Ainge out of the way in a scramble to get the souvenir game ball as players from both teams pushed through the mob to get to the tunnel in the middle of the arena. Treetop Lakers center Swen Nater punched *Globe* photographer Grossfeld in the face as Nater made his way off the floor.

In the winner's room, Auerbach grasped the championship trophy as he was interviewed by CBS's Brent Musburger and barked, "You guys were talking about a dynasty the Lakers had. But what dynasty? Here's the only dynasty right here! This team!"

It marked the first time the Celtics had won a championship in the Boston Garden since 1966, Red's final game on the bench.

After midnight, I ducked out of the champagne-soaked room, gathered my computer and notes, and made my way toward the Garden's upper-level pressroom, where I needed to file a late-edition story. Walking down the corridor toward the ancient, smelly stairwell, I heard a woman's voice and high-heel shoes clicking behind me. When I stopped and turned around, I was face-to-face with a super-agitated Nancy Parish.

"Dan Shaughnessy, let's talk," she spewed. "What are you gonna write about this game, huh, Dan? You made an ass out of yourself."

I hemmed. I hawed. "Um, gee. Chief sure had a good game. Okay, have fun. Gotta go."

Mrs. Chief still wanted a piece of me, but security approached and I was able to get on my way, hearing echoes of "You made an ass of yourself! You hear me?" I wasn't quite sure whether her grievance was specific or had to do with my coverage throughout the season.

While I was getting an earful from Mrs. Chief, Bird and Buckner were in a van driven by assistant equipment manager Joe Qatato, bound for Hellenic. Frustrated and impatient with the celebratory gridlock on Storrow Drive, Bird ordered Qatato to stop the van. The two players hopped out, vaulted the median, and started walking back toward Faneuil Hall amid the clogged traffic and honking horns. The Celtics stars were instantly recognized and picked up by astonished fans, who drove them to Chelsea's.

"I have a vague memory of that," said Buckner. "Storrow Drive is quite a place to stop a van, but we were going where we were going, and Larry got us there. Beating Magic was really important to him and that was a special night."

After Chelsea's, a group of Celtics players went to the Winchester home of former team promotions director Mike Cole for an all-night party. Bird stayed out until the sun came up, did a telephone interview with a Boston radio station, then went home to Brookline to sleep it off, telling friends, "If the president wants to see me, he knows where to find me."

Maxwell made it home to Cabot Estate near Jamaica Pond, then woke early and trudged downtown for a sunrise appearance on the *CBS Morning News*. Abdul-Jabbar was already on the set when Maxwell arrived.

"When Kareem saw me, he got up and said, 'You guys got the fuckin' winner here, so I'm gone,'" remembered Maxwell. "It was pretty cold."

After his TV gig, Maxwell went to Boston City Hall to get his marriage license, then got a haircut. It was his excuse for skipping the trip to the Reagan White House. Cedric and Renee Maxwell honeymooned in Nassau, where they ran into Magic Johnson. Years after his divorce, Max said, "I wish I'd gone to Washington with the team that day. It would have saved me a lot of money in the long run."

At 10:00 a.m. on Wednesday, June 13, nine members of the World Champion Celtics boarded the Eastern Airlines Shuttle bound for National. Casual inspection told me that Greg Kite, Wedman, and Ainge were the only players not hungover. Wearing Blues Brothers sunglasses, Ainge grinned and said, "I heard Nancy Parish went at you last night!"

I grabbed a seat near the front of the cabin and read my morning *Globe* while Celtics players and wives boarded. Lynn and Kevin McHale walked on, holding the couple's one-year old daughter, who was dolled up in a chiffon party dress. They were followed by Scott and Kim Wedman, and Mrs. Wedman paused when she got to my row.

"Hi, Dan," she said.

Oh, boy, I thought. *Mrs. Chief. Now this.*

"You know, in the last couple of weeks I've been unhappy with some of the things that have gone on," she started, as I slumped back into my seat. "But I read a lot and I've got to tell you, I love the way you write."

Nancy Parish wasn't on the trip. Neither was the Chief, Bird, or Maxwell. Little mention was made of it. In 1984, Red's cigar was just a cigar, and a no-show at the White House was no big deal.

"It was a late night and I'm sure they were very tired," Volk said with a shrug when I asked about it.

"If you look at those pictures from the Rose Garden, you can see that Quinn Buckner is sleeping standing up," said Joe DiLorenzo, a team official who'd been at Chelsea's and Cole's after-party. "We couldn't believe any of them made it there."

It was brutally hot in the Rose Garden as Reagan bumbled his way through a five-minute speech. Auerbach presented Reagan with a Celtics starter jacket, and DJ spoke, wiping sweat from his freckled face, concluding with "Mr. President, I just have one question. How do you stand out here and don't sweat?"

"The White House thing sounded like a good idea at the time, but I don't know if it was," McHale said decades later. "We'd never been to the White House before. We had a lot of fun at night, but we always got back at it the next day. We were a resilient group. So we went and did it, but I was never so happy to be flying back to Boston. Talking about the going to the White House was a lot better than actually doing it."

Six days after Game 7, *Sport* magazine presented Bird with a Pontiac Trans Am for winning the Finals MVP Award.

"It's always good to receive something that you feel you deserve, especially after they gave it to James Worthy after the second game of the series," Bird said after the presentation at the Boston Ritz-Carlton. He gave the car to his brother Eddie in exchange for Eddie's promise to cut Larry's lawn at the new house back home in Indiana.

Sport's MVP car presentation was a championship finals tradition, started when the magazine honored Brooklyn Dodger pitcher Johnny Podres after he was named MVP of the 1955 World Series. The NBA got in on the deal a decade later, and Bill Walton (1977 Trail Blazers) and Moses Malone (1983 Sixers) were recipients before Bird.

One Finals MVP who never got a car was the ever-disrespected Maxwell, MVP of the 1981 Finals.

"It was always a car or a trip to Disney or something like that," Max recalled in 2021. "I got a fucking watch. I actually had to go to New York to the Waldorf, and I thought I was going to get a car with a big bow on it, but I got a watch with *Seiko* on the back. I thought there was going to be more, but when I came outside the Waldorf, there was just a Yellow Cab waiting and I remember thinking, 'This is some bullshit!' I complained to David Stern years later and he said, 'Whoa, dude, we had a different sponsor then.' It should embarrass anyone in the NBA. Larry got a car. I got jack shit. That's what I got."

CHAPTER 8

"I WAS TRADED FOR A DEAD MAN"

There was little time to celebrate the 1984 championship. Twenty-three playoff games pushed the Celtics up against the draft and annual league Board of Governors meetings, both in late June.

The Celtics used their first-round pick on six-seven swingman Michael Young, who'd played at Houston with top overall pick Hakeem Olajuwon. The big story of the 1984 draft was Chicago's selection of Michael Jordan with the third overall pick. Leading up to the draft, there was debate about where Jordan would be selected. Olajuwon, a star at the University of Houston with the physical gifts and mental makeup to be an instant force in the NBA, was Houston's obvious top pick. Portland and Chicago had the second and third picks, respectively. Portland faced a dilemma. Kentucky's oft-injured seven-foot center Sam Bowie was at the top of many draft lists even though he was clearly a greater risk than Jordan, who appeared to be a sure thing, but Portland already had Clyde Drexler and Jerome Kersey, two leapers who were the same size as Jordan. The Trail Blazers believed Jordan would give them too many players with the same skills, while still leaving a hole in the middle. They announced their intention to select Bowie with the second pick.

"Taking Bowie over North Carolina's Michael Jordan is tantamount to picking Clemon Johnson over Sidney Moncrief," I wrote. "Granted the Blazers need a big man, but you can't pass up a sure thing."

It was not a daring take. Northeastern basketball coach Jim Calhoun told me, "Anybody with any brains would take Jordan. I don't see how there can be any doubt. Jordan might be the NBA's next Dr. J."

Nothing is guaranteed in any draft, but Bowie was a gamble and Jordan wasn't. Chicago's selection wound up being a move that forever changed the fortunes of the NBA, and David Stern. Bird already had two championships and the first of his three MVP Awards. Magic had two crowns, would be MVP three times, and play in nine Finals, winning five. The league was saved by Bird and Magic in 1979, and the '84 Finals attracted a new generation of fans. Jordan was next. With Stern's vision, Michael made the NBA a global attraction.

Ten days after the Celtics won their fifteenth banner, NBA executives gathered at the Salt Lake Sheraton for their annual meetings. Stern's first convention gave me a chance for some downtime with Marilou and our baby daughter, Sarah.

Marilou isn't a sports fan, which has always worked nicely. There's never any need at home to talk about ball screens or the 1-2-2 full-court zone press. She went to Michigan State at the same time as Magic and never bothered to see him play. When Bob Ryan first met my wife and learned of her Spartan connection, he asked what it must have been like to watch Magic and Greg Kelser all those winter nights at Jenisen Field House in East Lansing. Marilou interrupted, "I never went to a game, but I think I saw Magic in the infirmary once."

I introduced Marilou and one-month-old Sarah to all the NBA big shots in Salt Lake City. Pat Riley was surprisingly friendly and told me he thought the *Globe*'s coverage of the Finals was fair and well reported. Evidently, he'd forgiven my relentless Lakers hotel disclosures.

When Red waddled out of a board meeting while Marilou was in the lobby cradling Sarah, I pounced. "Red, can you come over to meet my wife and little baby girl I've been telling you about? You gave me the cigars when I told you we were having a baby. Marilou and Sarah are standing right over there."

Auerbach grunted and walked with me to where Marilou was standing.

Red wasn't the master of small talk. Bob Cousy's wife, Missie, told me Auerbach was at his worst when it came to chatting with players' spouses. According to Missie, the Celtics wives all hated the boss.

"We used to say that if he flicked cigar ashes on your jacket shoulder, that meant he liked you," said Missie.

Red stood next to Marilou, gazed down at little Sarah, and said, "Hmmm. Nice to meet you."

Motioning toward me, he added, "Do you think having that baby will make him more human?"

We all chuckled, awkwardly.

Before turning to leave, Red looked at my wife and said, "You know something? You got a lot of balls bringing that baby all the way out here. Yes, sir, a lot of balls."

Then he was gone.

"What was that?" asked Marilou.

"That was a compliment," I stammered. "That's Red's way of telling you he admires your toughness."

There was an awards banquet the next night and we expected Bird to collect his first MVP trophy.

I called Larry's mom the day of the dinner.

"I'm making Larry a sandwich," Georgia Bird said after picking up the phone at her French Lick home. "He's outside cutting the grass right now. He's flying out to Salt Lake City this afternoon. What's he going there for?"

On my follow-up call—after the lower forty acres were mowed—Ma Bird got her dutiful son to come to the phone.

"I heard Nancy Parish hit you with her purse after we won," Bird said. "Everybody loved that. You deserved it. What are you looking for now, Scoop? I'm tired. I just got through cutting eight acres of grass. And you can be sure I didn't use one of them push mowers."

We briefly discussed his MVP Award, but he had to shower and get a ride to the French Lick Municipal Airport, where Celtics owner

Don Gaston had arranged for a small jet to transport Bird and his agent, Bob Woolf, to Salt Lake City.

Woolf was sitting in Gaston's jet on the tiny tarmac when Bird arrived at the airport. It took a while to refuel the craft, and Bird had to push another small plane out of the way to clear the French Lick airstrip for takeoff. O'Hare, this was not.

"I didn't have it this bad in Vietnam," said Gaston's pilot.

The flight from French Lick to Salt Lake City took three and a half hours, and Bird arrived just in time for the trophy presentation. Wearing a bowling shirt and slacks, he accepted his MVP and addressed the NBA big shots.

"This will probably mean more down the road," Bird said. "It's not as big as the championship. It doesn't even compare."

Years later Bird told me a couple of his MVP Awards were rattling about in the back of a friend's pickup.

After Bird spoke, Stern announced that the league's Coach of the Year Award was officially going to be called the Red Auerbach Award, and each winner would be presented with a miniature replica of Red's Faneuil Hall statue. I've always wondered what Phil Jackson did with his Red statue after leading the Bulls to 72 wins in 1995–96. Auerbach loathed the Zen master. Jackson was an ex-Knick, and Red felt he shopped for easy gigs to make himself look good. Auerbach bristled when Jackson tied Red's record of nine championships from the bench in 2002. Red died in 2006 before Jackson won his tenth and eleventh rings with the Kobe Bryant Lakers.

In Stern's state-of-the-league address, he took a subtle shot at the *Globe*'s 1982 five-part series ("National Basketball Affliction") on the demise of the NBA.

"I apologize that we don't have any chaos, franchises folding, collective bargaining strife, or reports about drugs," Stern gloated. "But that's what happens when you start to get healthy."

Stern was on top of the sports world. His league was suddenly cool. The NBA was Fan*tastic*. Sponsors were calling. The league finally landed the US Army sponsorship deal it had lost to indoor soccer a couple of years earlier. There'd be no more Seiko watches for Finals MVPs.

Three significant changes were approved at the Salt Lake meetings, two arising from the exhausting '84 Finals. It was agreed that the travel format for the championship series would be switched from 2-2-1-1-1 to baseball's time-honored 2-3-2 World Series system. This was the Celtics-Lakers Rule. It was also agreed that a deliberate foul would result in two free throws and possession of the ball instead of two free throws. This was the McHale Rule.

Most important, in the wake of tanking allegations aimed at Chicago and Houston, who'd just come out of the draft with Jordan and Olajuwon respectively, a draft lottery for nonplayoff teams was approved by the owners.

"The lottery will once and for all eliminate the issue that has been raised that one can win by losing," said Stern. "Any suggestion that a team would forgo the playoffs to take a one-in-seven shot at the top draft pick doesn't hold water."

The lottery got Red's attention. He now had a team poised to make it to the Finals for several seasons. He wanted his 1984–85 Celtics to be the NBA's first repeat champions since the 1968–69 Russell Celtics. But the Celtics needed an infusion of youth to give Messrs. Bird, Parish, and McHale some rest.

Boston's roster was set with two exceptions: Maxwell and Henderson were free agents. Both wanted to get paid, especially Maxwell, who'd been on the team longer than anyone else.

Maxwell was always feeling unappreciated, ever comparing Larry's Trans Am with his tiny Seiko. He felt the same disrespect when he looked at his paycheck. Bird and McHale had signed new long-term deals, and Parish got an extension after his holdout. It bothered Max that he was making less money than McHale, who was still coming off the bench. Auerbach was friendly with Maxwell's agent, Ron Grinker, but signing Maxwell was going to be difficult. The seven-year veteran had no particular allegiance to Boston.

Like a lot of NBA players, Maxwell had a fondness for Atlanta, the only Southern city in the NBA in 1984. Atlanta was close to North Carolina, had a large upper-middle-class Black population, and was the home of Friedman's Shoes—a store that catered to African American fashion and NBA feet. Free agent Maxwell talked openly about playing for Atlanta and referred to the Hawks' owner, Ted Turner, as Uncle Teddy.

Before leaving Salt Lake City, I asked Stan Kasten—who ran the Hawks for Turner—about his level of interest in Maxwell.

"We have no interest," said Kasten. "I've gotten used to reading about it. I read about it once a week. I think Max must be chuckling, too, because he's the one who has planted the seed. We're loaded up front and committed to a youth movement. Believe me, if I had any interest, I'd tell you, 'No comment.' "

Still only twenty-eight, Maxwell was a link to the Celtics' past glory. He'd played with John Havlicek, who played with Bob Cousy, who was a rookie when Auerbach came to Boston in 1950. Maxwell was also an iron man. He'd played 72 games in his rookie year and no less than 78 games in any subsequent season.

Nobody who knew him called him Cornbread anymore. Cornbread was a character played by Jamaal Wilkes in a little-known 1975 film, *Cornbread, Earl and Me.* The nickname was all the rage when Maxwell was MVP of the NIT at North Carolina–Charlotte in 1976 and again when he led them to the Final Four in 1977. It was shortened to "Bread" when he came to Boston. Max was okay with "Bread," but pushed back on Cornbread and was insulted when Abdul-Jabbar referred to him as Cornbread during the '84 Finals.

A six-foot-eight Black man living in downtown Boston in the 1970s and '80s, Maxwell was uncomfortable with the racial climate in his professional home. Like Bill Russell before him, and so many after, he lived a life in Boston that was different from what he'd grown up with in Kinston, North Carolina. As a child, he'd experienced racism on driving trips through the South with his dad, Manny, a twenty-five-year marine veteran who'd been wounded in Vietnam. Cedric remembered being forced to use an outhouse instead of a restroom at a roadside gas station in Georgia. He saw barriers separating Blacks from whites at Atlantic Beach in South Carolina.

When Maxwell was a Celtics rookie in 1977, Boston was reeling from court-ordered school desegregation. Forced busing triggered enormous resistance in Boston's neighborhoods, and ugly scenes fortified Boston's racist image. Max noticed that he always stood out when he went to dinner or a nightclub in Boston—and not just because he was six foot eight. He felt little connection with his professional home or its fans.

"Boston is okay if you're an athlete," he said. "It's not an especially nice place in which to be Black. . . . Playing for the Celtics, it's like we were Uncle Toms. It's hard to be a Black guy when you play on a white team."

In 1983, when Maxwell learned that I grew up in Massachusetts, he nodded and said, "Uh-huh. There's another good reason for me to dislike you."

He admitted he had preconceived notions about his superstar white teammates.

"God is a funny God," Maxwell said. "He's got a bunch of jokes. I thought basketball was a Black game. In college, our assistant coach would tell me about the guy I was going to guard in the next game, and I would ask him one question—'Is the guy white or Black?' Cuz I knew I hadn't seen any white guys who could play. Then I come to the Celtics and I see John Havlicek and Dave Cowens and I was thinking, 'Damn, this may be some different shit right now.' And then God was even more funny. He didn't give me just the best white player. He gave me the two greatest white players ever to play together. Kevin McHale and Larry Bird. God, you have a funny sense of humor. Ha ha ha."

Maxwell tested Bird early:

"I remember Larry coming to the Garden in 1978 after he was drafted. We had a bad team, but I was a scoring machine. When they introduced Larry, fans were clapping like hell for Larry and I was like, 'Whatever. This is some bullshit.' I didn't know Larry and had never met him. When I first saw him at veteran camp, I was sitting up on

127

the stage at Hellenic. I was 'the Man.' When Larry came in the door, I gave him the slow clap: 'Oh, here comes the great white hope. I'm going to bust this guy's ass.' Well, we got on the court and I scored on him at will. Larry could not stop me. But there was two sides of the court. He kept making shots. When practice ended, I walked up to the first Black person I could find and I said, 'You know what—that fuckin' white guy can play.' That was my introduction to Larry Bird. Bill Fitch told me right away. He said, 'You're a smart guy. Who do you think is going to guard the other team's best forward from now on?' Me. I was going to have to play the pit. All that offensive array that I had? I was going to have to put that to the background. And I embraced it. I saw a path of winning."

Maxwell averaged 19 points per game the year before Bird arrived. His touches diminished in 1979–80, and again when McHale came to Boston the following season. By 1983–84 Maxwell was averaging less than 12 points per game. Bird and McHale got the shots, the attention, the credit, and the money.

Maxwell had a theory regarding the *Boston Globe*'s coverage of the Celtics:

"Scoop, do you ever notice what your paper does? Whenever we win, the front page of sports will have a big picture of Larry or Kevin or Danny looking all happy and celebrating some great play. Whenever we lose, your sports page features a big picture of me or Chief, lying on the court or making some goofy face."

Auerbach's rookie camp was uneventful in the summer of '84 because there wasn't any competition for jobs. Top pick Michael Young looked lost, while third-round selection Rick Carlisle of Virginia impressed. The best player in the night sessions at the Marshfield High gym was John Salley, a six-eleven "counselor" from Georgia Tech who looked like a future first rounder. Maxwell's agent, the affable Grinker ("The NBA's Broadway Danny Rose," according to Ryan), met with Volk a couple of nights in Marshfield and pledged, "We'll get a contract done. Max wants to stay here and we're really not looking to talk to other teams."

Maxwell and Henderson—40 percent of the 1984 championship starting lineup—were absent when the Celtics reported to Hellenic in late September. Red targeted Maxwell and Grinker on the first day, saying, "They used me. They jerked us around. I have moved for the last time. No more."

Everyone else was in a good mood. Parish said he thought criticism during the playoffs was "poured on a little heavy," but seemed rested and relaxed. We did not discuss my late-night, Game 7 exchange with Mrs. Chief.

McHale greeted me with his typical "Hey, Scoop. You had to eat a little crow after predicting that the Lakers would win, didn't you?"

One of the more discouraging and revealing moments of camp unfolded when veteran Celtics marketing/communications director Tod Rosensweig reluctantly fielded reporters' complaints about restricted access and told us, "Guys, the truth is that we don't need you anymore. If none of you covered us all season, we'd still sell out every game."

It was awful . . . and true . . . a blunt and brutal harbinger. Gone were the days when a successful team and its players needed newspaper write-ups to sell tickets and inflate interest. The Celtics had relied on the kindness of Boston newspapers for their entire existence. A panel of scribes had been summoned to help owner Walter Brown select a new coach when Auerbach was hired in 1950. Despite all their success, the Celtics were annually underdogs in their own region. They were never as popular as the bottom-feeding Red Sox and Bruins.

All that had changed by 1984 because the World Champion Celtics had Larry Bird. This was evident when retired Red Sox superstar Carl Yastrzemski came to Hellenic in his new gig as a TV reporter and groveled for access with the rest of us. The Celtics were top dogs and could do whatever they wanted. The importance of newspaper coverage was fading fast. Guys such as me would soon be completely irrelevant to the players and the team.

Henderson found little market for his services even though he had two championship rings and was a starter for the reigning champs.

129

The Celtics suddenly had backcourt depth. Ainge, who'd lost his starting job when DJ came on board in '83–84, looked terrific in preseason, and rookie Rick Carlisle was getting significant minutes even though K. C. Jones didn't seem to know the kid's name (Jones would routinely sneak a peek at the back of Carlisle's uniform jersey before summoning him—"Carlisle, get in there"). Eight-year NBA veteran Buckner was still around.

Henderson ended his holdout after three exhibition games, coming to terms on a four-year deal worth $325,000 per season, just in time for a preseason trip to Las Vegas and Houston. Before the ink was dry on Henderson's new contract, Auerbach traded him to Seattle for the Sonics 1986 first-round pick.

It was vintage Red. He felt the Celtics overpaid Henderson. He knew Ainge was ready to take back a starting position. Carlisle looked like an NBA guard. The Celtics had backcourt depth and needed to think about replenishing the frontcourt. Hoping Seattle would be a lottery team in the spring of '86, Auerbach made a deal with the southbound Sonics. Trading a starting guard from a championship team was a bold stroke, but Auerbach knew he was selling high. When he looked at Seattle, he saw a team that might have a spot in the NBA's second-ever lottery. Seattle had made the playoffs in six of the previous seven seasons, but was coming off a 40-42 season. Red took a shot at getting a lottery pick for a player he thought was overrated and overpaid.

Henderson's agent was livid. "We feel we have been deceived," said Scott Lang. "The Celtics negotiated in bad faith and were totally unethical. There's no way you decide you're trading a guard on a championship team in a three-day period."

Auerbach blamed Lang for not asking for a no-trade clause. It was the standard Otter-to-Flounder *Animal House* admonishment.

You fucked up. You trusted us.

"I've never broken my word, and I never will," said the Celtics godfather. "Gerald came in, in horrible shape."

Everyone knew this was false.

"Red was a liar," Henderson said in 2021. "The Celtics could have had more integrity in that one. For him to say I wasn't in shape . . . come on! I also thought it was racist. They wanted Danny to play. I got nothing against Danny, man. Danny had nothing to do with it, but they wanted Danny to play, and the only way for Danny to play was for me to leave."

Optics and honesty aside, it was a smart move. Henderson had played five seasons in Boston and made the play that delivered a fifteenth banner, but he was expendable. He went on to play for six teams after leaving the Celtics, but never replicated the success he enjoyed in Boston. The Celtics reached the NBA Finals in each of their first three seasons without Henderson. Meanwhile, the Sonics became NBA bottom-feeders with back-to-back 31-51 campaigns, which is how the 1986 World Champion Celtics wound up with the second overall pick in the 1986 draft. The pick turned out to be Len Bias, another Auerbach "camp counselor" and the best player in college basketball in 1985–86. Bias died of cocaine intoxication two days after he was drafted by Boston.

"Isn't that something?" Henderson said decades later. "I hate to say it, man, but anytime Len Bias's name comes up, I say, 'I was traded for a dead man.' It just wasn't right."

Moving Henderson made room for Carlisle, the third-round pick from Virginia, who appeared to have no chance when camp opened.

"On paper it didn't look very good for me," Carlisle recalled in 2021 as he was getting ready to return to the bench as head coach of the Pacers. "Championship teams rarely get broken up the following year. But Henderson and Maxwell holding out helped me. There was a lot of opportunity and I was fortunate. Things had worked out."

A native of Lisbon, New York, Carlisle played at Worcester Academy and the University of Maine before Virginia. Celtics teammates dubbed him Flipper, an homage to his size 14 feet.

What was it like for him to join the world champs after being selected in a round that no longer exists?

"Kevin McHale was the first one who took me under his wing

and was really nice to me," said Carlisle. "He was still coming off the bench. He and Ainge were great to me, and I got to know the other guys more gradually. Robert Parish was delightful, a wonderful guy. My locker was between Dennis Johnson and Kevin McHale. That's pretty good. I was surprised these guys even knew my name."

On the day before the Celtics flew to Detroit for the regular season opener of their championship defense, Grinker and Auerbach came to terms on a four-year, $3.2 million deal for Maxwell. When we asked Max if Grinker had negotiated a no-trade clause, the veteran forward said, "Ron asked for the clause and Red said it was too late. Guess that means I'm off to Seattle now."

Maxwell did not play the first game of the season in Pontiac. McHale, who'd been voted Sixth Man of the Year in 1983–84, started the first two games in place of Maxwell, then went back to the bench, but not for long. Maxwell had torn cartilage in his knee and would reinjure the knee in February. The injury changed everything for the 1984–85 Celtics.

The Celtics won their first 5 and 15 of their first 16. Included in this stretch was a 130–119 blowout of the 76ers on a November Friday at the Garden, a game best remembered as the night Larry Bird and Julius Erving had a fistfight, producing an iconic photo of the superstars with their hands wrapped around each other's throat.

Bird was at the height of his trash-talking game and gave Dr. J. an earful throughout the first three quarters. Dominating Erving would have been impossible a few years earlier, but Doc was playing his fourteenth professional season and was almost thirty-five, while Bird was in the middle of his three-year MVP reign.

Bird scored 29 in the first half, while Erving made only 1 of 9 shots. We heard the verbal assault from press row.

You better retire if that's all you got. . . . Get somebody else out here to guard me. You can't do it.

With Bird already at 42 points (17 of 23 from the floor), Larry and Julius traded elbows and insults in the third quarter. As they stood in front of the press table after an offensive foul on Bird, Erving cupped his right hand around Bird's waist, then went for Bird's throat with his left. Malone jumped in, and Sixers rookie Charles Barkley (playing his first game at the Garden) held Bird from behind as Erving landed a few punches, one to Bird's groin. Bird slipped and fell, then got up and charged the Doctor again—to no avail. Malone got into an undercard bout with M. L. Carr, and Chris Ford suffered a bloody nose when he tried to break it up.

Dick Bavetta was the only official working the game because veteran Jack Madden was in the trainer's room with a knee injury. Leaving Bavetta by himself in a Celtics-76ers game was like assigning Barney Fife to work solo during a jailbreak at Shawshank. Bird and Erving were ejected and fined $7,500, the second-highest fines in league history. It was the first ejection of Erving's career. Maxwell, who steered clear of all the action, said, "I was like a young Martin Luther King out there. Nonviolent."

The Celtics gathered the next morning at Logan's Delta terminal for an early flight to Washington. The 76ers were at an adjacent gate, and when Sixers coach Billy Cunningham passed the Celtics group, he said—in Bill Laimbeer fashion—"Good morning, men."

"Ain't nothing good about it," Carr muttered.

Bird has never publicly commented on the fight (Bird and Erving won't sign the famous photo), but was unhappy with my account in the paper.

"You made it sound like I started the thing by throwing elbows," he snapped. "Were you watching what was going on out there? What you write is important to what people in Boston think. How could you do that to me, Scoop?"

I knew why he was mad. He got a little beat up while he was being restrained by two Sixers, and he got hit in the nuts. It went against the code of fair fighting he'd learned as a boy in rural Indiana. I suspected Bird also had a problem with nonviolent Maxwell, and with Parish, who'd said he didn't come off the bench because he wanted to avoid the $500 fine.

These were largely good days on the beat. It was my third season, I was covering the most popular team in town, the Celtics were champions, and I'd established some trust and respect while not falling into the trap of making friends and delivering the party line for the team. In retrospect, I wish I'd smelled the roses a little more along the way. I was witnessing some of the best basketball ever played, but always had my head in the keyboard and vigilantly strived not to get close to the players.

"You've got to enjoy this more," *New York Post* hoop guru Peter Vecsey told me. "You should be giving half of your salary to Larry Bird. Guys in the business would kill to cover this team."

Carlisle certainly noticed my hard-guy approach at the keyboard.

"The running narrative with us was that you wanted us to lose," Carlisle said when I interviewed him for this book. "If something good happened to us at a road game, you'd throw your fist down on the table and say, 'Fuck!' You wanted us to lose so there'd be a different story other than 'The Celtics won again.' If you have any balls, you'll name this book *I Hope They Lose*."

Maxwell chuckled when I relayed Carlisle's comments, saying, "As a book title, that's not going to get the party going, but I think we did feel that way a little. You didn't like having to write 'The Boring Old Celtics Win Again.' You wanted there to be some shit happening. And I think we provided plenty of that. You just didn't realize how good you had it."

It *was* a sweet gig. On occasion, the lowly scribes even got to shoot hoops with the basketball gods. Hellenic practices were at 10:00 a.m., and I'd usually arrive with my notebook and stack of newspapers just before 9:30, when the gym floor was empty. There was no security. You parked your car, walked into the building, and took a seat at the top of the high-school-style wooden bleachers. The *Herald*'s Carey, the *Ledger*'s Mike Fine, and Peter May of the *Hartford Courant* were the other everyday scribes on the beat, and nobody objected if a couple of us wandered onto the empty court, grabbed balls off the racks, and hoisted a couple of shots before players came out from getting taped. I'd scram if Parish appeared early, but that almost never happened. Bird, DJ, and the rest didn't mind our presence in those final minutes before K.C. came out with the whistle and stretching commenced. Same with Greg Kite.

Kite was my Newton neighbor, and we sometimes carpooled to Logan. We were just two guys who knew that Monday was trash day in West Newton. He'd told me he couldn't believe Julius Erving knew his name when he first played against the Sixers. Kite didn't object when I noted that he had 42 personal fouls and only 65 points in his rookie season. Greg Kite was not going to kick me off the court before practice.

"Look at Scooper," McHale said when he redirected one of my misses back into my hands. "Scoop's got that high arc, like Purvis Short."

Purvis Short was a six-seven Warriors forward who shot rainbow jumpers and scored 59 points in a game against the Nets. Yup. I was just like Purvis Short.

Ball in hand, Bird took this opportunity to take money from the scribes, regularly uttering, "Shoot for money? Dollar?"

If you agreed, it meant that he was going to let fly from wherever he was standing. If the ball went in, you owed him a buck. If he missed, he owed you a dollar. I never made any cash when I agreed to this game, even if Bird was standing thirty feet from the hoop, but I took the pool shark concept home to my driveway hoop. In the 1990s, my six-year-old son would greet me in the driveway, holding a basketball, saying, "Shoot for money?"

"Shooting around" with the Boston Celtics was a once-in-a-lifetime perk, and every now and then I reminded myself how cool that was. All basketball players—NBA superstars and weekend ham-and-eggers—honor universal truths. When you are shooting around, you share the floor and retrieve stray balls for the other shooters. It's unspoken—like McHale pushing a stranger's car out of a snowbank in Hibbing, Minnesota.

"There was kind of an on-and-off relationship that we all had with each other," McHale said in 2021, when asked about reporter-player relationships of the early 1980s. "Half the damn bus was press, and we got very accustomed to that. There was an understanding, and I felt you guys didn't want to ruin that. I liked it when we had flight delays and you guys were looking to write something and you'd say, 'I'll buy you breakfast.' I'd always say okay to that. We didn't think twice about it. It was just stuff that happened. That's why you guys had insight into all the crazy shit we did."

Two days after Thanksgiving we flew to Kansas City for a nine-day, four-game trip through Dallas, Houston, and Richfield, Ohio. The Celtics played in Kansas City on a Saturday night, then flew to Dallas, where they had two nights off before playing the Mavericks on Tuesday. Two nights off in an NBA city is rare. In the winter of 1984, Bruce Springsteen's wildly popular "Born in the U.S.A." tour was visiting Texas at the same time as the Celtics. Springsteen was a national rage, a *Newsweek* cover boy, and it was almost impossible to flip on a radio without hearing "Born in the U.S.A.," "Dancing in the Dark," or "Glory Days." The Boss had shows scheduled in Dallas for Sunday and Monday, both nights that the Celtics were idle in the Hyatt.

The 1984 Dallas Mavericks played at sparkling Reunion Arena, adjacent to the Hyatt Regency, where the Celtics stayed. Late Sunday afternoon on our first off day, I was having a couple beers in the atrium lounge with the *Hartford Courant*'s Peter May when Bird and Buckner plopped themselves down at our table to mooch beers and break balls. While we were talking, the hotel lobby was suddenly overrun with young people streaming toward Reunion Arena. None of the young rock fans recognized Bird. When Larry asked what all the fuss was about, I told him that Bruce Springsteen was playing next door.

"Rick Springfield?" he asked.

"No, Larry, Bruce Springsteen," I said.

"Who's he?"

Long pause. Some chuckling and shrugs of shoulders.

"Let me put it this way, Larry," I said. "Bruce Springsteen is the *you* of rock 'n' roll."

"Where have I been?" asked Bird without a trace of embarrassment. "This Springsteen guy must be pretty good."

McHale was friendly with E Street Band guitarist Nils Lofgren and attended Sunday's four-hour show with Wedman. When the players gushed about Springsteen's performance, May and I committed to buying scalper tickets for the next night's show. Buying tickets for Springsteen in Texas was easier than we thought. The Dolphins and Jets were playing on *Monday Night Football*, which meant plenty of scalpers offering face value for the E Street Band at Reunion Arena.

McHale left tickets for Bird, who bailed halfway through the show.

"Not my type of music," Bird said before the Celtics played the Mavericks the next night. "But he works hard. Sweats a lot. I give him credit for that."

That winter the Celtics and the E Street Band played back-to-back shows several times in Dallas, Houston, and Atlanta. After McHale scored 19 against the Hawks in a 101–94 December win at the Omni, McHale grabbed me in the locker room and said, "Scoop, the Boss is over at the Marriott. Ray and I are meeting Nils over at their hotel. Want to come?"

McHale, Melchiorre, Lebeaux, and I cabbed from the Omni to the Marriott, where we were greeted by Lofgren and some roadies. We settled in the hotel atrium's soft chairs and ordered beers. I sat next to Patti Scialfa, a young singer from New Jersey who'd recently joined the band. Like me, Scialfa was a 1971 high school grad. She wore green socks, had played basketball as a teenager, and drank her beer straight from the bottle, Jersey-girl fashion. She married Springsteen in 1991 and raised three children with the Boss.

Late in the evening, Springsteen and his keyboard savant, Roy Bittan, visited our group when they returned from a local movie theater where they'd seen *The Cotton Club*.

Desperate to make conversation, I asked Bruce how he liked the film.

"I wouldn't give it no raves," he said. "But I'm not real judgmental."

When McHale and I shared a cab back to the Hyatt, I admitted being awestruck.

"I never get that way around anybody anymore," McHale said. "The only time I'm in awe of those guys is when I watch them play."

Melchiorre left the Celtics after the 1986–87 season and reunited with Bill Fitch as trainer of the Houston Rockets and Los Angeles Clippers. Lebeaux was let go by the Celtics when Rick Pitino took over in 1997 and has been Springsteen's road manager for fourteen years. McHale spent another six weeks coming off the bench for the Celtics in the winter of 1984–85, then joined Bird and Parish in the starting lineup to complete the greatest frontcourt in NBA history.

CHAPTER 9

"THAT GUY IS GONNA BE THE GREATEST PLAYER OF ALL TIME"

Professional ballplayers love routine. There's comfort in doing the same things at the same time every workday.

In the mid-1980s, on nights when the Celtics played games at the Boston Garden, Larry Bird would get to the gym early to work on his shooting. His game-night partner was assistant equipment manager Joe Qatato, also known as Joe Q or Corky. A public relations intern from Emerson College who started with the team in 1979, Joe Q was an everyday employee by 1985, handling equipment, driving vans, giving an occasional backrub, and rebounding for Bird. He didn't ask anything of Bird, which made him a Larry favorite. Bird kept in his locker Joe Q's high school football photo—a grainy image in which the balding Qatato had a full head of hair. Joe Q wound up being one of a handful of folks who attended Bird's wedding to Dinah Mattingly in 1989, and Larry brought Qatato with him to Indiana when Bird became head coach of the Pacers in 1997.

Hours before every game at the Garden, Bird and Joe Q could be found on the parquet for twenty minutes of perimeter shooting. There were no fans, and early-arriving media members knew to leave them alone. Anybody watching could log Bird making fifteen or twenty consecutive medium-range shots. If Bird missed, he'd blame the Garden's Bull Gang.

"If the basket was straight, that shot would have been nothing but net," Bird would tease after a rare miss.

Buckner and Bird occasionally played a shooting game called Knockout, and Buckner explained Bird's Knockout prowess to *Sports Illustrated*'s Jack McCallum:

"You'd be ready to win, and all of a sudden Larry would throw up a shot that would not only knock your ball away from the basket but would also *go in itself*. The man could play pool and basketball at the same time."

I was early to the Garden for every home game and knew enough to leave Larry and Joe Q alone. My press row seat was about ten chairs down from the Celtics bench. During his late-afternoon routine, Bird occasionally wandered toward my workplace to gossip or break chops.

When he was approaching an NBA record for consecutive free throws made, he came over to me and asked, "What you working on tonight, Scoop?"

"I'm working on your free throw streak for our early edition. Don't make me look bad by missing one. My story will look dated and stupid if you miss."

"Don't worry about that, Scoop." He went back to his pregame drill.

In the first half of that night's game, Bird went to the line for two free throws. After he drained the first attempt, he turned to his right and winked at me before making the second.

We were getting along well during these golden days of his three-year MVP reign. Still, he called me out when I reported that Maxwell ate a steady diet of McDonald's before home games.

"Scoop, I eat just as bad," said the man who claimed he'd eaten ten gallons of ice cream and seven wedding cakes during a long stretch when he was out with a back injury. ("I ate weddin' cakes 'cause you knew they was gonna be good," he told McCallum. "I mean, who would fuck up a weddin' cake?") "I love potatoes and french fries and potato chips. Staying in shape is one of the hardest parts of this job. You just wait till my playing days is over. I'll be the fattest fuck you ever saw."

Rookie Michael Jordan was all the rage in 1984–85, and as Jordan ascended, pundits pounded Portland for selecting Bowie with the second overall pick. Never one to resist a cheap shot, I compared Trail Blazer GM Stu Inman to Neville Chamberlain. Meanwhile, some NBA stars groused about Jordan's hype and his burgeoning brand. In an attempt to put Jordan in his place, Isiah Thomas and friends kept the ball away from Jordan at the 1985 All-Star Game.

Bird had no problem making room for a successor to the throne he shared with Magic. After Jordan scored 36 in his Garden debut, a 111–108 loss to the Celtics, Bird said, "That guy is gonna be the greatest player of all time."

This felt like false humility, never a Bird trademark, and I challenged him on it.

"I'm telling you," he insisted. "You watch and see what he does before he's through."

Swell. But it wasn't Jordan's time yet; it was still Bird's NBA. When the Celtics defeated the Trail Blazers 128–127 on a Bird buzzer-beater in late January, I wrote:

> You shoot it with frosted fingers from the side of the driveway as you fall into the neighbor's snowy hedges. Or sometimes you shoot it alone in the gym with an imaginary clock ticking down and an imaginary crowd roaring.
>
> Every basketball Jones who has ever played the game has practiced it hundreds of times, but it's rare that the opportunity arises, and even more rare when it works out exactly as it did in your mind games.
>
> It happened yesterday at the Boston Garden. Larry Bird, the homespun hick with the hungry heart, canned a fallaway jumper from the darkest corner of the Causeway Street gym with no time left, giving the Boston Celtics a 128–127 victory over the Portland Trail Blazers and sending K. C. Jones on an all-expenses-paid trip to Hoosierland as the Eastern Conference's All-Star coach.

It was life imitating art, straight out of *The Natural*. Bird's Kohoutek comet seemed to freeze in mid-flight. When it finally came crashing through the net (for his 47th and 48th points), Portland coach Jack Ramsay fell to his knees, Johnny Most went into dogwhistle delirium, the Garden organist struck up the Hallelujah Chorus, and 14,890 said, "There goes the best there ever was."

After that game, when Bird emerged from the showers, wearing a white terry-cloth bathrobe, ready to meet the press, his pal Jonny Miller broke the silence and asked, "Larry, did you want the ball at the end?"

"No, Jon," Bird said with a chuckle. "That's why you saw me out there hiding behind the bench."

Later that winter, in a quiet moment on the road, Bird spoke about his first days of wanting to take the last shot:

I missed every game my sophomore year of high school with an ankle injury. I was really coming on. Then we got to sectionals and I was on the bench and I heard my name called. I thought it was one of my friends in the stands. All of a sudden, my coach was in front of me saying, "Do you want to play or not?" Well, I was in that game and had the ball in my hands before I even thought about it. I turned and shot and it went right through. At the end of the game, I got fouled and had a one-and-one. I hadn't shot any free throws in a game all year long, and I knew everybody was thinking there was no way I'd make them. Well, I ripped both of 'em. The next day the headline in the [*Louisville*] *Courier-Journal* was "Bird Steals the Show." I'll never forget that. It was pretty eye-catching to me. I think me wanting the ball at the end was from that.

Two days after the Portland buzzer-beater, Bird did it again, against the Pistons in Hartford, canning a running one-handed shot from the left baseline as time expired to give the Celtics a 1-point win. He was at the height of his powers. When he learned that my game story from his Portland shot won an award, he said, "Scoop, you're winnin' all them awards because of me, ain't you?"

The Celtics beat the Lakers by 2 points in a Finals preview at the Garden in January and were 41-9 when Bird, Parish, DJ, and the coaching staff went to Indy for the All-Star Game. Bird spent his first two days of the break in French Lick, watching his baby brother, Eddie, score 24 with 17 rebounds in a high school game.

"He plays basically like I do," said Bird. "He's not real quick and he doesn't jump real well."

Bird bought fifty tickets to the All-Star Game at the Hoosier Dome and said, "I could have used three hundred, but at thirty-five dollars a pop, you got to draw the line somewhere."

The annual West Coast trip followed the All-Star Game. On a bus ride in Portland, Bird started going hard at veteran reporter Mike Fine. The *Quincy Ledger* scribe was generally a good sport, but when Bird dialed the abuse up to 11, Fine whirled around, got in Bird's face, and said, "Oh, yeah? Well, how come every time I see you talking on these television commercials you sound so smart and smooth, but in person, you sound like such a douchebag?"

"Because those guys pay me to talk," Bird retorted.

An exchange like this with a writer would have been unthinkable in earlier seasons, but the new Larry Bird was on top of the world, feeling comfortable even with folks in the media. Once described by his biographer Ryan as "willfully uneducated," Bird carried Arthur Schlesinger's Robert Kennedy biography on the Portland trip and told us, "I read a couple of books last summer. Shows you how bored I was."

He was loving the NBA life and could not believe how much free time he had on road trips. After game-day shootarounds he'd hop on the team bus and say, "Okay, we just got done shooting basketballs. Time now to go to our free hotel, eat a free meal, tap a nap, then come back to the gym tonight to play a basketball game. This sure is a tough life. If you don't like this life, you don't like life. Period."

Writers from the *Los Angeles Times*, the *Sporting News*, *Sports Il-*

lustrated, and *Time* joined us on the trip to write Bird features. Tom Callahan, who'd covered the ancient Baltimore Bullets and Cincinnati Royals, was crafting a cover story for *Time* on Bird and Wayne Gretzky.

Bird respected Callahan's early NBA experience and asked questions about what it was like watching Oscar Robertson, Elgin Baylor, and Wilt Chamberlain. Satisfied with the scoop on Oscar and Wilt, Bird asked Callahan, "What are you shooting for with this story?"

"Two things. True to me, fair to you."

Callahan told Bird he'd be going to French Lick for some background.

"Sorry," Bird said. "I've known Bob Ryan for six years, and I just let him go to French Lick last year."

"Larry," Callahan replied with a laugh, "it's not like I need a passport to get in."

But he did. Both men knew that if Bird turned off the faucets back home, *Time* would be shut out like Michael Jordan at the All-Star Game.

"If you leave my little brother alone, I'll have my big brother Mark pick you up at the airport," Bird offered.

With Larry's stamp of approval, Mark Bird picked up Callahan and took him to Ma Bird's house. Georgia welcomed Callahan into her kitchen, serving coffee, saying, "Red's kind of like the daddy who was never there for Larry. Larry thinks that Red is just it. . . . All my kids have been good, but to have a superstar, really. Well, I usually don't brag on him. He always played as though he had to be perfect. A lot of people say that's how it turned out."

Back out West, the Celtics lost their Finals rematch with the Lakers and also effectively lost Maxwell for the rest of the season.

Max had hurt his left knee a couple of weeks earlier, but he didn't sit until the nationally televised game in the Forum. While Worthy devoured Wedman in the closing minute, Max iced his knee and was sent back to Boston, where Dr. Robert Leach called for exploratory surgery. When Maxwell went under the knife on February 22, the Celtics said he might be back in ten days.

Maxwell started only one game for the rest of his Celtics career. He was unable to contribute, and his subtraction crushed Boston's quest to repeat. With Max on the shelf and no backcourt depth, Celtics starters played far too many minutes over the final two months of the regular season.

The day after Maxwell went home from LA, the Celtics crushed the Jazz in Salt Lake City. Bird scored 30 with 12 rebounds, 10 assists, and 9 steals over thirty-three minutes. At the end of three quarters, he was on the bench even though he was within one steal of a quadruple double, which had only been done once in NBA history (Nate Thurmond). When I saw the stat sheet, I got up from my seat, walked down the aisle that ran behind the Celtics bench, crouched behind Bird, and told him, "Hey, you need one more steal for a quadruple double."

"Get the hell out of here, Scoop."

K. C. Jones had already made the offer to put Bird back in the game, but the Celtics led 90–68 after three.

"I already did enough damage," Bird said. "Why go for it when we're up thirty? If it mattered, I'd have been out there trying to get it, but it wasn't no big deal."

A month after the Utah tour de force, Bird and McHale erased the Celtics' single-game individual scoring record twice within nine days.

Starting regularly for the first time in his career, McHale scored 56 against the Pistons on a Sunday afternoon at the Garden. Bird enjoyed seeing McHale abuse Kent Benson, the Indiana big man who ignored shy freshman Larry Bird back in the fall of 1974. Force-feeding McHale every trip down the floor, Bird compiled a triple double and got Benson fouled out of the game. Bird passed to McHale on nine straight possessions, setting up McHale's final 9 points. It was Babe Ruth helping Lou Gehrig set the single-season home run record.

When McHale came out with 56 points and a little bit left on the clock, Bird told him, "You should have stayed in and gone for sixty."

How long did Larry think the record would last?

"It might stand until the next game," Bird said.

Nine days after McHale vaulted over Havlicek's 54-point performance from 1973, Bird erased McHale's record with a 60-point performance against the Hawks at the Lakefront Arena on the campus of the University of New Orleans. This is how good and cocky the Celtics were in the spring of 1985.

The Hawks, who did not draw well in Atlanta, got promoter Barry Mendelson to guarantee $100,000 for each of twelve games played at Lakefront in 1984–85. Nobody liked playing there. Atlanta publicist Bill Needle said, "I was sentenced to all twelve games in New Orleans and opted for forty-eight hours of community service, but they wouldn't go for it."

Bird ran a 5K road race in Boston the day before the game and on the bus ride from the New Orleans Hyatt to Lakefront complained that his legs were sore. He was energized when the bus steered past Brother Martin prep, high school home of young Rick Robey.

"That's it right there," Bird said. "That's where Footer got all them bribes to go to Kentucky."

Bird was additionally inspired when he saw thousands of Celtics fans at Lakefront.

The Boston press corps was seated on an elevated platform directly behind the Hawks' bench, which gave us a great view of coach Mike Fratello arguing with his dissension-riddled team while Bird racked up easy baskets. As Bird made one preposterous long-range shot after another, Hawks benchwarmers laughed and high-fived. When Bird careened toward the Atlanta bench after draining another three, Hawks scrubs Antoine Carr, Cliff Levingston, and Eddie Johnson leaned into one another and fell off the bench with glee. Bird's final 2 points came on a buzzer-beater heaved from a few feet in front of the Atlanta bench. The NBA fined Hawks players for celebrating Bird's performance.

Hawks GM Stan Kasten came to the Celtics locker room after the game and presented Bird with the game ball.

"Lot of good scoop out there tonight, Scoop," Bird said as he exited the room.

Callahan's *Time* story hit the newsstands that same week, and Callahan sent Bird a thank-you note when Callahan learned that his cover boy had scored 60. A few weeks later Callahan got a letter from Bird.

"It was a piece of paper from a loose-leaf notebook with the circles torn out," Callahan recalled. "It had a candy smudge on it—like a piece of fudge or something. It read, 'Dear Tom, Fair to me. Larry Bird.'"

In the spring of 2021, after Celtics superstar Jayson Tatum tied Bird's record with a 60-point game against the Spurs, McHale said, "I was kind of glad Jayson stopped at sixty so Larry still shares the record. The NBA was different when we played. The money hadn't exploded and we were treated like basketball players, not rock stars. It was more of a 'we' league than a 'me' league."

A month after Bird scored 60, he agreed to a lengthy interview at the Richfield Holiday Inn (scene of my ham-handed attempt to buy him two beers). He was about to win another MVP, and my boss wanted a three-thousand-word profile to set up the playoffs and the inevitable Finals rematch with the Lakers.

The next day, I brought a bucket of ice and a couple of Cokes from the hotel's first-floor vending machine and pulled up a chair in Bird's hotel room, while he stretched across his bed, looked at the ceiling, and talked about shooting the basketball:

"I just aim for the big cylinder. The thing that helped me was when my high school coach told me you could squeeze two basketballs through there at one time. I always thought, 'Hell, if you can do that, you should be able to put one through there pretty easily.' And he always told me you need to have a good arc on your shot because, with a straight shot, it's hard to go in. It's better to miss long or short than sideways. The shot that bounces off the back rim is not a bad shot. When I get in shooting slumps, I have the ball going left on me a lot. It's hard to get out of it. You start aiming and then you're really in trouble. There's a flaw in your wrist when you're releasing it."

I asked him how a guy with his limitations managed not to be intimidated by the likes of James Worthy, Larry Nance, and other perfectly sculpted NBA pogo sticks.

"I can always outthink them," Bird answered. "I've made a living off guys who can run and jump higher. I'm never intimidated when I'm on a basketball court. Maybe in high school a little, but not in college and not now. In college I remember a guy on the other team trying to get into my head during layup lines before a game. He had his hair in cornrows and he was yapping during warm-ups. He was a big dude and I could tell he was intimidating our players. I went over to him and said, 'When this game's over, you're going to be kissing my ass.' I scored forty-eight on him.

"Guys who jump real high—they can do that when nobody's got their ass into them. You put your ass into them and box them out, and it takes away their legs and then you can jump as high as any of them. That's why I always try to put a body on people. I'm strong enough to hold them off. I've proven that a white boy who can't run and jump can play this game."

Buckner had an additional theory: "Larry is a lot stronger than people think. If he puts his forearm on me, I can't move. I think it's from throwing all that hay into the loft when he was a kid."

"I really don't need anyone to build my ego," Bird continued. "When I'm home in Boston, I want to go out and eat, pay my bill, and get the hell out. Back in French Lick, I don't have those problems, and that's why I go back there. It's the same with nice cars, Mercedes and all that. I can't see putting fifty thousand or sixty thousand dollars into a car when our house growing up was worth ten thousand dollars. I just can't buy that. And clothes never did catch my eye. I never really enjoyed 'em. I always wore what I felt comfortable in. I'll wear pretty much anything if I get it for free.

"When I was at [Indiana] State, finishing to get my degree, they had me teaching special needs kids in a high school. That was tough. It gave me a lot of respect for people who do that.

"I thought I'd wind up being a construction worker, pouring concrete. I wasn't very good at shop in school, but I'd been around construction. As far as basketball goes, I just wanted to be the best player on my high school team. None of the Birds went to college, and I didn't think I'd be going. I didn't take the SATs or college exams, or nothin'. Then everything was happening at once and I took those tests the last time they offered 'em. If I'd applied myself in school like I did to basketball, I'd have gotten straight A's. My kids definitely will have good grammar and be taught the right way."

I asked him about being a celebrity.

"I guess I understand it. When I was a kid, I felt that way about Mickey Mantle, but that's Mickey Mantle. Hell, I'm just Larry Bird. I mean, come on. I had one person come up to me in high school and ask for an autograph. He said his mom thought I was going to be famous someday. One thing that bothers me now is the staring. Everywhere I go, people stare at me. When you get to the airport and you find a quiet place where nobody sees you and then one guy says, 'Hey, it's Larry Bird!,' and then it's all over. If I worried about what people thought or wanted my ass kissed, I'd be out more. That's just not my nature. I just want to play the game, go home, watch the tape, and get ready for the next one."

In his early Boston days, Bird fumed when newspaper or magazine articles detailed his failed first marriage, his daughter from that marriage, and his alcoholic dad's suicide. He seemed at peace with that by 1985:

"The only thing I hate now is when they want me to talk about injuries. Other than that, I really don't care what's written if it's the truth."

We were going to put that one to the test before the summer was over.

Maxwell was not ready when the playoffs started. His "exploratory" procedure turned into serious knee surgery, and he made minimal contributions over the final six weeks of the regular season. His teammates and his boss didn't believe he was serious about his rehab program, and this perception wasn't helped when Dr. Leach, who performed the surgery, said, "The big problem was getting Max to do the work."

Suspicion about Maxwell's commitment to rehab crushed the Celtics' effort to repeat, damaged Maxwell's relationship with Bird, and infuriated Auerbach. Candid and ever jovial, Maxwell made things worse by appearing to take things lightly. He wisecracked about saving himself for "varsity games." Auerbach and Bird suspected that Maxwell was acting out because he'd lost his job to McHale. Max knew his starting days were over when he watched McHale score 56 against the Pistons.

Bird addressed the issue in his 2009 book *When the Game Was Ours*:

"Max was out of shape when he came back. He didn't do the rehab the way they asked. I was so pissed at him. . . . He got his money and he quit. . . . We were trying to win back-to-back, something no one had done in over 15 years, and Max is talking about laying down on us. . . . We could have won in '83, but we didn't because of all that bullshit with Bill Fitch. Then we could have won again in '85, but we didn't because of more bullshit."

The hard feelings never dissolved. In his twenty-first-century role as a Celtics color commentator, Max often takes subtle shots and mocks Bird's defensive skills. It bothers him that Bird was named to the NBA's second-string All-Defensive Team in 1984. Maxwell knows he was the player who nightly guarded the other team's best forward. When Dallas's Dirk Nowitzki retired in 2019, Max said Nowitzki was a better NBA player than Bird.

It took a long time for Auerbach to get over his anger. Red had a book in production in 1985 and had complimentary comments about Maxwell deleted before the tome went to press. He didn't allow Maxwell's number 31 to be raised to the rafters until 2003.

In the final month of the regular season, the '85 Celtics lost two straight for the first time when Bird and Ainge were given permission to skip a trip to Detroit and Milwaukee. This happens all the time

The foundation of the Celtics dynasty. Center Bill Russell won eleven NBA Championships in thirteen NBA seasons, all with Boston. Red Auerbach won nine rings as coach of the Celtics and another seven as team general manager. (Steve Lipofsky, LipofskyPhoto.com)

Larry Bird was drafted by the Celtics in 1979 and won his first NBA Championship in the spring of 1981. He took a puff on Red Auerbach's victory cigar to celebrate. (*Boston Globe*/ Frank O'Brien)

Under steadily accumulating championship banners, the "Bull Gang" at the ancient Boston Garden put down—and took up—the Celtics' fabled parquet floor hundreds of times through the decades. Celtics opponents complained about "dead spots." (Steve Lipofsky, LipofskyPhoto.com)

Sportswriters enjoyed great seats and access in the 1980s. Here, behind Danny Ainge driving the lane, the *Boston Globe*'s lineup excitedly watches the show. Left to right: author Dan Shaughnessy (the goofy-looking guy with the giant eyeglasses), Bob Ryan, and Leigh Montville. (Steve Lipofsky, LipofskyPhoto.com)

Celtics head coach Bill Fitch (left), who welcomed Larry Bird to Boston and won big with him, and his successor K. C. Jones, who continued the winning, were not close. (Steve Lipofsky, LipofskyPhoto.com)

Bird called DJ "the best teammate I ever had." (Steve Lipofsky, LipofskyPhoto.com)

Playing the Lakers in the Finals always meant more to Bird because of his rivalry with Magic Johnson. (*Boston Globe*/Stan Grossfeld)

Celtics vs. Lakers in the 1984 Finals. Jack Nicholson gets a reaction from the Garden crowd, including reporters (left to right) Peter May, Dan Shaughnessy, Bob Ryan, Leigh Montville, Mike "Smurf" Carey, and Joe Fitzgerald. Dinah Mattingly, Bird's fiancée, is pictured over Jack's left shoulder, wearing a blue dress. (Steve Lipofsky, LipofskyPhoto.com)

Sandwiched between Kareem Abdul-Jabbar and Magic Johnson, Cedric Maxwell fights for a rebound in the 1984 Finals. (Steve Lipofsky, LipofskyPhoto.com)

Tempers flared after Kevin McHale's takedown of Kurt Rambis in Game 4 of the '84 Finals. Here, James Worthy cocks his fist and threatens Bird, who is being restrained by Danny Ainge. (*Boston Globe*/Stan Grossfeld)

Overcome by oppressive heat in the old Boston Garden, Kareem Abdul-Jabbar sucks on an oxygen mask in Game 5 of the '84 Finals. (*Boston Globe*/Stan Grossfeld)

All flights were commercial for the 1980s Celtics. In the 1984 Finals, the team flew coast-to-coast five times, sometimes connecting in Chicago or New York. Here, Bird sleeps at LAX before boarding a red-eye after the Celtics lost Game 6 Sunday afternoon in the Forum. (*Boston Globe*/Stan Grossfeld)

Cedric Maxwell told teammates to "hop on my back" before Game 7 against the Lakers in 1984. Here, he gets a high five from Kevin McHale. Maxwell scored 24 points in the championship clincher. (*Boston Globe*/Stan Grossfeld)

Security around the Garden's perimeter was terrible in the closing moments of the 1984 Finals. Here, Bird tries to get fans off the court before the buzzer. (*Boston Globe*/Stan Grossfeld)

MVP Bird and young Michael Jordan reach for a loose ball. It was still Bird's league when rookie Jordan entered it in the fall of 1984, but Bird saw the greatness from day one, saying, "That guy is going to be the greatest player of all time."
(© Ted Gartland)

Julius Erving and Larry Bird face off in November 1984. Dr. J. had heard enough of Bird's trash-talking.
(© Ted Gartland)

A 1984–85 Celtics-Sixers brawl that started with Bird and Julius Erving erupts into a donnybrook. Moses Malone headlocks Bird while Quinn Buckner holds off Maurice Cheeks. (*Boston Globe*/Jim Wilson)

Bird is embraced by Quinn Buckner while M. L. Carr celebrates after Bird makes a buzzer-beating game-winner against Portland in January 1985. (*Boston Globe*/Stan Grossfeld)

Cedric Maxwell had a theory that the *Boston Globe* sports section would feature photos of Bird, McHale, and Ainge after wins, then use photos of Maxwell and Parish after losses. Not true, of course. However, this was our cover, May 20, 1985, after a playoff loss in Philadelphia. Max felt validated.
(*Boston Globe*/Janet Knott)

Bill Walton and Bird became a mutual admiration society when Walton came to the Celtics in the fall of 1985. (Steve Lipofsky, LipofskyPhoto.com)

A sense of ballet on the parquet floor with DJ, Bird, Ainge, Walton, and McHale celebrating after another easy basket. This may have been the best-passing NBA team of all time. (Steve Lipofsky, LipofskyPhoto.com)

Robert Parish, ready to break the no-drinking pact once the Celtics won the 1986 NBA Championship. (*Boston Globe*/Stan Grossfeld)

Danny Ainge, Rick Carlisle, Larry Bird, Bill Walton, and the 1986 NBA Championship trophy. (*Boston Globe*/ Bill Greene)

in 2021, but there was no "load management" in 1985, and Boston's failure to tell Detroit that Bird wasn't coming angered Detroit management. Michigan fans had bought tickets expecting to see Larry Bird in the Silverdome.

The *Boston Herald*'s Mike Carey scooped me on this story, quoting Bird and Ainge after calling them at home. When I next saw Bird, I confronted him with my journalistic outrage.

"This is horseshit," I started. "Smurf plays cards with you guys and writes whatever you tell him. You give him your phone number and then I get porked when you skip a trip and he calls you at home for all the quotes."

"You're right," Bird agreed. "That's not fair. I could tell Smurf tried to stick it to you by showing that he had the number and you didn't. He must have gotten it from Danny. I'm still not going to give it to you, but I will talk to him and Danny about it. That ain't right. I'm beginning to understand how all this works. We was all out downtown at Chelsea's the other night. Everybody was drunk, saying you're too negative and stuff, and I kept saying that it's okay if it's true. I defended you."

The Celtics won their first playoff game against the Cavaliers. Parish took 5 shots and scored only 8 points. When I characterized Chief as "pro basketball's Mr. October," teammates rallied to his defense.

"Mr. October," sniffed Ainge, who understood the baseball analogy (calling Chief basketball's Mr. October was like George Steinbrenner insulting Dave Winfield by calling him Mr. May). "That was horseshit."

A complicated fellow, never a friend of the media's, Parish was loved by his teammates. For good reason. They all knew he'd have been a bigger star on almost any other team. He didn't complain when he got fewer shots. He was the quarterback on defense and he was never out of shape. Everyone on the team went out of the way to pump Parish's tires.

"I love playing with Robert Parish because he is probably the most unselfish basketball player I've ever played with in my life," Bird wrote in his autobiography.

"As public as the rest of us were, Chief was private," said M. L. Carr. "He just wanted to do his job and didn't want publicity. He was a little different than me and Cedric. He never got as much of the credit, but he was as important as anybody."

"I think one of the gravest errors we made over the years was overlooking the contribution of Robert Parish," said K. C. Jones. "He was often criticized during the playoffs, which was ridiculous. The man came to play every night."

An elbow issue forced Bird to miss the third game of Boston's opening round playoff series against the Cavs at the Richfield Coliseum. He stayed back at the Holiday Inn while his teammates were beaten and 20,900 Cavalier fans chanted, "We want Bird!"

The next day at the local practice gym (Wedman skipped out, fearing asbestos), Bird, reenergized and feisty, answered questions about a variety of topics as he was surrounded by a couple dozen reporters. His elbow was feeling better and he welcomed the challenge thrown down by Cleveland fans.

"They want me?" he asked. "They're going to get me with both barrels."

Asked yet another question about his elbow, Bird sighed and said, "Like I said, it feels great. Really great. It's like that feeling you get just before you come."

The moment he said it, he looked up and noticed that a female reporter was present: Mary Shane of the *Worcester Telegram*. Bird liked Shane. She was a thorough professional from the Midwest, looked like a high school librarian, showed up every day, and did nothing to call attention to herself.

Bird was mortified that he'd used the vulgarity in front of Shane. What would Granny Kerns have thought?

"Mary, I'm so sorry!" he said. "I didn't see you there!"

Shane assured him it was okay. She had a son at home and told Larry she'd heard far worse. Inconsolable, Bird broke from the group and ran around the perimeter of the court with his hands in his face.

He got over his embarrassment before the next night's game, telling Cavalier forward Phil Hubbard, "I'm going at you tonight!" Hubbard was a Michigan man, and Bird loved to take down Big Ten players, who'd looked down on Indiana State. Booed every time he touched the ball, Bird scored 34 points with 14 rebounds and 7 assists as the Celtics closed out the Cavaliers and moved on to Detroit for the second round.

The conference semifinal was uneventful. There'd be epic Celtics-Pistons playoff series before the end of the decade, but Detroit wasn't ready to compete with Boston in 1985. The great rivalry was still two years away. The Celtics beat the Pistons in six games, and New England braced for a renewal of the Celtics-Sixers rivalry in the Eastern Conference finals.

The traditional beasts of the East hadn't met in the playoffs for three years, and Philly's 1983 championship team was crumbling. Dr. J. was thirty-five, and Malone could no longer run with the still-spry Parish. Two years removed from their dominant championship run, the Sixers came into the series much the way the Celtics limped into Milwaukee in 1983.

The Celtics won the first two at home easily. Parish, Bird, and McHale combined for 77 points in Game 1, while Erving was held to 12, scoring only 2 points in the second half. Malone had zero offensive rebounds in the first half, and Toney took only 11 shots. The Sixers committed 21 turnovers.

Boston took a 3-0 series lead with an easy Game 3 win in Philadelphia. Dr. J. shot 1 for 10, scored only 5 points, and was benched midway through the fourth quarter. Guarded by Dennis Johnson, Toney made 3 of 17 shots. Parish, easily the MVP of this series (perhaps inspired by my "Mr. October" comment?), devoured Malone for a third straight game. The Sixers were in complete disarray, bickering among themselves and ripping Cunningham.

The 76ers implosion disguised Boston's flaws. Bird's ever-crooked right index finger was newly mangled and swollen. He shot only 42 percent in the series, including games of 8 for 23, 4 for 15, and 6 for 18. Maxwell played no more than thirteen minutes in any of the first three games, scoring 2 points in each game. Every Boston starter played at least thirty-nine minutes in Game 3. The Celtics were on the doorstep of the Finals, but K. C. Jones had no bench.

The Celtics were unable to complete a sweep of the Sixers, owing in part to a particularly curious performance by Maxwell in a 115–104 Game 4 loss. Maxwell gave up on several plays at the end of the third quarter, then failed to enter the game with his teammates for the start of the fourth. The Celtics played four-on-five for twenty-one seconds.

"I felt like Wayne Gretzky playing in a shorthanded situation," said McHale.

In the Sunday *Globe*, I wrote, "Maxwell roamed the premises like a brother from another planet."

True to Max's theory that the *Globe* always blamed the Black players for a loss, the photo gracing the cover of our Sunday section featured a large photo of Maxwell wearing a goofy look on his face.

The day before Game 5, Bird practiced with his right hand taped in a weblike fashion. His ring and pinkie fingers were wrapped together, as were his middle and index fingers. At the end of practice, he stopped on his way to the locker room and took questions.

"Larry, you can't play in a playoff game with your hand taped like that, can you?" I asked.

"You never know," he teased. "It's a different feeling. I don't like anything taped because then it just doesn't feel like it usually does. It's difficult to shoot when you have something on your hand. Although I don't think Greg Kite has anything to worry about. He could wear a cast."

"But seriously," I pushed. "You're not going to tape it like that for the game tomorrow, are you?"

"Scoop, I could tape my whole hand up and make more shots than you."

"Well, yes, that may be true, but let's talk about tomorrow night and the playoff game."

It was too late. He wasn't letting this go.

"No, Scoop, let's go for it," he insisted. "You and me. I'll tape my whole hand up. One hundred free throws. Five dollars a throw. We'll see who can shoot free throws with tape on his hand."

"You're gonna tape all four fingers and your thumb?" I stuttered.

"That's right, all five wrapped up, and I'll still make more shots than you. What do you say, Scoop?"

I quickly did the math in my head. *Worst case: I miss one hundred and he makes one hundred and I'm out $500, plus the humiliation. But I'm a good free throw shooter and he's going to have trouble with this, and it will make for an easy off-day story to set up Game 5. Maybe I can even get the boss to forgive any losses.*

"You're on," I told Bird.

Shoot for money.

Bird got a roll of tape from Melchiorre and wrapped a long piece around the four fingers of his right hand, then folded the fingers over his thumb and wrapped another piece of tape over his balled fist. I inspected his hand and it looked as if he were wearing a soft cast. He would have to shot-put his free throws.

We agreed on three warm-up shots, followed by ten sets of ten. We would rebound for each other.

"You want to go first?" he asked.

Yeah.

"You don't like the pressure, do you?" He laughed.

I made 6 of 10 in my first round and felt pretty good about it. When Bird stepped to the line and hit 6 of 10 with his shot-put motion, I felt even better.

In round two I made 6 again. Larry made 7. As we switched places for the third round, he said, "You owe me five bucks.

I made 7 in my third round. When Bird drained his first attempt in round three, I heard him say, "I got this figured out."

And he did. Swish. Splash. Zing. He started making all of them.

155

"Couldn't you at least hit the rim?" I asked, not having to move to collect one made shot after another. This must have been what it was like when little boy Larry Bird rebounded for big brother Mark on the court across from the laundromat in French Lick.

Larry was in my head when I went back for round four. Suddenly I was standing at the free throw line in December of 1970, while Littleton fans jeered after I back-rimmed the first of two late-game misses.

At the end of five rounds my tab was up to $45.

"How about calling it a day?" I offered.

"Give me forty-five dollars, plus twenty-five dollars for a buyout, and we'll stop now."

Sheesh. He must have done this before. I was getting hustled by one of the great hustlers of all time.

I foolishly turned down the buyout, and the second half of the competition is a blur. I was Beezer Carnes. I saw $5 bills flying out of my hand every time I released a shot. I expected Jack Nicholson to pop up from under the floor and give me the choke sign.

The worse I got, the better he got. Bird made 46 of his last 50. He made 73 of 80 after figuring it out in the first two rounds. He made 86 of 100 free throws with a taped fist. I made 54.

"You owe me one hundred and sixty dollars," he said.

I told him he'd get his money before the game tomorrow. Then I went to the pay phone in the hallway outside the gym and called my boss.

"Vince, buddy," I started. "I've got this great story about Larry and his horseshit shooting in these playoffs and his busted-up finger, and how he can adjust to playing with tape on his hand. We sort of made a bet and I might have lost a little money, but I think it's a good story."

"How much did you lose?" Doria asked.

"A hundred and sixty," I whispered. "Think I can put in for it as a research expense and get reimbursed?"

"Write it up and we'll see how it goes."

I went to my West Newton BayBank ATM the next day and withdrew eight, crisp $20 bills. Later in the afternoon, as I was setting up my PortaBubble in the dark Garden, Bird interrupted his shooting ritual with Joe Q and darted to the press table, his greedy palm extended. I slapped the cash into his still-mangled hand.

"Thanks, Scoop," he said as he folded the bills and stuffed the wad into his Converse.

I expensed the $160, but it bounced back from *Globe* accounting with a note indicating that the IRS typically flags the word *wager* on expense reports. It was refiled as eight $20 lunches with Parish, and I was reimbursed by *Globe* accounting. Color me happy.

Larry Bird is no doubt worth north of $100 million today, but he's never forgotten the exact amount he took from me in 1985. More than a dozen years after our "Shoot for Money," I was part of a Boston radio broadcast in which three Boston reporters interviewed Larry after he'd been named head coach of the Pacers. There was a lot of teasing, and while answering one of my questions about his surprising foray into NBA coaching, Bird said, "Scoop, all I know is I got one hundred and sixty extra dollars in my pocket."

With no tape on his right hand, Bird made only 6 of 18 shots the night after our free throw contest, but stole the ball from Toney in the closing seconds to preserve a 2-point win and a Finals rematch with the Lakers. Parish, still not talking to the media, was easily Boston's best player in the series, and we heard about it nightly from Nancy Parish, who frequently stood over the exit tunnel and yelled at writers and opponents as they were ducking into the Garden's underbelly.

Setting up the epic rematch, I reported, "The Lakers are scheduled to arrive in Boston tonight. They stayed in three different hotels in last year's Finals. They're staying at the Copley Marriott again this year and hope to avoid a repeat of the fire alarms that drove them out last year."

Riley should have put a contract out on me.

The Celtics annihilated the Lakers, 148–114, in Game 1 of the Finals at the Boston Garden on Memorial Day. Boston made 11 of its first 12 shots in the second quarter, bolting to a 63–34 lead. Wedman came off the bench and made 11 of 11 shots, including 4 three-pointers.

"I was feeling it," Wedman recalled decades later. "I maybe had three or four games in my career like that when I was in Kansas City. I was always trying to make every shot, and every once in a while, it happened. That was certainly the biggest stage."

It was a miserable day for thirty-eight-year-old Kareem, who managed only 3 rebounds in the beat down. Jabbar looked like an aging Willie Mays stumbling around center field for the New York Mets in the 1973 World Series. Joyous Celtics fans mocked the soft Showtime Fakers and Tragic Johnson.

The drubbing triggered flashbacks to 1984 when Celtics stole the Lakers' lunch money, then kicked dirt in their faces. Carr, Maxwell, McHale, and Celtics fans taunted the Lakers, and security around the perimeter of the Garden floor was no better than it had been after the finale in '84. The rout gave the cocky Celtics twelve consecutive Garden playoff victories and a 21-1 postseason Garden record since Fitch had left.

Three days after the beatdown, Riley broke one of his own rules and allowed Ferdinand Lewis Alcindor Sr. to ride the Lakers team bus from the Copley Marriott for Game 2. In the tiny visitors' locker room, Riley talked to his team about his own dad, who'd once told him that there comes a time when you've got to plant your feet, stand your ground, and kick somebody's ass. This was that time.

The Lakers won Game 2, 109–102. Kareem scored 30 with 17 rebounds and 8 assists.

"I had people throwing dirt on my face," said Abdul-Jabbar. "That was a little premature."

After Kareem finished his media room obligation, Lakers publicist Josh Rosenfeld escorted Abdul-Jabbar back to the parquet for a late TV interview. Straggler Celtics fans, including the ubiquitous and ever-enraged Nancy Parish, hurled insults at Jabbar while he fulfilled his TV duty. When the interview was over, Rosenfeld flared as he steered Kareem back toward the locker room and pitched a wet towel into the jeering crowd. The towel hit Nancy Parish square in the face. Later in the night, Rosenfeld was told he'd hit Mrs. Chief.

"Nancy was a character in her own right," said Maxwell. "They used to give the wives popcorn in their row, and the popcorn would get passed down and stop with her, and then there was a fight because she didn't pass the popcorn. Nancy had her own agenda of being Nancy Parish."

"Nancy was a fireball," remembered Buckner.

We all flew to Los Angeles the next night (*Beverly Hills Cop* was the in-flight film), and the Celtics hunkered down for a week at the Los Angeles Airport Marriott. Early Saturday the Celtics practiced at the Forum, and when Parish walked into the arena, he was approached by a somber and chagrined Rosenfeld. They walked into the stands to get away from reporters, and Rosenfeld fumbled through an apology, telling Parish that he'd been unaware Nancy Parish was in the line of fire when he tossed the wet towel after Game 2. According to Jeff Pearlman's *Showtime*, Parish listened to Rosenfeld's apology, smiled, and said, "I've been telling that bitch to keep her mouth shut for ten years, and you're the first guy to finally get her to do it."

Nothing about any of it was amusing more than a decade later (1998) when *Sports Illustrated* published a thoroughly documented report in which Nancy Saad Parish—divorced from Robert Parish in 1990—accused the Celtics center of multiple instances of physical abuse. She claimed she spent a week in St. John's Hospital in Santa Monica after a beating she said Robert Parish administered at the LA Airport Marriott during the 1987 playoffs. She told *Sports Illustrated* that during her marriage to the Celtics center, she'd taken shelter at the homes of Scott and Kim Wedman, and M. L. and Sylvia Carr. Both players declined comment when approached by *Sports Illustrated*. Robert Parish has never commented on the allegations.

When I bumped into Bird at the hotel bar late in the afternoon on the eve of Game 3, we didn't talk about his shooting woes.

"I think we're gonna kill 'em," he said. "I got a real good feel now."

I asked him if he was picking up our tab since he'd just taken me for $160.

"Funny thing about that, Scoop. Dinah and I went out for a nice dinner on you after you gave me all that money. When we was finished, she said, 'Okay, Larry, we had a great meal, but there's still money left and you should give the rest back to that writer.'"

I laughed.

He laughed.

"Can you imagine her sayin' something like that?" he said.

"Right. Yeah, what a sap." I sighed, then remarked how unusual it was for us to be in one hotel for a full week.

"I can't believe it either. I hate it. Dinah never comes on the road with me, but this trip is so long—and I've been able to save up some of them frequent-flier miles—so she's flying out here for a few days."

"Yeah, good thing for those miles, you cheap bastard. Guess it would have been Amtrak for Dinah if you couldn't fly her out here for free."

He was bothered by the 2-3-2 format and echoed the complaint of his boss, Red Auerbach.

"We earn home court advantage and we got to play three of the first five out here. It ain't right."

The Lakers demonstrated their superiority the next day, running to a 20-point lead in the fourth and crushing the Celtics, 136–111. Abdul-Jabbar had 26 with 14 rebounds, and Bird missed the mark (8 for 21) all afternoon. The Celtics again got nothing from their bench.

Bird was discouraged, telling *Globe* columnist Leigh Montville, "I can't play any worse than I did today. You could play better than I did today. I don't know what it is. I shoot well in practice and then . . ."

This wasn't one of those normal shooting slumps when his shot would start hooking left. It wasn't a mechanical flaw in his wrist that would make him start aiming. This was different.

Reminded that one year earlier he'd called his teammates "sissies" after a Game 3 blowout in the Forum, Bird shook his head and said, "I can't say that now because I'm the only one playing like a sissy."

Two nights later, DJ canned a buzzer-beater from the top of the key to give the Celtics a 107–105 series-squaring victory. Johnson's shot capped the best game of the series, demonstrated that the Celtics weren't going down easily, and gave hope to the Celtics fandom. Suddenly, it felt like 1984 all over again. It was a best two out of three, with two of those games potentially played at the Boston Garden. All the familiar themes were in place for the Celtics. The only problem was that this Celtics team wasn't as deep as the 1984 Celtics.

The Lakers won Game 5 at the Forum, 120–111. Four Celtics starters played forty-four or more minutes, and only six Boston players scored. Maxwell pitched a shutout in five feeble minutes, the final appearance of his brilliant eight-year Boston career. The in-flight film on the Celtics final coast-to-coast trip was *The Mean Season*.

The Celtics returned to the Garden Sunday, June 9, for a Game 6 matinee with the Lakers. Lakers GM Jerry West, tortured in seven Finals losses to the Celtics dating back to 1961, made his first Boston Garden appearance since 1979. The Lakers knew it was their time. Messrs. Abdul-Jabbar, Johnson, Worthy, and Riley were on a mission to do what they should have done in 1984.

The Celtics staggered to a 55–55 halftime tie. In his final act as a Celtics player, M. L. Carr got in Riley's face at intermission, but Riley called for security and had Carr taken away. The Lakers were no longer backing down in the Garden gulag.

The fatigue of Boston's starters was obvious in the second half as DJ and Ainge each made only 3 of 15 shots and Bird clanged the rims to the tune of 12 for 29. The Celtics shot 38 percent, second lowest of their 103-game season. Boston's starters played 214 of a possible 240 minutes. Carr, Buckner, Ray Williams, Carlos Clark, and Cedric Maxwell were all DNP-CD—as in Did Not Play—Coach's Decision. None ever played another game for the Celtics.

The Lakers won, 111–100.

Cooper, who was born in LA and had an uncle who was a Celtics fan, said, "It always bothered me to see Jerry West and Elgin and Wilt constantly lose to the Celtics, so this wasn't just for us. We cleaned house in '85 and got to shut M. L. Carr's ass up."

Abdul-Jabbar and Riley had settled all family business.

"Nobody wants to hear about history anymore," said the Lakers coach. "They can no longer mock us."

CHAPTER 10

"I LIKE THIS COACH"

With their season over, the 1984–85 Celtics gathered at the Garden late Monday afternoon to pose on the parquet floor for the official team picture.

It was like taking a wedding photo after the divorce.

Traditional and somewhat mandatory, team photos are filler for media guides and sometimes featured in lobbies and corridors of a team's executive offices. They're like junior high class photos: nobody wants to pose for them, but they sometimes come in handy years later.

The Celtics originally planned to pose for their group photo in February, but McHale missed the shoot and it was rescheduled for March. When they gathered before a home game in March, one of the team owners was missing, so it was postponed until the playoffs. Once they got to the playoffs, K. C. Jones thought it would be bad luck to take the shot before a postseason game, so it was agreed that they'd do it after the last game. After they won the championship.

Monday was supposed to be the eve of Game 7. It was supposed to be the season's last practice day. Instead, the Celts assembled for their grim group shot as the Lakers were visiting Reagan in the Rose Garden.

The Garden's baskets had already been taken down when Celtics players arrived for the shoot. A forklift rested where one of the hoops had been a day earlier. Waiting for the last of the owners to arrive, Bird stretched out on a hockey dasher. When everyone was present—

players in uniform, suits in suits—they posed. Smiles were in short supply.

After the session, players filed into the locker room with the doleful trudge of prison inmates. An exhausted and still-silent Parish gathered his belongings and cleared out first. DJ and Wedman piled some of their things into trash bags. Bird refused to talk about potential surgery on his elbow, ducked out of the room, and bounced a basketball on the corridor floor as he walked toward the exit.

Speculation about his finger, elbow, and poor shooting was rampant. Some of the buzz was rooted in a rumor about his alleged participation in a barroom fight in the middle of the conference finals against the Sixers. I'd first heard the rumor during the Philly series. Larry was supposedly involved in a fight outside Chelsea's on a night off between games. I'd approached Bird about the rumor while he was stretching on the court before Game 5 at the Garden, and our exchange was brief:

"Larry, there's a story going around that you busted up your hand in a fight outside Chelsea's on one of the off nights after Game Two. Is it true?"

"No. And you can tell whoever made that up to go fuck themselves."

I let it go, but kept hearing about it and watched Bird's shooting deteriorate. A 52 percent shooter in '84–85, Bird shot 43 percent in nine playoff games after the night at Chelsea's. Incredibly, the brawl rumor never made the papers—not even the *Herald*'s juicy Page Six–type gossip column.

After watching Bird miss 17 shots in the final loss to the Lakers, I figured it was time to at least cover myself. I asked Dr. Silva about the rumor, and he acknowledged he'd been approached about it by the NBA's director of security Jack Joyce. GM Jan Volk said, "As far as I know, nothing happened. It's a rumor."

I composed a small story that ran under the headline "Bird Fingers a Falsehood." Larry's colorful denial was cleaned up for the newspaper.

Before going home to Indy for the summer, Bird stopped by Red's office, and Auerbach asked him what he thought about bringing Bill Walton to Boston.

"Get him if you can," Bird answered.

Red's final reload was underway.

The Larry Bird Celtics had won two championships and appeared in three Finals since 1981. They'd just won a league-best 63 games and made it to the Finals for a second straight season, but Auerbach needed to bolster his bench. Before the summer was over, he'd replace Maxwell, Buckner, Carr, Clark, and Williams—the five DNPs from Game 6—with Walton, Jerry Sichting, David Thirdkill, Sam Vincent, and Rick Carlisle. Red's final masterpiece would go on to win 50 of 51 home games—a record that still stands—and deliver the franchise's sixteenth championship. Along the way, they'd have more fun than the Russell Celtics, the Jordan Bulls, or the Curry Warriors.

A few weeks after the Finals, I connected with Bird when he came to the San Francisco Hyatt Embarcadero to collect his second MVP. The ceremony was sponsored by Allstate Insurance, and Bird quipped, "The way I was shooting the ball in the championship series, I must have owned a piece of the rock."

We discussed the rumor that the Celtics were trading Maxwell for Walton.

"If we get Bill Walton, we're gonna be three times the team we were this year," Bird gushed. "He clogs up the middle, he's a great shot blocker and intimidator. And he can shoot and pass. He won't need to score with us, but he could give Robert some rest. When he's feeling good, there's nobody better than Bill Walton."

We didn't talk about the Chelsea's rumor.

The Chelsea's fight is something of a Loch Ness Monster in Boston sports lore, our version of the booze-fueled Copacabana Brawl involving Yankee stars Billy Martin, Mickey Mantle, and Co. in 1957. Only a few people know anything about the Chelsea's brawl, and the principals agreed to settlements that seal their lips forever. What is known is that Bird punched former Colgate football player Mike Harlow and later settled out of court. Other people at the scene included Buckner, a nefarious Bird associate named Nick Harris, and Harlow's girlfriend, Lola (it's always Lola with these things, right?).

More than a month after the '85 Finals a *Globe* advertising executive told me she knew of a bartender who worked at Little Rascals, near Chelsea's, and was telling people he'd been struck by Bird outside Chelsea's. I went to Little Rascals the next night.

The place was quiet and the rugged bartender had time to talk. Harlow grew up in Falmouth, and had been a defensive lineman and hockey player at Colgate. I told him I'd gone to Holy Cross and had seen multiple Colgate-HC games. When I informed him that I covered the Celtics for the *Globe*, he claimed Bird sucker punched him after an argument at Chelsea's in May.

According to Harlow, he was enjoying a night out at Chelsea's with his girlfriend when he was joined by Bird, Buckner, and Harris, a thirty-nine-year-old Somerville car dealer from Winchester who identified himself as Larry's bodyguard. Drinks were consumed, voices were raised, and folks took things outside to the corner of State Street and Merchants Row. Harlow fought with Harris, then with Bird.

Jim Roque, the manager of Clarke's saloon, across the street from Chelsea's, witnessed the fracas and told me, "I don't know what happened inside, but there was noise and a scuffle as they came across [State] Street. Larry went 'boom,' a nice swoop over the top with his right hand to the left side of the [Harlow's] face. . . . He hit him, then a couple of guys from Chelsea's grabbed him and pulled him back inside."

"He [Bird] sucker punched me," Harlow told me in 1985. "But there's a lawsuit and I really can't tell you any more about it."

I called my boss the next day and told him what I had. It was almost August. Was this still a story?

"Yeah, it's a story," said Doria. "It's Larry Bird and a barroom fight and he lied to you. You've got the guy he hit and another guy who saw Larry hit Harlow. Work it up on Monday, call Bird for a comment, and we'll run it Tuesday on page one."

"Are you sure you want me to be the one to write it? Larry's going to cut me off over this. I can give the information to one of our other guys, and the *Globe* will still have the story and I won't lose Bird."

"No. You write it."

My call to Indiana the next day was not high yield. Dinah answered and summoned Larry to the phone.

"It's about the Chelsea's fight," I told him. "I found the guy who says you hit him. Name's Mike Harlow. I've got an eyewitness from across the street. Care to comment?"

"Fuck you, Scoop. You'd better never write that. I won't be talking to you anymore."

Click.

Globe editor Jack Driscoll wasn't totally comfortable with my witness, Roque, who needed to go nameless or risk losing his job. I told the bosses that Roque (a friend from my college days) was real and reliable but needed to be protected.

"Okay," said Driscoll. "But if this goes to court, you could be subpoenaed and asked to produce your witness. And if you don't talk, you'd risk going to jail."

That sounded ridiculous. We had the guy Bird hit, and an independent witness. Massachusetts General Hospital had a record of treating thirty-nine-year-old Nick Harris in the emergency room on the night of the incident.

The story ran on the front page of the July 30 *Globe*, under the headline "Bartender Says Bird Hit Him during Playoffs—Celtics Star May Have Injured Shooting Hand."

The story stated that Harlow was seeking an out-of-court settlement, and that an unidentified woman was seeking damages from both Bird and Chelsea's.

"The incident arose out of a situation involving her," said the woman's attorney, Dan Harrington.

No charges were filed.

The day the story broke, Kevin Cullen, a young *Boston Herald* reporter, got a call from a source at the Massachusetts State Police, who told him Harris was trouble. The cop told Cullen that state police had urged the Celtics to have Bird stay away from Harris. Cullen thanked his source, hung up, and walked across the *Herald* newsroom to Mike Carey, who was seated at a typewriter, smoking a cigarette and nursing a Coke. Cullen introduced himself, extended his hand, and said he was looking into Larry Bird's relationship with Nick Harris. Did Carey know anything?

"Mike Carey never even looked up," recalled Cullen (a *Globe* metro columnist in the twenty-first century). "He just turned away and pretended I wasn't there."

Two days later, Cullen and Charles P. Pierce coauthored a front-page *Herald* story disclosing Harris's criminal record, which included a $20,000 fine for altering odometers, a 1979 conviction on two counts of possession of a controlled substance with intent to distribute, and a raft of pending charges including conspiracy and fraud. The *Herald* reported that the Celtics had asked law enforcement to run a background check on Harris and that the team had urged Bird to distance himself from his friend.

Through the decades, Bird has refused to discuss the Chelsea's incident. When he dictated his 290-page autobiography to Bob Ryan in 1989, he spoke emotionally and eloquently about his failed first marriage, his daughter from that marriage, and his father's suicide, but he wouldn't talk about the Chelsea's fight. Harlow and Harris aren't mentioned in any authorized Bird biography.

Roque died in 2019. Harlow, who still lives in Falmouth, has been telling friends for thirty-five years that Bird sucker punched him while Harlow was being restrained by a bar employee.

Buckner was traded to the Pacers before the start of the 1985–86 season and played only thirty-two more NBA games before settling into a life of basketball broadcasting. In 2021, when I asked him about the Chelsea's fight, he said, "I didn't see anything. I don't know anything."

In the late 1990s when Bird was coaching the Pacers, he let his guard down after we'd shared a few postgame beers in a Boston Garden locker room.

"Scoop, I hit that guy with my left hand!" he said with a laugh.

When Bird spoke to the *Ringer* about me in 2016, he said, "I always told him [Shaughnessy] that if he got fifty percent of his stories right, that was pretty good for him. . . . To this day, he says I'm lying, that I'm not telling the truth about it. He just won't admit he's wrong."

Sigh.

In late August of 1985, Auerbach, still entangled in negotiations for Walton, welcomed camp "counselors" and a few veteran Celtics to his annual free-agent/rookie camp. The big news on the first night of camp was the retirement of M. L. Carr, a ten-year veteran who'd come to the Celtics the same season as Bird, in 1979.

Carlisle, the second-year guard who'd been hurt during the '85 playoffs, arrived in Marshfield driving Mike Carey's car. Decades later, when I asked Carlisle about his cozy relationship with the *Herald*'s beat reporter, the coach said, "That era of the NBA made situations like that possible. Mike was a unique guy. In today's NBA it simply wouldn't be possible."

The best basketball player at Red's 1985 camp was "counselor" Len Bias, a six-eight forward from Maryland who could shoot, rebound, defend, and run the floor.

"He's the best player in the country," said Carlisle, who'd played two ACC seasons against Bias. "That's the guy we should take if Red wins the lottery with the Seattle [Henderson] pick."

Maxwell declined a request to play at the rookie camp. The Celtics no longer had Max's phone number and had to communicate through his agent. Incensed, Auerbach ordered Volk to renew trade talks with the Clippers for Walton. When the cost-conscious Clippers learned of Boston's heightened interest, they told Walton they'd only make a deal with Boston if Walton agreed to forfeit eighteen months of deferred salary. Walton surrendered the future payment in exchange for the freedom to play with Bird. The trade was consummated on September 8, and Walton forever insists, "The Celtics gave me my life back."

Bill Walton was born in La Mesa, California in 1952, the second of four children of William "Ted" Walton and Gloria Anne Hickey. Ted was a six-four social worker/music teacher, Gloria a five-eleven librarian. Ted and Gloria's firstborn son, Bruce Walton, grew to be a six-six, 250-pound NFL offensive lineman who played in a Super Bowl with the Dallas Cowboys. One year younger than Bruce (George Brett syndrome), Bill grew to be a seven-foot giant—one of the best basketball players of all time. The Walton home wasn't a sports-mad household. Ted Walton was an accomplished musician with a degree in English from Cal Berkeley. Ted and Gloria encouraged independent thinking and filled their home with music. Ted formed his children into a teen band when they were in high school, but Bruce and Bill quickly abandoned the stage for the hardwood court.

Shy and skinny, with a significant stutter, Bill played his first basketball as a fourth grader, impressing his coach with dribbling and passing skills. He was unusually coordinated and could trigger fast breaks with quick outlet passes after grabbing defensive rebounds. He possessed rebounding instincts and timing that couldn't be taught. As an adult, Walton told people he believed his stuttering made him a better basketball player. The basketball court was a place where he could express himself.

Walton chose La Mesa's public high school, Helix, over the local Catholic high school. At Helix, he played alongside brother Bruce, who protected him. Freshman Bill was only six-one, but grew to his adult height while at Helix. By 1970, Helix coach Gordon Nash was blessed to have a seventeen-year-old high school star who cared more about rebounding, passing, and defense than scoring. The Highlanders won 49 straight games and back-to-back state championships in Walton's final two seasons.

Teenage Bill Walton got an education in NBA 101 when the expansion San Diego Rockets set up shop near his La Mesa home. Bill had the keys to the Helix gym and invited Pat Riley (who'd been a first-round pick for the Rockets in 1967) and other NBA talents to his high school for scrimmages. In the years the Rockets played in San Diego, they employed basketball coaching legends Jack McMahon, Pete Newell, Tex Winter, and Alex Hannum. It was a lot for a young ballplayer to absorb.

Every college coach in the country wanted high school senior Bill Walton, but UCLA was the natural landing spot. The Bruins were coached by the legendary John Wooden, a humble son of the Hoosier hoop heartland (Martinsville, Indiana) and a stickler for fundamentals and discipline. Sixth-grade Bill had been hypnotized when he heard Wooden speak at a University of San Diego clinic. Two years later, eighth-grade Walton sat in front of the family TV and watched underdog UCLA beat Cazzie Russell's Michigan Wolverines for a second straight NCAA championship. Wooden's Bruins built their game on ball movement, teamwork, and quickness. When Walton came of age as a high school star, UCLA had seven-foot center Lew Alcindor, who won 88 of 90 college games and three national championships. Helix junior Walton was in Pauley Pavilion for Alcindor's last home game, a West Regional Final demolition of Santa Clara that vaulted the Bruins into another Final Four. Walton loved the UCLA band and cheerleaders, and the way the Bruins conducted themselves. The Westwood campus was only two hours north of La Mesa.

Coaches recruiting Walton had to make their pitches over dinner at the family home and a parade of flashy promise-makers passed through La Mesa offering assorted perks, including—in some cases— jobs for Walton family members. This offended Ted and Gloria. Wooden promised nothing, not even a starting spot. The regal coach was patient, caring, did not react to Bill's stutter, and wisely asked for a second helping of Gloria's potatoes. He assured Bill's thoughtful parents that anything their son achieved at UCLA would be earned.

The Wooden-Walton pairing was near perfect. UCLA's coach stressed fundamentals and had no time for selfish, flashy players. Winning basketball was about preparation and details. Each year Wooden spent a portion of his first practice demonstrating the proper way to put on one's socks. In Walton, he found a rare teen star who wanted only to rebound, defend, make his teammates better, and win.

Still, Walton was somewhat rattled when he learned he was going to be a "high post" center. He wasn't a ball hog, but admitted, "When you're six-eleven and you're playing against all these stiffs eighteen feet away from the basket, you start wondering, 'When is it going to be my turn?'"

The master knew better. UCLA's high-post offense allowed Walton's game to evolve, encouraging him to develop passing skills that helped make him a Hall of Famer. As a Bruin, Walton learned footwork, positioning, and offensive moves that he was later able to use against Abdul-Jabbar, Artis Gilmore, and Ralph Sampson. Walton learned to always hold the ball high, elbows extended.

Walton's arrival at Pauley Pavilion occurred in the middle of a years-long effort by UCLA to establish itself as the greatest college basketball dynasty ever. Over twelve seasons the team compiled an 88-game winning streak and won ten national championships. The Bruins went 86-4 in Walton's three varsity seasons, winning two national championships. Walton made 21 of 22 shots in the 1973 championship final against Memphis State. The only more decorated player in NCAA history is Abdul-Jabbar.

Larry Bird was an impressionable high school basketball player when Walton was winning championships for UCLA. When Larry and Mark Bird played one-on-one in West Baden, Mark sometimes pretended to be Bill Walton.

"I wasn't much of a [basketball] fan when I was growing up, but the one player I was aware of was Bill Walton," Bird wrote in his autobiography. "I loved the way he passed and rebounded, and his technique was flawless. He did everything exactly the way Coach Jones [Bird's high school coach, Jim Jones] had taught us to play. He was just so sound, right by the book. . . . I loved the way he held the ball up high and I loved the way he used the glass on his turnaround jumpers. If you can say I had anything close to an idol in basketball at the time, that player was Bill Walton."

Walton arrived in Westwood one year after the summer of Wood-stock, during a time of free love, drugs, rock 'n' roll, and campus unrest. Richard Nixon was in the White House and America was in Vietnam. Still shy about his stutter and height, Walton was newly famous, and people were suddenly interested in what he had to say. He embraced the counterculture and joined campus protests. He brought Transcendental Meditation to UCLA practices, smoked marijuana in his apartment after games, and said no when he was asked to play in the 1972 Olympics. He wrote a letter to Nixon, asking the president to resign (Wooden refused Walton's request to sign the document). One of Walton's everlasting regrets is not being included on Nixon's enemies list.

Wooden defended Walton's right to protest peacefully, but wouldn't bend team rules regarding personal grooming. The Wizard of Westwood wasn't pleased when Walton showed up for the first day of his senior season looking like one of the Allman Brothers.

"I should be allowed to grow my hair as long as I want," Walton told his coach.

"Is this something you feel strongly about, Bill?"

"Yes."

"Well, then, we're going to miss you, Bill. But it was nice having you here."

With that, Walton hopped on his bike and went for a haircut. Long hair could wait until he became a professional basketball player.

Walton let his freak flag fly after UCLA. He wore a flannel shirt and blue jeans when he collected the prestigious Sullivan Award, presented to the nation's top amateur athlete. He had a full ponytail by the time the Trail Blazers selected him with the number one overall pick. When he got to Portland, his roommate was radical Jack Scott, a former ath-letic director at Oberlin College, an author, and an advocate for Black athletes. Scott was involved in the 1974 kidnapping and harboring of newspaper heiress Patty Hearst. Living with Scott made Walton a tar-get. Pulitzer Prize–winning historian David Halberstam reported that Walton's Portland house was a center for local radicals, "watched off and on by the FBI because of a strong suspicion of a Scott–Symbionese Liberation Army–Patty Hearst connection . . . a center of both basketball and politics, the two main forces in Walton's life."

"Jack and Mikki [Scott's wife] were, much to my surprise, quietly and secretly recruited to help keep Patty and some of the SLA members safe and alive," Walton wrote in his autobiography, *Back from the Dead*, in 2016, ". . . which brought the FBI calling, convinced I was involved. My phones were tapped, my mail intercepted. I was trailed. Everywhere I went, there were federal agents with guns and binoculars."

In 2021, Walton says, "I have never met Patty Hearst, but would love to say hello sometime."

Knee issues and a broken leg shortened his first two NBA seasons, and Portland fans and teammates wondered if Walton was brittle because of his vegetarian diet. In 1976–77, Portland won its only NBA championship, when Walton was healthy for sixty-five games and the entire postseason. Coached by Jack Ramsay, the Blazers beat the Sixers in a six-game Finals, and Walton was named Finals MVP. Walton had 20 points, 23 rebounds, 7 assists, and 8 blocks in the clincher. It was the NBA equal of his near-perfect game in the NCAA Finals against Memphis State. It has been argued by many—including Pat Riley—that a healthy Bill Walton in 1976–77 was the greatest center in the history of basketball. He could shoot, rebound, defend, run the floor, and pass. He was the best fast-break outlet-pass man since Bill Russell.

Ultimately, Walton's brittle feet prevented him from being the greatest NBA center of all time. The Blazers were 39-8 in their title-defense season when Walton felt pain in his right foot in 1978. His fragile bones were protected in thirty-game college seasons, but there weren't many nights off in the NBA. He broke his left foot while playing on painkillers in the 1978 playoffs, then missed the entire 1978–79 season. Angry with Portland, he signed as a free agent with the San Diego Clippers.

Walton's six-year San Diego/Los Angeles Clipper experience was a nightmare, owing to injuries and buffoonish owner Donald Sterling.

The Clippers never made the playoffs and Walton was rarely healthy enough to play. He retired and started law school, but returned to the court after LA surgeon Tony Daly performed reconstructive surgery on his foot. He was able to play in sixty-seven games for the Los Angeles Clippers in the 1984–85 season, but desperately wanted out when the season ended.

He first reached out to the Lakers, but Jerry West had seen Walton's feet and said no thanks. That prompted the call to Auerbach. Medical experts in Boston looked at Walton's feet and agreed with West, but were overruled by Auerbach. Boston was motivated to make a deal. Red wanted Maxwell gone, and a part-time Walton would be enough to keep Parish rested for the playoffs.

When Walton flew into Boston to join his new team, Celtics front office employee M. L. Carr suggested he drive Walton to Robert Parish's house in suburban Weston. Carr knew that the sensitive Chief might be threatened by his new "backup" and correctly figured the Celtics could pacify Parish by having Walton announce his non-threatening intentions. The summit meeting went well (when Parish was inducted into the Hall of Fame in 2003, he asked Walton to deliver his presentation speech) and confirmed the NBA's worst-kept secret: Walton was a footer. Always listed as six-eleven, Walton was taller than seven-foot Parish, but believed a stigma was attached to seven-footers, so his true height was forever falsified.

After satisfying Parish, Walton visited Boston orthopedic specialist Robert Leach.

"He came in, smiled, said, 'Nice to meet you, and this will be the last time you see me,'" Leach recalled. "He was right. I didn't see him as a patient that whole year."

The arrival of Walton abruptly ended Maxwell's ten-year career in Boston. The man who'd been MVP of the 1981 Finals and won Game 7 in '84—the senior Celtic in continuous service—was suddenly gone with zero ceremony. Enthusiasm over Walton's arrival marginalized Maxwell's significant contributions. Max never fully got over the hurt of being so quickly erased.

"When I left, I just wanted them to say, 'Good luck,' or some-thing," said Maxwell. "Instead, I was getting blamed for us losing. I've always wondered how the 1985 team lost because of me. I must have really been a bad man. We had Larry and Chief and Kevin and DJ, and they're all Hall of Famers, but when we lost to the Lakers, it was all my fault. I was the scapegoat and that hurt. I was the fallen angel. I was very soured by what I felt to be total disrespect for how I'd played. The undertones about how I didn't try . . . I mean, we got a guy who gets his hand busted up in a barroom fight. That wasn't me. But I'm never going to win this one. He's Larry Bird."

To this day, anytime Walton sees Maxwell, the big redhead hugs Max and gushes, "You saved my life! You fell on the sword for me!"

A month after the Walton trade, the Celtics acquired veteran In-diana guard Jerry Sichting for a couple of second-round picks. To close the deal, the Celtics guaranteed the Pacers a preseason game in Indianapolis. The cash-strapped Pacers knew their fans could never get enough of Bird, and Red was happy to make the guarantee. It reminded Auerbach of 1956, when Walter Brown gave Rochester the Ice Capades in exchange for promising not to select Bill Russell with the first pick of the draft.

Sichting was a twenty-eight-year-old, five-year NBA veteran who grew up in Martinsville, Indiana, hometown of John Wooden. He was a real-life Jimmy Chitwood (the phenom in *Hoosiers*), a quiet, flaw-less jump shooter from a tiny town in rural southern Indiana (Sicht-ing's younger brother auditioned to be an extra in *Hoosiers* but was deemed too stocky for the silver screen). Sichting played high school home games in the five-thousand-seat gym where Martinsville won state championships with Wooden as its star from 1926 to 1928. The Garfield Avenue building where Sichting attended high school is now the John R. Wooden Middle School. Like French Lick, Martinsville is known for mineral-water spas, sanatoriums, and high school basketball stars. At Purdue, Sichting matched up against Bird's Indiana State Sycamores.

Walton.

Then Sichting.

It was as if Auerbach was assembling a supporting cast of players born to play with Larry Bird.

"That's what a great leader does," Walton said. "You identify where the strength is—where your ultimate edge is. We had Larry Bird and nobody else did. Our job was to help a guy like Larry be himself. Red and John Wooden talked about this. For them, building a team was all about the complementary aspects. What are the elements of a team? Friendship, loyalty, and cooperation, supplemented by sacrifice, discipline, and honor. That's what we were all into. We wanted Larry to be the best. We wanted Larry to be the MVP. We wanted him to be the champion. It wasn't like any of us were ever freezing him out or hoping he'd have a bad game so we could go in there and play. We had a collective sense of effort and purpose."

Bird wasted no time pranking his new teammate, inviting Sichting to join him at a gay bar on Boylston Street. Bird said they'd watch the Red Sox game on TV.

"I didn't know it was a gay bar," Sichting remembered. "There was nobody in the place when I first got there, so I left and walked back across the street to the Howard Johnson's, where I was staying. Carlisle was my roommate and he asked, 'Did you see Larry?' And I said there was nobody in the place. Rick said, 'Larry just called to say he's running late. You should get back over there to meet him.' So I went back, and after about twenty minutes some guys started coming in, and I finally figured out what the place was. Larry got me."

Seeing me interviewing Walton on the first day of practice, Ainge said, "Watch out for him, Bill. He'll be your friend one day and drive a pipe through you the next."

When most of the reporters had left, I approached Bird while he was riding a stationary bike. We had eight months ahead of us. I figured I might as well take the temperature.

It was subzero.

"Scoop, get the fuck away from me and stay the fuck away from me all year," he snapped. "We're thinking of suing you and your paper. You'd never see Mike Carey write nothin' like that."

Boston played a whopping four preseason games against the Lakers in autumn of '85, and the familiarity fueled emotions. The first game in LA featured multiple ejections and 8 technical fouls. When the rivals played again a couple of nights later, Maurice Lucas—who'd been Walton's bodyguard in Portland—triggered a bench-clearing mini-melee that pushed Parish over the press table.

During the rumble, Sichting noticed K. C. Jones had Michael Cooper in a headlock.

The image stayed with Jerry Sichting. Reminded of the episode decades later, he said, "I remember thinking right then, 'I like this coach.'"

CHAPTER 11

"OBVIOUSLY, I JOINED THE RIGHT TEAM"

Danny Ainge will someday see his number 44 Celtics jersey raised to the rafters at the Boston Garden and will likely join the rest of the 1985–86 Celtics starting lineup in the Basketball Hall of Fame in Springfield, Massachusetts. Short of being a team owner, Ainge has served the Celtics and the NBA in every possible fashion. He played fourteen NBA seasons, appeared in six NBA Finals, and won two championship rings. He has been an NBA head coach and network television analyst. Following in the large footsteps of Red Auerbach, who drafted him when he was a Major League Baseball player in 1981, Ainge was president of Celtics Basketball Operations for eighteen seasons and in 2008 delivered Boston's championship banner number 17 after trading with his pal Kevin McHale to acquire Kevin Garnett.

This is what Ainge remembers about Bill Walton coming to the Celtics in the fall of 1985:

"Larry, Kevin, and I all really looked up to Bill. I grew up watching him on the West Coast at UCLA. He was a great, great player. I was a senior in high school in 1977 when I watched him come back from oh and two and beat the Sixers, and I still think it was one of the greatest individual seasons of all time. He was a very special player, and on top of that, he was such a character. In 1985 we knew we weren't getting the Bill Walton superstar we'd seen when we were young, but he was a guy we looked up to, one of the greatest players ever, and we knew he would help us if he was healthy. I think it was his character that impressed us the most from the start. I'd been the guy everybody picked on—the little brother—but as soon as Bill joined us, Bill became that guy. He was sort of the rookie of our team.

"We had some informal workouts at Boston College before the start of the season, and we were developing some good chemistry and then Bill came in one day and said, 'Hey, I'm not going to be around next week. I've got to go to South Dakota for a sit-in. And I said, 'You mean you have to go to South Dakota to smoke a peace pipe.'"

Celtics stars made fun of Walton's music, his retro bell-bottoms, his big American cars, his halting speech, and his years of inactivity. Ainge, who was twenty-six years old and had played only four NBA seasons by '85, insisted that he'd already played more minutes than Walton, who was about to turn thirty-three and had been in the NBA for eleven years.

McHale, who'd grown up with a Walton poster on his bedroom wall, said, "Bill, no one's ever actually seen you play basketball. I've just seen you on that grainy black-and-white footage from your college days."

They teased Walton about his fabled Patty Hearst connection.

"Come on, Bill, you were hiding her, right?" Ainge said. "You can tell us."

"If I didn't tell the FBI, think I'm going to tell you guys?" Walton said with a smile.

"My wife's from California and Bill was her favorite player when he was at UCLA," recalled Wedman. "I was thrilled that he was on our team. We all knew he was a great player who'd had injuries. Oh my gosh, did we have fun in practice."

"It didn't take long for us to realize that we had something special going on with Bill," McHale said. "He had a really high basketball IQ and he had the talent. I'm not sure even at the time if I realized how unique it was."

"I was young, so I was in no position to be a ringleader when they were teasing Bill," said Carlisle. "But the truth was that everybody on that team had huge respect for Bill, and they loved the fact that he wanted to be in Boston. He was an opinionated guy who had a big personality, and they made it clear to him that he wasn't going to run the locker room or run the team."

"I liked being part of the team," said Walton. "I wanted it to be fun, and I know that when you're on a team, there's a lot of teasing and it's got to go both ways. It was fine and it just inspired me to be better."

There was drama at the end of camp when Jones selected Carlisle over Carlos Clark and David Thirdkill for the final roster spot. This gave the 1985–86 Celtics a highly unusual racial mix of eight whites and four Blacks. No NBA team since the 1969–70 Warriors had featured eight white players on its roster. That K. C. Jones was the coach figured to insulate the Celtics from criticism, as did the presence of Auerbach, who'd drafted the NBA's first Black player, fielded the league's first all-Black starting five, and hired the first Black head coach in North America. Still, there was backlash.

Dennis Johnson was tight with Clark and Thirdkill and believed Thirdkill was a better player than Carlisle. DJ had a hard time controlling his emotions when I caught up with him before the Celtics' annual B'Nai B'rith kickoff dinner on the eve of the team's first regular season game.

"Scoop, somebody's always going to think we have too many of something," DJ admitted. "This year, I guess it's too many whites. It's sticky for a player to get involved in. I have a friend in David. I have a friend in Carlos. I hung around with them more than I did Rick, but I'm for anybody who can help us win."

In their 1992 book, *The Selling of the Green*, New York reporters Harvey Araton and Filip Bondy characterized Carlisle as "untalented" and "a very white, third-round savior—one who could not push the ball down court, but could play piano."

"I thought Carlisle was the best man for the team," said K. C. Jones. "The race issue was a nonissue. The only issue for me was winning. . . . I thought it was strange that I was criticized or at least needled by Black people for keeping a white player in preference to one of their own."

Thirdkill wound up coming back to the Celtics early in the season when Sly Williams was released after a fitful five weeks in which he missed games with dental issues and hemorrhoids.

"That 1985–86 team was the best I ever played on by far," Bird said later. "But if we'd had Sly Williams, we'd have been even better."

Wearing new black sneakers, the Celtics kicked off their fortieth NBA season at the Brendan Byrne Arena in East Rutherford, New Jersey, in late October. The Greatest Team Ever blew a 19-point lead to the atrocious Nets and committed 28 turnovers in a 113–109 overtime loss. DJ missed a pair of free throws that would have sealed victory late in regulation. Bird made only 5 of 15 shots, and Parish and McHale both fouled out.

Walton scored 4 points and grabbed 5 rebounds in nineteen minutes, but also committed 5 fouls and 7 turnovers. Behind closed doors, he was overly contrite with his new teammates.

"It was unbelievable," McHale remembered. "We play a million of these games and this was just another one and we knew we were okay, but Bill was really taking it hard. I remember Larry bending over taking off his shoes, and all of a sudden Bill was standing up and saying, 'I'd like to apologize to all of you for losing the game tonight. I was a disgrace to the game of basketball.' None of us had ever heard anything like it, and Larry just snapped at him and said, 'I sure as hell hope we play better, because I can't stand hearing this eighty-one more times. Go have a beer and forget about it.'"

When the room finally opened to the media, as we made our way to Walton's stall, we heard Bird asking, "Why'd we trade for this guy?"

"It was exactly the way not to play basketball, and no one knows that better than me," said Walton. "I played a terrible game. I was a disgrace to my team and to the sport of basketball."

Postgame gold. I knew in that moment that this was going to be a great season on the beat.

I'd written a couple of features on Walton when he was a Clipper and found him quiet, uncooperative, almost rude. He was intimidating and he knew it. He did not suffer fools. So imagine my surprise when Walton joined me as I ate breakfast at a hotel coffee shop during one of the early-season trips.

"Hey, Dan, okay if I sit down?" asked the redheaded giant.

He talked for ten minutes without interruption. He told me he'd grown up a Celtics fan and always wanted to play for Red Auerbach's team. He said the La Mesa Waltons didn't have a television until the mid-1960s, when his folks procured a tiny black-and-white model that had no sound. He remembered seeing pro basketball games on the parquet floor on it and picking out number 6 (Russell) who was rebounding and blocking shots. He read Russell's *Go Up for Glory*, when his librarian mom brought it home from work. He'd been impressed at the way legendary Lakers announcer Chick Hearn spoke of Russell. Walton was a baseball fan and wanted to know about my years covering the big leagues. He was a fan of the *Globe*, asked me about where I grew up and how I became a sportswriter. He said he hadn't read David Halberstam's iconic *The Breaks of the Game*, an homage to the 1979–80 Trail Blazers.

Famous athletes go through life like *Sports Illustrated* swimsuit models—always the center of attention. Most lose all instincts for reciprocation. If a famous athlete or supermodel sat next to the Person Who Cured Cancer on a coast-to-coast flight, the athlete/supermodel would grudgingly tolerate questions from the Person Who Cured Cancer without ever thinking to ask, "And what is it that *you* do?" The athlete/supermodel would exit the plane five hours later never knowing he or she just sat next to the Person Who Cured Cancer.

Walton wasn't like that in 1985 and he's not like that today.

He told me that he and his wife (Susan) and four boys were living on Avon Hill Street in Cambridge near Porter Square—a recommendation from Halberstam. He'd purchased the home from Gunther and Karen Weil, who'd used it as a classroom for psychology courses taught with Dr. Timothy Leary in the early 1960s. A playground was near the Walton homestead, and the *Globe*'s Jackie MacMullan, a weekend hoopster, said that during a Sunday-morning pickup game she'd witnessed a pair of sneakers—thrown from inside the house—crash through a window and onto the Waltons' lawn.

Adam, Nate, Luke (named after Maurice Lucas), and Chris Walton were between ten and five years old in 1985. Tall boys with giant heads of curls, they loved going to games and practices.

"Those kids were hilarious," recalled Greg Kite. "They were everywhere, knocking over the ball rack, jumping into the Jacuzzi with muddy feet after playing football outside, going over to the cooler and cracking open a beer. A couple of them [Adam and Chris] were born on Halloween, and we called them Halloween One and Halloween Two."

The boys were inadvertent stars of a Celtics charity fashion show at a downtown Boston hotel.

"All the boys were dressed in tuxedos with tennis shoes," Bill Walton recalled. "They were about to go onstage and they started fighting. Adam reached over and punched Luke in the face and bloodied his nose. Blood everywhere. The team doctor was there and he wanted Luke to lie down, and Luke said, 'No way! I'm with the Celtics! I'm going out on that stage.' With blood all over him, little Luke Walton went out there and basked in the glory of Larry Bird, Red Auerbach, K. C. Jones, and the legendary Boston Celtics."

Walton saw his first Grateful Dead show when he was still in high school and was an unofficial member of the group by the time he came to the Celtics. He sometimes introduced the band before shows and toured with the Dead in Egypt, playing drums during a show at the foot of the Pyramids. He attended Jerry Garcia's funeral in 1995 and claims to have seen more than six hundred Grateful Dead concerts. He plastered Grateful Dead stickers on teammates' lockers at Hellenic.

In early November, most members of the Celtics team—even the reclusive Parish (Chief always called Walton "William")—met at Bird's house in Brookline and hopped in a couple of limos bound for Worcester, where the Grateful Dead were performing.

"We pulled up to the arena and just walked in the door," McHale remembered. "We had no tickets. Nothing. Bill just said, 'I'm with the band and they're with me.' We got to a room and next thing you know Jerry Garcia and the entire band walk in, and they can't start the concert until they get a chance to talk to Bill and the promoter's trying to get them out there, and they're like, 'Bill's here. We're not done talking to Bill yet.'

"Hanging out with those guys before a show was a lot different than the E Street Band. The Dead were a little more loose in their hanging-out abilities."

Bird and Garcia talked at length.

"They really are the same person," said Walton (he still speaks as if Garcia were alive). "Very quiet guys. They don't like the limelight other than when it's the job at hand. Larry doesn't like all the peripheral stuff. But when he's on the court, he wants the ball and wants the light on him. That's the way it should be. Jerry is the same way. They're not self-promoters who worry about the world knowing how great they are. They're very kind and humble in their lives. They're selfless, make other people happy, and are incredible talents who work well in a team concept. They acknowledge, respect, and appreciate the contributions of their teammates. They see things that nobody else does, and they're able to accomplish things that nobody else can."

The morning after the Worcester show, Dead drummer Mickey Hart and some roadies were sitting with us frumpy scribes in the Pappas Gym bleachers when Walton and Bird emerged for practice. Bird fired a two-handed chest pass off the back wall six inches above Hart's head and laughed when his bullet pass bounced back into his hands on the fly. We asked Bill if Garcia was coming to practice, and Walton said, "Jerry hasn't seen daylight since 1968."

It was November 5, Walton's thirty-third birthday.

Toward the end of practice, a woman dressed like a belly dancer stood in the corner of the gym, holding a boom box. When K.C. brought the players into the center circle for the end of practice, the woman walked toward the group, carrying her portable stereo. After Jones placed a folding chair in the middle of the circle, the woman motioned for Walton to sit in the chair, hit the play button, and started to dance and disrobe.

As soon as they realized what was happening, Mormons Ainge and Kite half sprinted toward the locker room.

Shaking his head, Kite muttered, "In the old days people just brought cakes."

The rest of the players howled, and Walton blushed as the woman's clothes came off.

When the show was over, the near-naked dancer gathered clothes strewn around the hardwood and dashed toward the corner of the gym, out the door.

With the same apparent satisfaction Sichting had felt when he saw K. C. Jones holding Michael Cooper in a headlock, Walton smiled and said, "Obviously, I joined the right team."

Susan Walton had arranged the prank, and K. C. Jones signed off on the plan. Parish was particularly impressed that Walton's wife planned the party.

Given that this was the first practice session in professional sports history that could have been covered by *Sports Illustrated*, *Rolling Stone*, and *Playboy*, I went to the pay phone outside the gym and called my boss looking for permission to write the story. Permission granted. Headlined "Grateful Shed" and accompanied by a cartoon of a stripper popping out of a cake, the article was a major hit.

If any of this had happened in 2021, the coach of the Celtics, the sports editor of the *Globe*, the paper's beat reporter, and the cartoonist would probably all have lost their jobs.

In 1985, it was just another day in the life of the Greatest Team Ever.

Walton led his teammates back to the Centrum in Worcester later that night. Ainge didn't attend but requested a cassette and spent some time at home listening to the Dead's music.

"I tried, but I just wasn't feeling it," Ainge concluded. "I challenged Bill and asked him to name his favorite Grateful Dead song. He said, 'When you're a Grateful Dead fan, it's all one song.'"

Walton's arrival brought Bird and McHale closer than they'd been since McHale's rookie year.

"Larry and I got on Bill a lot, and it was fun," McHale said in 2021. "It was fun because Bill loved it. After everything that had happened in his career, there was a joy about this for him. He really liked playing basketball and the style we were playing. Bill would stutter his way through, telling us, 'You . . . you . . . you guys are unbelievable. You don't even call plays. Everybody just moves.' He was startled at the IQ and how we played."

"Life on the team was fun again . . . ," Bird wrote in his autobiography. "The focal point was Walton. Kevin and I would call him at home, just to bust his chops. I'm talking about every day. We loved to call Bill up and trash talk to him. We never let up. We even got Susan involved. She called us up, asking us to let up on her poor Bill. He loved it. I don't think Bill has ever been on a team in the pros where he was more comfortable.

"We couldn't wait to get to practice every day. All we wanted to do was scrimmage. We had a much better attitude from the year before. Everybody was talking and laughing."

Practice jerseys identified who started and who came off the bench. The starters wore white, the subs green. Walton's Green Team roster of Wedman, Sichting, Carlisle, Kite, Thirdkill, and Sam Vincent had enough talent and energy to regularly beat the White Team, aka the Stat Rats. Assistant coaches Jimmy Rodgers and Chris Ford (Walton called them Chris Rodgers and Jimmy Ford) officiated the scrimmages and took as much abuse as Jake O'Donnell and Jack Madden.

"There was a tremendous rivalry between the White Team and the Green Team," Walton insisted. "But bear in mind, the White Team was playing forty minutes a night and they were just trying to get through practice. When you have Larry Bird, Kevin McHale, and Danny Ainge on one team, there's a lot of trash talk going on."

"Only time in my life I ever called technical fouls during practices," recalled Rodgers.

"The acquisition of Walton really changed the complexion of the second unit," Carlisle said. "Because of the mounting campaign to go after Bill every day, it became very competitive between the first and second team. A lot of the impetus of that was his presence and how good he was."

"Scott Wedman was a great basketball player," Walton said. "He guarded Larry every day in practice. There were times when Scott Wedman was the second-greatest player in the world and he couldn't even get in our games. What a teammate."

Walton and Bird regularly stayed after practice for a little friendly one-on-one. Same with Ainge, McHale, and Wedman.

"It was the best time of my life," McHale told Jackie MacMullan in 2009. "Of all the things we did, what stands out is how naturally we gave of ourselves to the team. No one person was bigger than the rest of us."

It was even fun for the sportswriters.

Sarah Shaughnessy—born during the 1984 playoffs the day after I'd been out drinking with McHale at Major Goolsby's in Milwaukee—was eighteen months old at the start of the 1985–86 season. Her Michigan-based grandparents were in need of a visit when the Celtics left Logan for a Saturday game in November, and I struck a deal with my in-laws that they could take Sarah overnight if they'd meet us when we landed in Detroit.

As I carried my little girl through first class for a Saturday-morning flight, McHale reached for Sarah.

"Shank, how can you bring this cute little girl on a plane by yourself?" he asked. "Where's her mom? I'm going to call social services. First baby, right? That's when you're nervous about everything and you sterilize the pacifier. You loosen up a little after a while. By the time you've had your second one, you just let the dog lick the pacifier before you give it back to the baby. You'll see."

McHale, soon to be father of five, passed Sarah over to Walton, dad of four boys. Walton's huge head was bigger than Sarah's whole body. After everybody had a good laugh, I scooped up my daughter and made my way back to coach.

Sarah grew up to play softball at Harvard and today has two children and a husband who closely follows the twenty-first-century Celtics. When clips of classic games from the 1980s were rebroadcast regularly during the COVID-19 shutdown of 2020, I reminded Sarah that she once flew on a plane with the greatest basketball team of all time.

CHAPTER 12

"I'M NOT DRINKING
THE REST OF THE SEASON"

It was not all babies, strippers, wisecracks, and easy wins. I was still playing the role of objective narrator, breaker of news, never emotionally attached to players or the team. And there was still plenty of edginess in my final months covering the Larry Bird Celtics.

Early in the season, I wrote a story that called out Bird for failing to appear at a team-mandated reception hosted by the Celtics' flagship television station. Nobody had any comment on Bird's no-show at the Copley Westin.

"You were invited there as a guest, not a reporter," scolded Volk.

"What's this about you goin' at Larry?" charged Ainge.

"Why are you writing about that, Shank?" asked McHale. "He's our leader, man. Lay off him."

I contacted Bird's agent to ask if Larry would discuss the topic, or anything else.

"I think Larry's exasperated with everything that's been happening," said the always-available Bob Woolf. "He's getting a little paranoid. But I wouldn't read anything into it. I don't think he's going to become a hermit or anything."

Bird settled the Chelsea's matter out of court and, after paying Harlow and Lola, addressed the incident with Mary Shane, the *Worcester*

Telegram reporter who'd been a good sport when he'd made his crude joke in Cleveland.

"I made a mistake," Bird told Shane. "I embarrassed the Boston Celtics. I was in the wrong place at the wrong time. I really don't care about my image as far as grown-ups are concerned. Most grown-ups are a pain anyway. But in my heart, I feel bad about the kids. I regret all of this because kids should be able to look up to athletes, and my mom took it pretty hard. She said, 'You know better than that.' That bothered me a lot. . . . I really regret the whole thing because it reflects on the Boston Celtics. I'm really sorry about that. The good thing about all this is that maybe people finally understand that I'm human. I make mistakes. I've made a lot of mistakes. I like to drink beer and go out and have a good time—I'm human. It isn't easy being Larry Bird."

"We wish he hadn't been in there that night because you can get hurt," M. L. Carr said in 2021. "Everybody wanted to hang out with Larry, so he had to be a little careful. But none of us were upset with him. We just didn't want him to hurt those hands because they were our ticket to the promised land."

My next run at Bird came after I read a nasty passage about him in Dan Issel's book, *Parting Shots.* The retired Nugget characterized Bird as rude when Issel attempted to get some professional courtesy after a game in Denver. According to Issel, he'd escorted a teenage girl to the corridor outside the Celtics locker room to get Bird's autograph. Issel characterized Bird as rude and insensitive toward the young fan and wrote, "I don't think I'll ever forgive him for that."

I figured Bird would tell me to bleep off when I read him the unflattering vignette. Instead, he laughed and said, "You know where I learned how to be like that? I learned that from Dan Issel. When I was in the eighth grade, I went with a friend to see an ABA game, and I got Artis Gilmore's autograph and Louie Dampier's, but Dan Issel wouldn't sign."

With Chelsea's off-limits, Bird found plenty of alternative watering holes. Celtics players taped a cornball commercial with the Scotch &

Sirloin restaurant near the Garden and cut a deal with the owner to make the place a personal hangout for team members and families. Bird got his older brother Michael a job at Dockside, a Faneuil Hall Marketplace bar owned by the owners of Chelsea's. Dockside had a downstairs bar that was closed weeknights—unless Larry Bird needed a place to hang out. Bird occasionally visited his brother, hiding out in the downstairs bar, where he could watch sports, smoke cigarettes, drink Bud Lights, and not be bothered.

Another favorite hangout was the Fours, a classic sports bar/restaurant on Canal Street in the shadow of the Garden. Bird would sometimes close down the Fours, then invite the waitstaff to after-hours dinner in Chinatown, where he demonstrated a generosity not known to teammates and media members.

"He'd be there when we closed, then ask six or eight of us if we wanted to go eat," said Paige Renaghan, a Fours waitress for thirty years. "Of course, we said yes. It would be three in the morning, and he'd go to this place where we'd walk down like twelve steps and the waiters would come up and say, 'Mr. Bird, Mr. Bird, we have your lobster.' And Larry Bird would buy us dinner. It was fabulous."

Bird tweaked his back shoveling gravel for his mom in the summer of '85. In the early weeks of the 1985–86 season, he drove daily to the office of physical therapist Dan Dryek, where he'd get treatment to minimize pressure on compressed nerves. He was feeling much better as the holidays neared.

In those weeks, Walton developed a cultlike fascination with Bird—staying after practice for one-on-one games, then watching Bird's mastery from the Celtics bench. In Walton's mind, Bird knew exactly what was going on with every player on every play. Bird knew the strengths and weaknesses of all of his teammates. He knew when they were in good moods or bad moods. He knew when McHale was working for position and when McHale was coasting. Walton believed that Bird was the only basketball player who could control an NBA game while playing the forward position. Who else besides Larry Bird could lead his team in shot attempts *and* assists?

"To be able to play basketball with someone who thought and dreamed about it the way Larry did—he was always ahead of every-thing—was amazing," gushed Walton. "Our four boys would come to practice every day, and they loved it. It was so exciting for them after seeing all the disappointments of my career. And then they were able to be part of something fun and what sports is all about. Larry drove that. He could not have been nicer to our children. He took Adam and Nate with him to the All-Star Game as his guests. He bought them their plane tickets, got them a suite, took them everywhere, and introduced them all around."

"Larry was our idol," Luke Walton told me when he came to Boston as a member of the Lakers for the 2008 NBA Finals. "Even though my dad played on the Celtics, we all had the Larry Bird shirts on, and we'd go over to his house for dinner and play Nintendo with him."

"Luke got to see Larry play," said Bill Walton. "And if you were ever in the Boston Garden when Larry Bird was playing basketball, your life was never the same. The level of inspiration, dedication, and motivation—to go along with his remarkable talent—it was some-thing that changed people forever, and Luke saw that at the earliest of ages. His determination is a direct result of Larry Bird's brilliance."

Bird and Walton shared roundball telepathy on the court. Dusting off his UCLA high-post game, Walton conducted nightly clinics on the old-fashioned backdoor, pick-and-roll, and give-and-go plays. Bird would dribble from a spot out top, signal for Walton to flash from the low block to the foul line, then fire a pass to the giant redhead. Walton would catch the pass, hold it chest high, extend both elbows, then nod left or right. Bird would take the suggested route and explode to the basket, leaving his man behind while Walton feathered a no-look pass over his shoulder. Bird would catch the pass in stride and bank it in for a reverse layup. It was Wooden-esque, Straight Outta Hoosiers, fundamentally perfect basketball from the Picket Fence Playbook. Don't get caught watching the paint dry.

"When you threw that pass to Larry, you knew he was gonna catch it and turn it into gold," Walton said with a satisfied smile.

Bird loved working with Walton at the defensive end.

"Bill always tells me to set him up a couple of times so he can block the shot," said Bird. "My man will come driving in there, and I'll cut right in front of him so when he jumps, he can't stretch all the way out. Then Bill will smack it."

When the Celtics played an early-season game in Indianapolis, Jones gave Bird and Walton permission to visit Bird's hometown. Quinn Buckner, then a Pacer, tagged along and Tom Hill, Bird's state policeman friend, drove the trio to French Lick in the dark of night. Walton suggested a detour to Bobby Knight's home in Bloomington, but Buckner refused to give up the phone number. The players arrived in time for late beers, stayed over at Bird's new home, and had breakfast the next morning at Georgia Bird's house. Walton peppered Larry's mom with questions, then asked her if she could spare an empty canning jar. Walton went outside and scooped dirt from the area where Larry first practiced as a young boy. Walton placed the Indiana driveway soil in his equipment bag and kept it throughout the 1985–86 season, occasionally sprinkling some of the magic dust on his body for inspiration and strength. When the championship was won, Walton brought the jar to his parents' driveway in La Mesa and stomped Bird's driveway dirt into the soil where he'd learned to shoot hoops with his brother Bruce.

"That ground is now sacred," Walton declared.

"I love history and I wanted to see where Larry grew up," Walton said in 2021. "We had a break in the schedule, so I asked, K.C., 'Please, can we just have a couple of days? We'll be back on time. Tom Hill was the coolest dude. Larry called him Dr. Root. He was always around and he always had a gun, which was terrifying. He took us after the game and drove like a hundred miles an hour, calling ahead, telling cops, 'Clear the road, Larry Bird's coming home.' When we got there, we started at a place downtown—the Jubal—with a bunch of Larry's buddies. It was the most interesting place; sort of a combination of a church, library, parlor, roadhouse, health club, museum, psychiatrist's office, and innovation hub. It was like Alice's Restaurant.

It seemed everything you might need was there. Then we went to an exquisite ranch home Larry had built on the outskirts of town. It had an outdoor basketball court, golf course, bar, everything. There was more Miller Lite in that place than I've ever seen in my life."

The night before Bird's twenty-ninth birthday the Celtics were beaten at home by the Trail Blazers, 121–103. The Celts committed 26 turnovers and 4 technical fouls while K. C. Jones earned his first ejection. It was Boston's only home-court loss of the season, an NBA record that still stands.

Then came Christmas in New York.

In 2021 the NBA on Christmas Day is a highly promoted, daylong extravaganza: five dream matchups stocked with star power. It has evolved into an American TV sports holiday ritual on a par with the Detroit Lions playing on Thanksgiving. In 1985, the NBA on Christmas Day was pedestrian afternoon programming, not worthy of prime time. The Knicks were usually featured because New York's large Jewish population regularly filled Madison Square Garden on Christmas.

The Celtics asked permission to arrive in New York on Christmas Day for the 3:30 start, but the league deemed that too risky due to the television commitment and the ever-present prospect of a winter storm.

McHale didn't care and stayed home while the team flew to New York Christmas Eve. When his grumpy teammates awoke in the Summit Christmas morning, McHale was home in Weston opening presents with Lynn and the kids. He took a 9:00 a.m. shuttle from Logan, made it to Madison Square Garden plenty early, and played a whopping fifty minutes of an overtime loss, scoring 29 points with 14 rebounds. The Celtics blew a 25-point third-quarter lead, giving them three losses in five games.

When they returned home Christmas night, Sichting met up with Bird in Brookline.

"Our families were back in Indiana," Sichting recalled. "So I went to Larry's house and we went out for Chinese food and tried to wash away the memory, which we did pretty well."

When I reached K. C. Jones the next day, the coach said McHale would be fined. McHale said he was okay with that.

McHale was never fined (Auerbach wouldn't hear of it), and everybody with the exception of Bird understood why a player would want to be with his young family on Christmas morning, but the Celtics didn't appreciate a reporter going public with a family squabble, and I got the stink eye when I strolled into the visitors' locker room in Salt Lake City two days after Christmas.

"Don't even think about coming near me or the trainer's room," snapped Melchiorre. "Come to think of it, how about if you just come tap me on the shoulder to let me know that you're in the locker room? Next time I read something about one of my players that you shouldn't know, we're coming after you."

Things were more relaxed on the floor. Bird's back was feeling better and the Celtics closed out 1985 with road wins over the Jazz and the Clippers. Walton celebrated his return to the Los Angeles Sports Arena with 13 rebounds in seventeen minutes against the Clippers.

There were no games New Year's Eve or New Year's Day, and Jones told his players they were off until January 1 in Indianapolis. Walton flew to San Francisco, where he was master of ceremonies for the Grateful Dead's New Year's Eve concert featuring Ken Kesey, Al Franken, Father Guido Sarducci, and the Merry Pranksters.

"Kesey was on fire that night," Walton recalled. "Tommy Heinsohn [known for being animated in his then TV color-commentator role] would have fit right in."

Bird and Sichting left LAX on a red-eye, bound for Indianapolis, connecting through St. Louis.

"We didn't sleep all night," said Sichting. "When we arrived, it was New Year's Eve, so I went home and saw a bunch of high school buddies. I got back to the Hyatt in Indianapolis New Year's Day and went out for a good run. I figured we weren't going to have a very hard practice that night. Well, when we got to practice, K.C. tried to kill us. He knew what we'd been up to, and he ran the crap out of us. Most of us were just dead because we'd all been out on New Year's Eve.

"When we finally got back to the hotel, we were hanging out in the atrium area, standing outside our rooms trying to recover from practice. Nobody was feeling too good, and Larry said, 'I'm not drinking the rest of the season.' And everybody was on board."

Celtics teammates have different memories of the birth of the no-drinking pact.

"It had to have been much later than New Year's," Walton said. "Nobody would have committed to six months! I just remember we were sitting around toasting another great victory for the Celtics and somebody saying, 'Let's make a pact that we won't take another drink till we win the championship.' That's when Kevin chimed in and said, 'Well, we're going to win the championship this year, aren't we?'"

"It happened around the first of the year," McHale remembered. "I can't tell you whose idea it was, but I can assure you it wasn't Larry's idea. I just remember someone saying we're not going to drink until we win a championship, and I remember saying, 'Well, I hope we're planning on winning it this year because I will break my vow if it goes longer than this June.' Of course, we all had some hall passes."

Ainge said, "It wasn't like it was enforced, but everybody made a commitment to get more sleep, stop drinking, work harder, and get more shots after practice every day."

Bird wasn't going to let another championship get away. He'd been on teams that wasted opportunities—1982–83 and 1984–85 specifically. Walton knew for sure that he was not likely to have many more opportunities.

In January, the Celtics temporarily shared the Boston sports stage with the New England Patriots, who advanced to their first Super Bowl with road playoff wins against the New York Jets, Oakland Raiders, and Miami Dolphins.

Hours before the Patriots played the Bears in New Orleans January 26, the Celtics beat the Sixers by 2 points in a CBS-televised Super Bowl Sunday warm-up. Bird scored 28 with 14 rebounds and 6 assists, while Walton added 19 with 14 rebounds and 6 assists in just twenty-five minutes. Bill and Susan Walton hosted a Super Bowl party at their Cambridge home after the game.

"We had a grand time," Walton said. "Everybody was there and they brought their wives and children. Instead of watching the pre-game football show, we watched our game, which I'd taped on my VCR. Larry had this monster game, including two half-court shots. We were celebrating as we watched it in my house, and then the broadcasters came on at the end and said, 'We want to honor the Chevrolet Player of the Game—Bill Walton!' Larry was sitting right there on my couch and he said, 'Wait a second, what's going on here? Dinah, let's go right now!' So Larry got up and left, but we continued on."

"That party was probably one exception to our drinking pact," recalled Sichting. "But it was pretty mild by Bill Walton's standards."

The Patriots were demolished by the Bears, 46–10, putting the local sports spotlight back on the Celtics.

After Super Bowl Sunday, the Celtics won games in Chicago, Washington, and Milwaukee, and fans were waiting for them at every arena. By 1986, if you played for the Celtics or merely rooted for them, you never walked alone. Bird and Co. were tracked and trailed by "Green People"—transplanted New Englanders who pledged allegiance across America. There were no empty lobbies like the one I'd experienced at the Richfield Holiday Inn four years earlier. Green People knew where the team stayed and found them in airports, hotel lobbies, and on sidewalks getting off the team bus. The Celtics had tradition, banners, and most important—Bird. If the Celtics were coming to town, they'd sell out your building, even in Atlanta.

"They never have a road game," said Hawks GM Stan Kasten.

The 32-7 Lakers made their annual trip to the Garden in January.

Walton, who'd spent his basketball life tracing Kareem's footprints, was ever inspired by the Lakers and Abdul-Jabbar. Walton had only praise for his treetop rival, even though Kareem sometimes hinted that Walton's reputation was inflated by white media.

"Kareem was the standard of excellence and still is," Walton said in 2021. "I wanted to be great. I wanted to be the best. So everything I did was in preparation to try to be him. I raged in my work all the time, saying to myself, 'Jabbar! Jabbar!' I'm going to get this guy. 'Jabbar!' I'd be hiking the John Muir Trail. 'Jabbar!' I'm riding my bike from Oregon to Mexico. 'Jabbar! Jabbar!'"

Walton blocked Kareem's skyhook from behind and was the center of attention when the Celtics thrashed the Lakers, 110–95, at the Garden in January. Walton rang up 11 points, 8 rebounds, 7 blocks, and 4 standing ovations in only sixteen minutes. Abdul-Jabbar made only 6 of 20 shots.

"The only word which describes the way Bill Walton plays against us is *maniacal*," noted Riley.

Riley knew a lot about Walton, going back to the days when he'd scrimmaged against teenage Bill in the Helix gym. Riley's wife, Chris Rodstrom, was a senior at Helix when Bill Walton was a sophomore (Danny Ainge's wife, Michelle, also went to Helix).

In 1986, Riley could see that Walton had tipped the scales in Boston's favor. Parish was getting more rest, and Walton was on his way to playing 80 games and shooting a career-high .562. Walton was also the happiest man in sports.

"It's impossible to overstate how better than perfect our life was in Boston," he said. "When you're on a special team, it changes your life forever. The thing about the Celtics is that they've always been about the family, the group, the team. That's all I ever wanted in my life—to be part of a special team. There was that sense of community that you live for on a team, and Boston-Cambridge had the same thing as a city. To expose our children to that at such an early age, it had a phenomenal impact and left an indelible impression on their souls.

"I rode the T to the Garden for most games. Red Line to Green Line to North Station. On some of the rare occasions when I'd drive to the Garden, Luke and his brothers would hide in the back of the car and I'd have no idea they were there. I'd have Jerry Garcia and the Grateful Dead blaring, and I'd pull into that back parking lot, and as I was getting out, the boys—led by Luke—would jump out, saying, 'We're here! We're going to the game! We don't care about going to school tomorrow!'"

A few days after the Lakers left town, Bird learned that he was going to participate in the first-ever "Long Distance Shootout" at the All-Star Game in Dallas. First prize was $10,000, and Bird was slated to compete with seven other NBA sharpshooters. He reacted to this news like a puppy who'd been served a heaping bowl of raw hamburger meat.

The three-point shot in 1986 was largely a gimmick, never the focus of a team's offense. Bird led the NBA with 194 three-point attempts in 1985–86. In 2018–19, James Harden launched 1,028 threes. NBA teams today routinely take more than 40 percent of their shots from beyond the arc. In the 2021 NBA All-Star Game, 133 three-pointers were chucked, almost three per minute.

The three-point contest was an opportunity for Bird to showcase his talent and earn $10,000 for ten minutes of shooting. It rained threes at the Pappas Gym in the days leading up to the event, Ainge and Wedman challenging Bird, while Bird logged bets from any teammate who doubted he'd win.

"When that contest was announced, there was no question who was going from our team," remembered Wedman. "Danny and I were good from out there, but Larry was in his own category when it came to threes under pressure. Hands down. I still remember the day he [K.C.] ended practice for us and K.C. said we could go home if anybody could make a half-court shot. Before K.C. even finished talking, Larry said, 'I'll take it.' And of course he made it."

The All-Star Game launched Boston's West Coast trip, annually Bird's favorite stretch of the season. The '86 trip featured flights to Sacramento, Seattle, Portland, Los Angeles, Phoenix, Oakland, and Denver. Counting the All-Star Game, it was eight games in twelve days in eight cities in six states, stretched across three time zones. There were three trips in and out of California. Small wonder the Celtics got along so well with the E Street Band and the Grateful Dead.

By the time the 1986 Celtics West Coast trip was over, the Celtics would be NBA championship favorites, Bird would be the Three Point King and consensus MVP, and I'd be finished as the *Globe*'s Celtics beat reporter.

This Last Waltz started at Reunion Arena in Dallas, where Bird had bailed midway through his first Springsteen concert a year earlier. Reporters warned Bird that Bullets guard Leon Wood had made 28 of 31 three-point attempts in practice.

"That was when he was all by himself and there was no pressure," said Bird, chuckling. "On Saturday there'll be people screaming and ten thousand dollars on the line and Leon Wood probably won't hit a shot. I'll be out there hollering at him."

The next day Bird walked into the tiny dressing room, looked at the other seven contestants, and asked, "Which one of you guys is going to finish second? Leon, I saw you warming up out there, and your shot looks a little different to me."

Wood darted out of the room and wound up being eliminated in the first round. He was out of the league five years later, then had a long career as an NBA official.

The contest was pure and simple. Twenty-five basketballs (five racks, five in each rack) were placed around the three-point stripe. Each shooter had one minute in which to release twenty-five shots. The fifth ball in each rack was an old-timey red-white-and-blue ABA ball, which counted for two points instead of one.

Without even taking off his warm-up jacket, Bird advanced to the finals easily. In the championship round he drained 18 of 25 attempts, including 9 straight, adding a preposterous banker for good measure. This was his Apollo 11. When it was over, he danced into the interview room and shouted, "I'm the new Three Point King! And the ones who didn't think I could win can go to hell. Put that in your paper, Dan Shaughnessy!"

"Larry has that Muhammad Ali kind of approach," said K. C. Jones. "He gets to you and your mind before the fight begins. By the time you step in the ring, you're forty points down."

Atlanta's five-six Spud Webb won the slam dunk contest after Bird's three-point mastery.

"Spud gives everyone who is short an incentive to live," said McHale. "Inner-city kids identify with Isiah and Magic. Middle-aged people identify with Kareem. Middle America identifies with Larry."

En route to Sacramento for the start of the trip, I asked K.C. how he thought his team would fare on the seven-game Western trip.

"The best you can ask for is a split," said the coach.

There was no quarreling with the math of "splitting" seven games. K.C. had a little Yogi Berra in him and never got hung up on details.

"There couldn't possibly be another NBA coach in the past two decades less knowledgeable or less interested in pursuit of NBA minutiae," wrote Ryan.

In this spirit, Jones's pregame interviews with Johnny Most produced broadcast gems. Before the first Celtics-Lakers game of 1986, Most asked K.C. how he planned to stop veteran forward Jamaal Wilkes. Most didn't know that Wilkes had been waived by the Lakers and signed by the Clippers over the summer. Fortunately for Johnny, the coach of the Celtics didn't know either. Thus, listeners to the broadcast were treated to a discussion in which the voice of the Celtics and the head coach of the Celtics plotted ways to contain a player who no longer played for the Lakers. Radio gold.

When the Celtics checked into Sacramento's finest Red Lion Inn to start the junket, Bird patrolled the lobby with a mini-golf pencil and small notepad, collecting cash from teammates who'd made the mistake of betting against him in the three-point contest. No one was allowed to postpone payment.

"If you don't have your money, I'll wait right here while you go back to your room and get it," Bird told teammates. "The bus will wait for me. I'm the Three Point King."

Bird was feted with a minute-long standing ovation before the game versus the Kings, but the Celtics lost, snapping their 13-game winning streak.

I wasn't paying close attention. I was about to walk away from the best sportswriting gig in America.

The *Globe*'s iconic baseball writer, Peter Gammons, was headed to *Sports Illustrated*, no small transaction in our industry. *Sports Illustrated* was a monster media entity with a stable of great sportswriters and an unlimited budget. Gammons's departure meant that the *Globe* needed a baseball columnist on the eve of spring training. With five years of experience covering big league ball and a native's understanding of what the Red Sox mean to Boston, I was a strong candidate. I raised my hand for the Sox gig, and Ryan, who'd returned to the *Globe* after a short shift in local TV, agreed to jump back on the Celtics beat he'd invented.

My boss informed me of the switch when I called him from a pay phone at the Sacramento airport the morning after the Kings game. I was instructed to finish out the trip, fly home from Denver, then pack for Florida. I was on my way to Winter Haven to cover the 1986 Red Sox—a snarly, mediocre bunch that had underachieved to the tune of 81-81 in 1985. The Sox didn't figure to be very good, but they were still the most important team in our town—even if they didn't have Larry Bird and fifteen championship banners.

I hung up the phone, took a deep breath, and walked back to our departure gate, where half-asleep Celtics were sprawled across airport furniture—eating muffins, drinking coffee (a jug of water for Wedman), and waiting to board the flight to Seattle. The *New York Post*'s ubiquitous Vecsey (McHale called him Ears) was chatting with Bird and Parish when I walked over to tell them my news.

"Well, boys, this is it," I told Bird, Parish, and Vecsey. "I just talked to my boss. I'm leaving you guys to go cover the Red Sox. When this trip is over, you won't have Scoop to kick around anymore."

"Things won't be the same, that's for sure," Chief said, slowly shaking his head.

Bird stood up, took out his wallet, cracked it open, and said, "I'll pay your way if you go right now."

Ainge, the only Celtic who understood the importance of the Red Sox beat in Boston, said, "That's great, Dan. I can't believe you're leaving, but this will be good for you. I'll warn Bruce Hurst [about to have a breakthrough season as one of the Sox's starting pitchers] about you."

Vecsey couldn't believe it. "You'll never have another team like this. I've only been here a few days, and this is the most fun I've ever had with any team."

We were on to Seattle, where there was big buzz about the Celtics owning the Sonics' first-round pick in the 1986 draft. Red had correctly projected Seattle's demise. The 18-33 Sonics were lottery-bound. The Celtics beat Seattle easily, moving ever closer to their coveted lottery pick.

At this juncture in their brief time together, Bird and Walton were the NBA's Lennon and McCartney—Bird registering triple doubles nightly while Walton played with abandon for the first time since his Portland days. Their give-and-goes were hardwood poetry, and in my final days on the beat I was finally appreciating some of the basketball ballet I'd been watching for four seasons. The ball movement was glorious. Bird and Walton formed the core, but Parish, Ainge, McHale, and DJ were veteran champions who enjoyed the artistry of going from baseline to baseline without putting the ball on the floor. We saw no-look passes, behind-the-back passes, and give-and-go passes feathered perfectly through traffic. Ainge asked Jones if he could stay on the floor with the Green Team late in games. Everyone wanted to be part of the ball-sharing mosaic.

"We were the greatest passing team ever," said Ainge.

"We decided we had to ramp things up," recalled McHale. "So we started hitting stride, and it was ridiculous. At the start of the third quarter I'd say, 'We got to quit beating everybody this bad because then we don't even play in the second half. That's not fun. It was like a scrimmage for us. I wanted the games to be closer. We'd just put it on people in a terrible way and beat the shit out of them."

We flew from Seattle to Portland, where the local papers were peppered with photographs of Walton's ponytail days with the Blazers. While McHale and Ainge crushed Walton over the photos, Walton walked around the room and asked if anybody had extra tickets. He needed fourteen.

"Management won't give you any?" Parish asked.

"I'm not really tight with them anymore." Walton laughed.

Walton had sued Portland's team physician after the 1978–79 season; the case was settled out of court for an undisclosed sum. The Blazers announced that they'd never retire Walton's jersey number 32 (they changed their minds in 1989).

"I remember coming here to watch you play," said Ainge. "They used to sell ten thousand tickets for people who couldn't get in. They'd watch on closed-circuit television at the Paramount."

On the night the Trail Blazers' sellout streak reached 386, Bird torched the locals with 47 points, 14 rebounds, and 11 assists, winning the game with a 14-foot shot with three seconds left in overtime. He made at least seven of his baskets with his left hand.

"I'm saving my right hand for the Lakers," he said.

He was never more bold, or more receptive to the media. In LA, Bird answered a hypothetical Magic question that would have drawn an icy stare in earlier seasons: "Who would do better if the roles were reversed? Bird in LA or Magic in Boston?"

"I don't think I could do the things Magic does, but I'm sure they'd still win a lot of games with me there. I think Magic would fit in better with Boston than I would with LA. I'm not a great individual defensive player, but I can run my guy into Robert and Kevin all night."

Bird had something extra for a reporter from Salt Lake, telling the startled scribe, "Danny and Greg Kite should be heroes in Utah. Instead they get cursed. They put Utah on the map. People would have never heard of Utah if it weren't for BYU—and maybe Gary Gilmore."

The nationally televised Sunday Lakers game at the Forum was a homecoming for Walton, an opportunity to play in front of his parents and friends and prove himself against Jabbar one last time. He scored 10 points with 7 rebounds in twenty-six minutes of a 6-point Celtics win that gave Boston a sweep of the season series. He even guarded superhuman James Worthy over the final three minutes.

"I think Bill is the difference," ceded Magic.

"They're deeper than they were last year," admitted Abdul-Jabbar.

Winners of 20 of 22 since Christmas, the Celtics followed their victory over the Lakers with four games in four cities in just five days: Sunday, LA; Monday, Phoenix; Wednesday, Golden State; Thursday, Denver.

Wedman vanished after a loss in Phoenix.

"Scott Wedman has a personal problem he's dealing with in Kansas City," publicist Jeff Twiss explained.

Personal problem is a red flag in the sportswriting world. In the 1980s NBA, it was code for "drugs." Wedman was the last candidate for a substance abuse scandal, but Twiss's unfortunate phrasing put me on the trail of one final controversy before leaving the beat.

When I reached Volk over the phone, he said, "It's a routine problem. There's not a Communist under every rock."

We were on the way to the Bay Area, where the Celtics had just switched hotels due to a series of NBA drug-related problems at an infamous hotel. Long since demolished, it was a drug/prostitute haven in the 1970s and 1980s when it housed NBA teams and Major League Baseball teams. Located a couple of miles from the homes of the A's, Raiders, and Warriors, the "Hotel California" was the site of bad news involving professional athletes. Some players labeled the hotel's lounge "the Star Wars Bar."

Ainge had his four-year-old son, Austin (now Celtics director of player personnel), on the trip, which made him happy that the Celtics were done with the Edgewater Hyatt. Seeing Austin with his dad reminded me of how much had changed since Fitch wouldn't allow five-year-old Michael Carr on the team bus during the '83 playoffs.

Also along on this trip were friends of Bill Walton's: Arthur Heart-felt, a social worker from San Diego, and Mokie Ruiz, who owned a liquor store in Santa Monica. Arthur and Mokie rode the bus and showed up at practices and game-day shootarounds. Overnight, they crashed on the floor of Bird's room.

"That was another example of how K. C. Jones was the perfect coach for our team at that time," Walton said. "He could have been like, 'Who are these guys?' But he was told, 'They're with Bill.' And that was all he needed."

Even without McHale and Wedman, the Celtics beat the Warriors, then trudged to the Oakland airport for the next morning's flight to Denver. I'd discovered that Wedman's "personal" problem was back spasms, but that didn't stop Bird from needling me as we sat waiting to board the flight to Denver.

"Scoop, I hear Scottie's on drugs," Bird teased.

Secretly, he was going to miss me, I deduced.

He had reason to be in a good mood. He was having the greatest road trip of his life and I was leaving. When our inevitable flight delay was announced, Bird approached again.

"Got a blank stat sheet on ya, Scoop? I want to mail in my stats for tonight and go home. "Put me down for twenty points, eighteen rebounds, and no assists."

When we arrived at the lobby of the Denver Marriott, Scott and Kim Wedman were standing near the front desk, accompanied by Wedman's chiropractor friend, Steve Krischel—the same guy Melchiorre said looked like a plumber when the Celtics barred him from the locker room during the 1984 Finals. Wedman received a standing ovation from his teammates as he boarded the bus for McNichols Arena, started the final game of the trip, and scored 14 points in a 2-point loss to the Nuggets.

Bird exceeded his projected totals, scoring 27 with 16 rebounds and 4 assists, but missed a couple of free throws down the stretch (the ghost of Beezer Carnes). On the seven-game trip, he averaged

31 points, 13 rebounds, 7 assists . . . and picked up ten grand while becoming the Three Point King.

We didn't go straight to the airport from the gym. Red-eye Ray Melchiorre arranged for the team to return to the Marriott, rest for two hours, then hop back on the bus for a trip to the Denver airport and a 3:00 a.m. flight that would connect with another aircraft at O'Hare and deliver the team back to Boston at 10:40 a.m. This was NBA travel in the 1980s.

Riding in the pitch-black team bus after midnight in Denver, it struck me that this was my final moment with these guys. Players were silent, exhausted, and half-asleep. Certainly I was the only one aware that this was it for me with the Celtics. Everybody else just wanted to get home.

When the bus pulled to the curb and the lights came up, I stood and went to get my bag in the overhead rack.

Bird was standing in front of me, hand extended. "Good luck, Mr. Shaughnessy."

I was on my way to baseball.

The Celtics were on their way to history.

CHAPTER 13

"A LITTLE BIT OF A LETDOWN WHEN IT ENDED"

Walking into the Red Sox locker room in Winter Haven, I felt young and tall again.

That was the good part.

The 1986 Red Sox were a star-laden, star-crossed pack of tortured personalities, carrying sixty-seven years of franchise failure, a curse they'd upheld with a sad symmetric season (81-81) in 1985. They had twenty-three-year-old, tight-lipped Roger Clemens, who'd won 16 career games and was coming off shoulder surgery. They had Hall of Fame–bound Jim Rice, who'd threatened me when I made fun of his defensive struggles in 1982. The Sox had gruff former NL batting champ Bill Buckner, and Hall of Fame–bound Wade Boggs—a hit machine who'd one day claim to have willed himself invisible to escape a knife fight in a Florida parking lot. They had Oil Can Boyd, a combustible starting pitcher with cocaine issues, and another pitcher who hurled an anti-Semitic epithet at a rookie reporter from Hartford.

These sullen Sox were appropriately managed by John Francis McNamara, a traditional "good baseball man" with a tragic thirst who received new media representatives as if he'd caught them breaking into his home. Mac was a company man who treated his stars royally and had friends around the game from his many decades in baseball. He hated to be second-guessed and routinely challenged young reporters, asking, "Where are you from?"—which was more accusation than inquiry. The Sox manager reacted to lofty preseason predictions with "A lot of people pick you to finish first just to see you get fucking fired."

The Red Sox in '85 had been embroiled in scandal when it was learned that the ball club allowed the Winter Haven Elks Club to distribute free passes to white ballplayers, but not to Blacks or Hispanics. Institutional racism was a Red Sox trademark going back to the 1940s, when Jackie Robinson was insulted at a sham Fenway tryout and again when the team passed on signing Birmingham minor leaguer Willie Mays. The Red Sox were the last major league team to put a Black ballplayer on the field.

In this arena of superstars and churls, I found a kindred spirit in Bruce Hurst, a polite twenty-seven-year-old left-handed pitcher from St. George, Utah. Hurst was Danny Ainge's best friend.

Mormons from the Far West, Ainge and Hurst met in 1980 when they were competing in the International League—Ainge with Toronto's minor league affiliate in Syracuse, Hurst with the Pawtucket Red Sox. Ainge hit a double and a single in four minor league at bats against Hurst. By the time Hurst was good enough to come north with the Sox in 1982, Ainge was a Celtics rookie, living in Newton with his wife and two young children. Bruce and Holly Hurst moved in with the Ainges when they first came to Boston, and the couples socialized with the McHales of Weston and the Kites of Newton.

Hurst—who'd come within one strike of winning the World Series MVP in October of 1986—knew all about the Celtics culture of winning, camaraderie, and fun.

"Near the end of baseball season we had more off days because of weather and travel, and I'd go to the Celtics practices at Hellenic with Danny," Hurst remembered. "Sometimes they'd let me play a little with them, but mostly I'd just rebound and watch. The interaction between those Celtic players was just beautiful. They had a riot together. There was nothing sacred. They were hard on each other, but they were hilarious. Is there a better teammate in the world than

Kevin McHale? Same with Danny. He had this unique personality and he was unflappable and never took anything personally. They were all like that. No matter what was thrown at those guys, they just moved on. They were so honest in the way they approached their game. Criticism of them could be harsh, but they handled it well. In baseball, we don't handle criticism so well. The Celtics were always around media people because they played major college basketball with TV and everything that comes with that. When you grow up in baseball, you never see reporters until you're in the big leagues.

"In baseball, just getting to the big leagues puts you in conflict with your teammates. In the minors, you're competing against your teammates because there are only so many spots in the big leagues. The development process puts a wedge between you and your teammates. If another guy did good, you'd think, 'Well, now he's going to take my spot.' And that would carry over to the big leagues. So you were almost trained to pull *against* each other instead of *for* each other. It created jealousy instead of teamwork. The Celtics had none of that. When Danny would talk about his teammates, there was none of that jealousy. They were always pulling for each other. They all had their roles. Bird, McHale, and Chief were stars, but Danny, DJ, Flipper, Kite, and Wedman all had roles to fill. There was such a difference between the two environments and a real contrast to what I was experiencing with the Red Sox. I wanted to find a way to take that positivity I saw with the Celtics and keep it around me."

Celtics players liked Hurst. When the big lefty lost his arbitration case versus the Red Sox, Bird quipped, "The Mormon Church will be on the front steps, picketin'."

Hurst understood my plight and in Florida was good to me from day one.

"I can sympathize with what that must have been like for you to leave those Celtics and then try to cover us," he said. "You had to be dragging your tail. We weren't very good at dealing with the media, and we weren't very good at dealing with each other. The roles in baseball aren't as defined. We were all pretty new to each other. We were trying to figure each other out and who we were. We were confused. There was a lot swirling about us. There were storms and little tornadoes everywhere. The pitchers and the everyday players didn't mix. It was a tough crowd. We all felt it.

"Eddie Lynch tried out with us in '86, and he'd pitched six years with the Mets and even he couldn't believe it. He'd never seen anything like what we had with the Red Sox. You had to have thick skin because it was no-holds-barred. Those Celtics were tough on each other, but they never, ever took it personally. That wasn't the case in our clubhouse. We were tough on each other and it was personal. Feelings were harbored."

"I was around those Red Sox a lot," echoed Ainge. "In baseball, there are more players, so it's a little harder to be connected to everybody. There wasn't the cohesiveness like there was with us. McNamara seemed on edge and responsive to criticism. Not many guys on our Celtic team were sensitive like that. Nobody really cared. I think if we got mad at you, it was just busting your chops, as opposed to actual anger."

"We had a lot of intensity around us, but there was an unbelievable amount of looseness and fun," remembered McHale. "It was a bunch of characters with everybody giving each other a ration of shit, and that was the fun vibe of it. I remember one night Jerry Sichting scored thirty for us, and after the game we were sitting around and Larry said, 'That's three times your average. That would be like me getting one hundred.' We all laughed. We enjoyed each other's success."

The 1986 Celtics won their first eight games of the post-Shaughnessy era and finished 67-15, the second-best record in franchise history, and fourth-best in league history at that time. The final four months of the 1986 Celtics season were more performance art than competition. Bird was named Player of the Month in both February and March as the team won fourteen in a row. They went 39-5 in one stretch, including 11-0 against the Lakers, Sixers, Bucks, Hawks, and Rockets, beating them all on the road. They clinched a playoff spot on February 28, then an NBA record for earliest invitation to the postseason. Of their 15 regular season losses, only 5 came against teams with winning records. McHale said they could have won 70 if they felt it mattered.

Almost bored, Bird started to bank three-pointers, just for the fun of it. When Knicks trainer Mike Saunders bet $10 that Bird couldn't do it against the Knicks, Bird banked a three late in the fourth quarter and put his hand out when he passed Saunders on the bench while running back down the floor.

The man was playing Shoot for Money in real NBA games.

"It was the best time of my life and I'll never forget it," Bird said.

On April 8 in Milwaukee, the seventy-ninth game of the regular season, K. C. Jones went with a starting lineup of Walton, Wedman, Kite, Carlisle, and Sichting. The Green Team beat the formidable Bucks, 126–114.

On the final day of the regular season, the Celtics played the Nets at the Garden. Bird had a chance to cash a $30,000 bonus from a sporting goods company if he finished with the league's best free throw percentage. The only player capable of finishing with a higher percentage was Ainge, who needed at least fifteen attempts just to qualify. Ainge hurled his body into Net defenders all afternoon, and by the middle of the fourth quarter he was 13 of 14 from the line, on the cusp of passing Bird.

"I just wanted to make Larry sweat it out," said Ainge. "My goal was to get to the line set to pass Larry and make the first one, and then negotiate for some of his bonus in exchange for missing the second one. But the whole team was telling K.C. to get me out of the game, so I never got to do it. K.C. took me out. So Larry stole my free throw title, basically."

The Celtics won and the Three Point King picked up an extra $30,000.

They swept the Chicago Bulls three straight in the first round, a series remembered only for Michael Jordan's 63-point performance in Game 2 ("the day Jordan and I combined for sixty-three," according to Kite). It was Jordan's coming-out party as the Future of the NBA. Sixty-three is still an NBA playoff record.

The Celtics beat the Hawks in five games in round two, painting a parquet Picasso in the 132–99 clincher—a 36–6 quarter that included a 24–0 surge. Ryan termed it a "scintillating display of interior defense, transition basketball and Globetrotter-like passing which transformed the game into something bordering on legitimate humiliation. The Hawks could not avoid being an accident of basketball history."

It was mildly reminiscent of the 1965 NBA Finals, when Russell's Celtics beat the Lakers by 33 points in a clinch game. Boston scored 20 straight to open the final quarter, and Russell wrote, "We simply took off into unknown peaks. . . . We were on fire, intimidating, making shots, running the break and the Lakers just couldn't score. . . . We had taken sports out of the realm of the game."

The Celtics swept the Bucks in a conference final that lacked drama, closing out the series May 18, which meant a week of rest before the Finals. Celtics-Lakers III was all teed up, until Ralph Sampson canned a twisting 12-foot buzzer-beating miracle shot over Jabbar that eliminated the Lakers. *Boo.* This meant no Ali-Frazier III in the spring of 1986. (The Celtics and Lakers met again in the '87 Finals, but McHale played with a broken foot, Walton was almost totally sidelined, and the Lakers won in six.)

"I would like to have played the Lakers in '86," McHale admitted. "But as weird as it sounds, after the All-Star break I didn't think it mattered who we played. I just didn't see any chance for another team. The stuff we did was unguardable."

"We always wanted to play the Lakers," said Bird. "There's no question about it."

Asked about Houston, Walton channeled the Grateful Dead, saying, "Too close to New Orleans."

The 1986 Rockets were coached by old friend Fitch and had the Twin Towers: seven-four Sampson and emerging superstar Olajuwon.

"I'm not into opponent selection," Walton said. "But if you're really good, the opposition, they're irrelevant. Houston had a lot of good players, but we were better at every position."

Nancy Saad Parish performed the national anthem at the Finals, and Boston won the first two games, at home, easily. After his Rockets were routed in Game 2, Fitch snapped, "We were humiliated. It's embarrassing to get to the Finals and play like this."

Olajuwon led the Rockets to a pair of victories in the middle three games in Houston, giving the 1986 NBA Finals a veneer of competitiveness. Game 5 produced the only fire of the series, when Sampson unleashed a flurry of punches at six-one Sichting.

"Ralph Sampson showed his true colors," Johnny Most howled. "He is a gutless big guy who picks on the little people."

"Everybody wants to take a shot at Jerry," Bird said, smirking. "Hell, my girlfriend could whup him. . . . Ralph will have a tough time in Boston. He better wear his hard hat. . . . I expect this to be over with Sunday."

Before Game 6 in Boston, K. C. Jones sent his players home after only ten minutes of Saturday's practice. He could see that his team was ready and was afraid somebody might get hurt if he kept the session going.

The clincher was a forty-eight-minute, Sunday-afternoon Garden party. Bird said he felt his heart pounding through his chest when he came out for the opening tip, and he changed jerseys at halftime so he would have an extra souvenir shirt. The Celtics led 97–67 in the fifth minute of the final quarter, when Jones commenced with the curtain calls. Bird finished with 29 points, 11 rebounds, 12 assists, and another car from *Sport* magazine. Kite made it off the floor with the game ball.

"There were a few beers had after that game," said Carlisle.

"It was everything I hoped for and better, and it all came true," said Walton. "From the people to the place to the game to the court to the Garden. It changes your life forever. It was a fantastic period in the NBA. Just to be with all the players, all the reporters, the broadcasters, in the hotels, at the airports, at the gym, in the restaurants, and in the bars, and just having the time of our life."

"When it was all over, it was a letdown, it really was," added

Sichting. "You just wanted to go out the next week and play another series. We were almost having too much fun, and it was a little bit of a letdown when it ended."

Hours after the final buzzer of the final game of the '86 season—late Sunday night—Walton rang the bell at Bird's home on Newton Street in Brookline. Dinah answered the door, invited Walton inside, and woke Larry. Rubbing his eyes, Bird came out of his bedroom and told his tall friend that the party was over. He was going back to bed. This didn't discourage Bill Walton. He sat down in Bird's kitchen with a bottle of Wild Turkey, put on some Grateful Dead, and soaked in the moment. All night long.

"Larry went back to sleep and I didn't want to wake him up, so I just sat there and listened to the Dead and I prayed," said Walton. "When you're part of something that special, it changes you. You spend the rest of your life trying to get that back. When you're doing it, it seems like it's going to last forever. When it ends, you realize how fragile, how tenuous, and how fleeting it all is."

When Bird woke up in the morning and peeked into his kitchen, Walton was still there, ready to talk more about the glory days of 1985–86.

No team had more fun. We all wish it could have lasted forever.

CHAPTER 14

"I GOT A TEAMMATE WHO NEEDS A HUG"

When Celtics management gathered the '86 champs for a thirty-year reunion in 2016, Sichting was struck by how little had changed.

"We were together for three or four days and it all came back," said the shooting guard, who lives near McHale in Arizona and regularly goes to Wyoming for fishing trips with his tall teammate. "Everybody carried on the same way we always did. It was like we'd just been playing games last week. The one-liners and the trash-talking. It all comes back anytime we're together. I guess it had something to do with Red. He knew how to put the right guys together."

Auerbach died at the age of eighty-nine in 2006.

The '86 Celtics had five Hall of Famers Bird, Chief, McHale, Walton, and Dennis Johnson, plus Hall of Fame GM Auerbach and Hall of Fame coach K. C. Jones. They had six players who went on to become NBA head coaches. Carlisle, one of the players at the end of the bench, will probably be a Hall of Fame coach when his career is over.

DJ wasn't at the 2016 reunion. After coaching stints with the Celtics and Clippers, he died at the age of fifty-two in 2007 while coaching the Austin Toros of the D-League.

Maxwell and Walton flew to Texas for Johnson's memorial service.

"DJ died of a broken heart," said Walton. "He wanted to get back to coaching in the NBA in the worst way. I loved Dennis Johnson and I wanted the best for him. He was always very protective of me, especially in 1987 when I had a broken foot and couldn't play when everybody wanted me to play. I remember DJ walking over to me while the crowd was chanting my name and whispering, 'Don't do it, Bill.'"

"Dennis was one of my best friends," said Maxwell. "When I got to the church for his service, his wife, Donna, came up to me and told me she wanted me to speak. I wasn't ready for that, but I got up there and said, 'Dennis, I know you're up there looking down, and you're thankful I'm speaking and not Bill Walton, because if Bill was up here, you would never get buried.'"

Days after the service in Texas, Ainge, Bird, and McHale attended DJ's funeral in Gardena, California.

Five years later, Ainge and Walton made a sad trek to Shoreview, Minnesota, for the funeral of Alexandra "Sasha" McHale, one of Kevin and Lynn's five children. A college basketball player like her dad, Sasha succumbed to lupus at the age of twenty-three. Sasha's dad was still coach of the Rockets, and her funeral was attended by family, friends, and NBA royalty.

Asked about that gray Minnesota afternoon, Walton stuttered, "Kevin McHale. What a player. What a human being. What a spiritual force of nature. I remember the overwhelming sadness. Kevin is this incredible ball of energy and hope and laughter, and then, to lose your daughter . . . oh my God."

After McHale returned to his coaching duties in Houston, his quiet stroll outside the Rockets' locker room before a regular season game was interrupted when a large man stepped into his path, prepared to take a charge, and yelled, "Defense!"

"Froggy, what are you doing here?" McHale asked.

"I got a teammate who needs a hug," said M. L. Carr, who'd called McHale's secretary, arranged for a pass, and requested secrecy.

"We had the biggest hug," Carr said years later. "That's just what teammates do, and it was a closeness that we had. Everybody needs a hug sometimes, and Kev needed it then."

In 2021, some of the reunions come without effort. Ainge ran the Celtics from 2003–21, Bird still works with the Pacers, and Carlisle just returned as head coach of the Pacers after thirteen seasons with the Mavericks. Maxwell and Buckner regularly tour the league circuit for their broadcast work. No longer a coach or GM, McHale works for TNT and NBA TV. Walton is a broadcaster, podcaster, activist, honorary member of Dead & Company, and says, "I'm busier than I've ever been."

Others are far out of the NBA loop. Parish moved back to Louisiana, somewhat bitter that none of his teammates hired him to coach in the league. Chief occasionally appears at autograph events, but chose not to attend the 2016 reunion, even though he was signing for cash just a few miles from the team-sponsored event. Wedman manages apartment buildings and sells real estate in Kansas City and has never set foot in the new Boston Garden, which was built in 1995.

Bill Fitch was inducted into the Basketball Hall of Fame in 2019. Gerald Henderson lives in Charlotte and watched his son play eight NBA seasons. Rick Robey sells real estate, goes to the track, and spends some holidays drinking beer with Bird. Sam Vincent had a one-year stint as head coach of the Charlotte Bobcats and is head coach of the Bahrain national team. Greg Kite is a financial adviser in central Florida who oversees the lives of his ten children and seventeen grandchildren. Mike Carey was a groomsman at Carlisle's wedding, wrote books after he left the *Herald*, and died after suffering a stroke in April 2020. Carlisle was one of Smurf's last hospital visitors and gathered tributes from famous ex-Celtics before Carey's funeral.

M. L. Carr is seventy, lives in New Jersey, cares for his grandchildren, makes occasional prank calls to Bird, and hops on an airplane when he has a sense that one of his teammates needs a hug.

K. C. Jones stepped down as Celtics head coach after the 1987–88 season, continued to coach professionally until the turn of the century, and retired to Connecticut with his wife, Ellen. When Jones died of Alzheimer's disease on Christmas Day 2020, Bird said, "K.C. was the nicest man I ever met."

Bird has scaled back his workload, spends a lot of time in Naples, Florida, and became a grandfather in December of 2020.

Were the '86 Celtics the best NBA team of all time?

It's a fun but fruitless debate. How would Mike Trout fare if he batted against Walter Johnson? Could the 1985 Chicago Bears have stopped Jimmy Brown's ground game? Would Bobby Orr be the best player on the ice in 2021?

Sports evolve. We don't know if Bob Cousy would dazzle and dominate if you put him on the court in the 2022 NBA playoffs. Would Bill Russell have the physicality to stop Anthony Davis or Giannis Antetokounmpo?

The 2016–17 Golden State Warriors won 67 games, went 16-1 in the playoffs, and had Kevin Durant, Stephen Curry, Klay Thompson, Draymond Green, and Andre Iguodala. The 1995–96 Chicago Bulls went 72-10, 15-3 in the playoffs, and had Michael Jordan, Scottie Pippen, Dennis Rodman, and Toni Kukoc. The 1962–63 World Champion Celtics had nine Hall of Fame players and a Hall of Fame coach.

The 1985–86 Celtics had size, speed, skill, and five Hall of Famers (so far).

"It's hard to compare different generations, for sure," said Wedman. "But one thing I think we'd have an advantage on today would be our inside presence. When you got Chief and Kevin and Larry, we were tough inside. There aren't many people in this day and age who could guard Kevin, and DJ was such a good defensive guard. We were a very unselfish team. We had a couple of good shooters coming off the bench. Sometimes I watch these teams today and see how much guys celebrate when they make a shot. When you played with Larry Bird, you celebrated when you won a championship. Period."

Carlisle, a coach in the league since 1989, won a championship as head coach of the Mavericks in 2011.

"I don't argue against the position that our Celtics team might have been the best ever," he said. "It certainly would be up for debate. That team would win in any era. We controlled the game with inside-out play. We were a low-turnover, high-rebound team that controlled possession. We had the size, intelligence, and highly skilled players."

Jimmy Rodgers, who won three rings as an assistant with the Bird Celtics and three more with the Jordan Bulls, said, "I get asked this a lot. I'll tell you, that Celtic team was so deep I think they could take on anybody today. They were big and deep and competitive and versatile. Kevin could defend smaller guys, and Larry could defend bigger guys. And in the process, it worked to the advantage of mismatches at the other end. In Chicago, I don't think we had the depth that we had in Boston. We played that triple-post offense that was effective. In Boston it was more classic-type offense, setting screens. I think if you were going to start any team to try to build a winner, you've got to pick Larry Bird."

"I don't think any of us thought about best team of all time or anything like that," said Ainge. "It was just about redemption from our '85 loss. But when people talk about the greatest team of all time, I think the '86 Celtics belong at the top."

"If it was the rules of 2020, half of us would foul out in the first five minutes," said McHale. "But if they would allow us to bang and push and shove the shit out of people and offensive rebound and be bigger, stronger, and faster than the other team, yeah, we win that. If you told me you could put us out there against anybody with the rules of 1986, I'd say, 'Let's go play.'"

ACKNOWLEDGMENTS

When the world changed and we all locked down during the COVID spring of 2020, there were predictions that there'd be a baby boom in 2021. Not true. This book is a stone in a massive literary wall inspired by the coronavirus. Hunkered down in our bubbles, writers and journalists found the uncertain times of 2020 and 2021 good years to reflect, and to reconnect with people and events from our past.

Literary agent/Master of the Universe David Black motivated me to write this story, and it proved to be more fun and satisfying than I envisioned.

Thanks to all those who helped: Megan Wilson, Stan Grossfeld, Sean Mullin, Bob Waterman, Globe librarian Jerry Manion, Celtics publicist Jeff Twiss, Steve Lipofsky, Bill Greene, Chloe Grinberg, Ian Browne. NBC Sports Boston's Jim Aberdale was probably more help than anyone else. Thanks to Bob Ryan, Jackie MacMullan, Leigh Montville, Peter May, Mike Fine, Steve Bulpett, Adam Himmelsbach, Gary Washburn, Tom Callahan, Bill Tanton, Dave Smith, Vince Doria, Don Skwar, Joe Sullivan, Matt Pepin, Brian McGrory, Mike Barnicle, Jonny Miller, Kyle Draper, Joe Amorosino, Liz and Joel Feld, Chris and Christy Lemire, Lesley Visser, Kevin Dupont, Stephen Stills, Peter Goddard, Steve Sheppard, Paul Comerford, John Horn, John Iannacci, Coach John Fahey, Annie Shannon, Mike LaVigne, Dick Johnson, Bill Shaughnessy, Ann Martin, Bruce Hurst, Gary Tanguay, Trenni Kusnierek, George Regan, Francis Storrs, Jill Leone, Bob Waterman.

The great Susan Canavan helped every step of the way. Thanks to Rick Horgan at Scribner for believing in the project. Thanks, also, to Rick's colleagues Beckett Rueda, Ashley Gilliam, Brian Belfiglio, Paul O'Halloran, Olivia Bernhard, and Tracy Woelfel.

Eleven family members and three dogs populated my home when the bulk of this book was written, and I thank them for their patience when I locked myself away in the second-floor office. I won't forget that day when an appliance repairman—making an appointment to keep our thirty-year-old warhorse fridge alive—innocently asked me, "Will there be anyone home?" For more than four months, there was never a moment when there was no one home in my house. Out of that chaos comes this book.

The voices of the 1980s Celtics bring the old story to life, and I thank them for enduring my questions. Cedric Maxwell, M. L. Carr, Bill Walton, Kevin McHale, Danny Ainge, Quinn Buckner. Gerald Henderson, Rick Carlisle, Rick Robey, Greg Kite, Sam Vincent, Jerry Sichting, Scott Wedman, Dave Cowens, Jimmy Rodgers, Ray Melchiorre, and Jan Volk all agreed to be interviewed.

Sarah Shaughnessy was my in-house IT expert, and the edits and recommendations from Kate, Rob, Griff, and Sam are appreciated. We watched a lot of *Jeopardy!* and 1980s Celtics classics together.

The biggest thanks goes to Marilou, who has put up with me for forty years and remains a good sport when we tease her for having gone to Michigan State while Magic was there and having never once seen him play. Who else could take me on a trip to Quebec City, forcing me to miss a playoff Game 7 between the Celtics and the Bucks, and then console me with "Well, you can always go to Game Eight"?

LIST OF SOURCES

Araton, Harvey, and Filip Bondy. *The Selling of the Green*. New York: HarperCollins, 1991.

Auerbach, Arnold "Red." *Basketball for the Player, the Fan and the Coach*. New York: Simon & Schuster, 1952.

Bird, Larry, Magic Johnson, and Jackie MacMullan. *When the Game Was Ours*. Boston: Houghton Mifflin Harcourt, 2009.

Bird, Larry, and Jackie MacMullan. *Bird Watching*. New York: Warner Books, 1999.

Bird, Larry, and Bob Ryan. *Drive*. New York: Doubleday, 1989.

Boston Globe newspaper articles, 1979–86.

Boston Herald newspaper articles, 1979–86.

Callahan, Tom. "Masters of Their Own Game." *Time*, March 18, 1985.

Carey, Mike, and Jamie Most. *High Above Courtside*. New York: Sports Publishing, 2003.

Carr, M. L., and Bob Schron. *Don't Be Denied*. Boston: Quinlan Press, 1987.

Celtics/Lakers: Best of Enemies. Bristol, CT: ESPN Films, 2017.

Curtis, Bryan, "Dan Shaughnessy Roots for Himself." *Ringer*, August 5, 2016.

'86 Celtics, The. Burlington, MA: Comcast SportsNet New England, 2016.

'86 Celtics, The. Interviews from the podcast. Burlington, MA: Comcast SportsNet New England, 2016.

Halberstam, David. *The Breaks of the Game*. New York: Alfred A. Knopf, 1981.

Jones, K. C. *Rebound*. Boston: Quinlan Press, 1986.

Levine, Lee Daniel. *Bird*. New York: McGraw Hill, 1988.

May, Peter. *The Big Three*. New York: Simon & Schuster, 1994.

———. *The Last Banner*. New York: Simon & Schuster, 1996.

McCallum, Jack. *Dream Team*. New York: Ballantine Books, 2012.

———. *Unfinished Business*. New York: Simon & Schuster, 1993.

Ostler, Scott, and Steve Springer. *Winnin' Times*. New York: Macmillan, 1986.

Pearlman, Jeff. *Showtime*. New York: Gotham Books, 2014.

Ribowsky, Mark, and Bill Feinberg. "The Pride of the Celtics." *Sport*, March 1984.

Russell, Bill, and Taylor Branch. *Second Wind*. New York: Random House, 1979.

Ryan, Bob. *Scribe*. New York: Bloomsbury, 2014.

Schron, Bob, and Kevin Stephens. *The Bird Era*. Boston: Quinlan Press, 1988.

Shah, Diane K. *A Farewell to Arms, Legs & Jockstraps*. Bloomington, IN: Red Lightning Books, 2020.

Shaughnessy, Dan. *Ever Green*. New York: St. Martin's Press, 1990.

———. *Seeing Red*. New York: Crown, 1994.

Simmons, Bill. *The Book of Basketball*. New York: Ballantine Books, 2009.

Walton, Bill. *Back from the Dead*. New York: Simon & Schuster, 2016.

———. *Nothing but Net*. New York: Hyperion, 1994.

INDEX